Alternative Perspectives in Assessing Children's Language and Literacy

Alternative Perspectives in Assessing Children's Language and Literacy

edited by

Kathleen Holland
Amherst-Pelham Public Schools

David Bloome
University of Massachusetts–Amherst

Judith Solsken
University of Massachusetts–Amherst

Ablex Publishing Corporation
Norwood, New Jersey

Printed in the United States of America

Library of Congress Cataloging-in-publication Data

Alternative perspectives in assessing children's language and literacy
/ edited by Kathleen Holland, David Bloome, & Judith Solsken.
    p.   cm.
   Includes bibliographical references and index.
   ISBN 0–89391–864–4.—ISBN 0–89391–914–4 (pbk.)
   1. Language arts—Ability testing. 2. Reading—Ability testing.
3. Literacy—Evaluation. I. Holland, Kathleen E. II. Bloome,
David. III. Solsken, Judith W.
LB1576.A6156 1994
372.6′044—dc20
                                      93–40230
                                        CIP

Ablex Publishing Corporation
355 Chestnut Street
Norwood, New Jersey 07648

Contents

Acknowledgments

Many of the chapters in this book were originally presentations at sessions at various National Council of Teachers of English conventions. Some of the sessions were sponsored by NCTE's Committee on Alternative Ways of Assessing Children's Language. We are grateful to the Committee for the impetus it provided for the book and for the insights of the Committee members when the book was being conceptualized.

We also want to acknowledge numerous teachers who helped with the book but whose names are not listed as authors. They shared their classrooms and stories about their students, they discussed issues and perspectives, they reacted and responded to chapters and ideas. We gratefully acknowledge the support and assistance of Lauretta Baldwin, Toby Curry, Debra Goodman, and the Detroit T.A.W.L. group (Teachers Applying Whole Language).

We also want to thank Carolyn Hedley and Catherine Walsh for comments and feedback on an earlier draft of the book. We want to thank the University of Massachusetts, School of Education, for providing support to prepare the book.

Of course, whatever flaws remain in the book are the responsibility of the authors and the editors. The views and opinions expressed in the book are those of the authors and do not necessarily reflect the views or policies of the National Council of Teachers of English, the Committee on Alternative Ways of Assessing Language, the University of Massachusetts, School of Education, or any of the people above or others who so generously helped with feedback, insight, and support.

Kathleen Holland
David Bloome
Judith Solsken

Introduction: What Is An Alternative?

An assessment is a public judgment.

A child listens to a story and tells her friends that the story wasn't very good. A young man rereads a story he has written and tells his teacher that he is not satisfied with it, and that he has decided to start all over again.

But the examples above are not what people think about when they think about assessment. They think about tests: tests used for grading and tests used for getting into college and careers, tests used to place students in ability groups and tests used to evaluate how well students, teachers, and schools are doing. Assessment is linked to power, the power to exclude and to control.

Language and literacy are a major target of assessment. Tests are used to evaluate how well students talk, listen, read, and write. But even when language and literacy are not the focus of testing, they play a hidden role in assessment. With rare exceptions, assessments in schools are either oral or written tests. Language and literacy are both the means and the object of assessment. But the language and literacy of school assessments is not the language and literacy of our everyday lives (DeStefano, 1990; Emihovich, 1990; Hill & Parry, 1989; Lytle & Schultz, 1990). It is a register all to itself, with its own forms, uses, and ways of making meaning (Aronowitz, 1984; Cambourne, 1982; De-Stefano & Kantor, 1988). Regardless of a child's cultural background, to do well in school assessments, whether they are formal written assessments or merely responding to teacher questions, a child must code-switch, must use the language of school assessment (Bloome & Nieto, 1989; Scollon & Scollon, 1984; Trueba, 1988). A language that is linked to power, the power to exclude and to control (Goodman, Shannon, Freeman, & Murphy, 1988; Lemke, 1988).

Many educators, parents, and others have become dissatisfied with the tests used in school. Too often, children's ability with language and literacy is underestimated (Emihovich, 1990; Meier, 1972; Wilkinson & Silliman, 1990). The tests too often deny what children know and what they can do, and discount their abilities to use language and literacy in their everyday lives at home and in communities and classrooms (Cheng, 1987; Taylor, 1988; Wilkinson & Silliman, 1990). Too many children of color score low on the test (O'Neal, 1991) and are denied access to educational opportunities that, seemingly, the tests reserve mainly for White and middle-class children (Arewa, 1977; Labov, 1976; Pullin, 1985; Smitherman, 1981). Too often, the tests control curriculum (Goodman, Shannon, Freeman, & Murphy, 1988; Harman, 1991; Heath, 1983) and instruction (Goodman, Shannon, Freeman, & Murphy, 1988; O'Neal, 1991; however, see Hammersley & Scarth, 1986, for counterevidence about tests influencing instruction). Many educators and parents are no longer willing to tolerate the way tests change life in classrooms and life at home and in the community (e.g., Fitzgerald, 1980; Harman, 1991; Irvine & Elsasser, 1988).

The dissatisfaction with school assessment has led educators, parents, and others to call for changes in assessment (e.g., Genishi & Dyson, 1984; Goodman, Goodman, & Hood, 1988; Harman, 1991; Heath, 1983; Jaggar & Burke-Smith, 1985; Lytle & Schultz, 1990; Olson, 1980; Rhodes & Shanklin, 1993; Valencia & Pearson, 1987). Test makers may respond by increasing efforts to eliminate cultural bias, by using longer reading passages and texts taken from children's literature (to make them more like reading in the real world), by developing holistic writing tasks and new formats and packaging, such as portfolio assessment. Administrators and other educators may respond by seeking multiple sources of assessment information, usually a series of test scores (more testing) combined with teacher assessments, grades, and student achievement in basal reading series. Parents may respond by seeking additional testing of their children by experts outside the school and by teaching their children's test-taking skills.

The response to the dissatisfaction with school assessment has primarily been technocratic—an attempt to fix the mechanisms of assessment (e.g., Wixson, Peters, Weber, & Roeber, 1987). However, a technocratic response is unlikely to assuage the dissatisfaction because the dissatisfaction goes to the very heart of school assessment— its linkage to the power to exclude and to control. To get to the heart of the matter, it is necessary to examine the basis for the public judgments of assessment—the underlying theoretical and conceptual perspectives which inform judgments about language and literacy (see Street, 1984, 1993, for discussion of technocratic stances—which he calls the *autonomous model*—versus *ideological* stances; see also Hill & Parry, 1989; Lytle & Schultz, 1990).

ALTERNATIVE PERSPECTIVES

The dominant perspective on educational assessment during the 20th century has been that of educational psychology, with its emphasis on learning, motivation, and individual differences. Learning, motivation, and individual differences do not seem to be such terrible things to emphasize. They seem to make sense as a basis for assessment and teaching—and that is part of the problem. Educational psychology has become a hegemonic perspective, making it seem as if it is the only common sense, driving other perspectives to the margins.

There has lately been criticism of educational psychology and its underlying assumptions. In Chapters 2 and 3, Barrett and Emihovich examine some of the assumptions of educational psychology and how they are translated into assessment. Other criticisms can be found in Emihovich (1990), McDermott and Hood (1982), and Taylor (1988). While critical examination of educational psychology is important, we do not need a new improved version of the old, nor do we need one dominant perspective to be replaced with another; what we need is something fundamental and substantively different.

We argue the need for alternative *perspectives* rather than the need for *an* alternative perspective. We do so because it is not just the current perspective that is problematic, but its hegemony as well—the way it forces everything to be understood in its own terms, the way it makes it seem as if there are no alternative ways of understanding and acting. We take it as axiomatic that there are multiple and competing realities and interpretations. More simply put, there are many ways to understand what children are doing with language and literacy; and sometimes the interpretations we get from different perspectives do not complement each other; instead, they conflict.

THE ORGANIZATION OF THE BOOK

After an introductory section that describes the need for alternative perspectives, the chapters are grouped under three broad headings: anthropological, sociopsycholinguistic, and reader response to literature. The three headings reflect the disciplinary or theoretical 'starting point' shared by the authors of the chapters in each section. We have chosen anthropology, sociopsycholinguistics, and reader response to literature as headings, in part because they represent our own starting points, but more so because these disciplinary and theoretical perspectives are deservedly gaining wider acceptance and prominence in education.

The three sections should not be viewed as three coherent alternative perspectives on assessment. Even within a section, although authors may have the same starting point, they do not necessarily end up with the same perspective. Nor need they. The differences are informative and should not be rationalized away to create a false harmony. There are conflicts, tensions, and diverse agendas in education, in our communities, and in our society; differences in perspectives on assessment reflect differences in how we see education. Some of these differences result from our different positions within education, and we include chapters written by university professors and researchers as well as chapters written by K–12 classroom teachers. Each section begins with an overview by one of the editors and concludes with a reaction by one or more classroom teachers.

Holloway and Barritt, in the first two chapters of the book, provide an introduction to the need for alternative perspectives. They raise themes that reappear throughout the book. They insist that assessment always be seen as contextualized. Barritt emphasizes the local context of individual actions, knowledge, and intentions. Holloway emphasizes the broader cultural and social context. They both see alternative assessment procedures as social processes leading to changes in traditional power relationships, with more respect for diversity in language and literacy practices and with students and teachers taking greater responsibility for choosing the criteria and procedures for assessment.

The tension between a focus on the individual and the group reoccurs throughout the book. In some chapters, the individual is viewed as a member of the group, for example, as a member of the peer group, classroom, or broader community of readers and writers. In other chapters, the group is viewed as a collection of individuals, each with their own agendas and each making their own contribution to the whole. The tension between focusing on the individual or the group reflects a real tension in students' and teachers' everyday lives, where simultaneously they are individuals and group members, influencing and influenced by the group. And it is not just one group to which they belong, but many and often with different agendas. There is no way to focus on both the individual and the group(s) simultaneously—and yet they are both real.

Underlying the theme of assessment as a social process which involves power relationships is another tension which reoccurs throughout the book—the relationship between change and the status quo. Whether the focus is testing, schooling, teaching, or thinking, teachers and students must deal with the situations they are in, even while recognizing the need for change. Educators recognize the need to help students make it through and achieve within the status quo, yet at the same time it is clear that there are some fundamental problems with our educational system that make it difficult, if not impossible, for many children to succeed. For some educators, this tension is explicitly acknowledged in decisions about teaching and assessment methods. They find ways of compromising, not confronting the status quo directly, but in small ways that, over time, produce change, or, if not change, at least greater opportunity for teacher and students to grow and to enjoy learning. For others, the tension is implicitly expressed in conflicting visions of themselves and their students. Frustrated with the judgments made about them by tests, they try to create more opportunities for students and teachers to tell their own stories, make their own interpretations.

The alternative perspectives presented in this book challenge traditional assessment by challenging its underlying assumptions about language and literacy and its visions of children and teachers. They also challenge each other, and the very idea that a single perspective is sufficient. If assessment is going to work *for* children and teachers, then we need to understand a multitude of perspectives and consider carefully which assumptions and criteria to use in making public judgments about children's language and literacy.

David Bloome
Kathleen Holland
Judith Solsken

REFERENCES

Arewa, O. (1977). Cultural bias in standardized testing: An anthropological view. *The Negro Educational Review, 28*(3-4), 153–171.

Aronowitz, R. (1984). Reading tests as texts. In D. Tannen (Ed.), *Coherence in spoken and written discourse* (pp. 245–264). Norwood, NJ: Ablex.

Bloome, D., & Nieto, S. (1989). Children's understandings of basal readers. *Theory Into Practice, 28*(4), 258–264.

Cambourne, B. (1982). Test results and the real world: A study of incompatibility. *Australian Journal of Reading, 5*(3), 129–141.

Cheng, L.L. (1987). English communicative competence of language minority children: Assessment and treatment of language "impaired" preschoolers. In H.T. Trueba (Ed.), *Success or failure? Learning and the language minority student* (pp. 49–68). Cambridge, MA: Newbury House.

DeStefano, J.S. (1990). Assessing students' communicative competence using a linguistic analysis procedure. *Linguistics and Education, 2*(2), 127–146.

DeStefano, J.S., & Kantor, R. (1988). Cohesion in spoken and written dialogue: An investigation of cultural and textual constraints. *Linguistics and Education, 1*(2), 105–124.

Emihovich, C. (1990). Ask me questions: Sociolinguistic issues in experimental and testing contexts. *Linguistics and Education, 2*(2), 165–183.

Fitzgerald, S. (1980). What are the effects of tests? *Childhood Education*, pp. 216–217.

Genishi, C. & Dyson, A.H. (1984). *Language assessment in the early years*. Norwood, NJ: Ablex.

Goodman, K.S., Goodman, Y.S., & Hood, W.J. (1988). *The whole language evaluation book*. Portsmouth, NH: Heinemann.

Goodman, K.S., Shannon, P., Freeman, Y.S., & Murphy, S. (1988). *Report card on basal readers*. Katonah, NY: Richard C. Owens.

Hammersley, M., & Scarth, J. (1986). *The impact of examinations on secondary school teaching: A research report*. Milton Keynes, UK: The Open University.

Harman, S. (1991). National tests, national standards, national curriculum. *Language Arts, 68*(1), 49–50.

Heath, S.B. (1983). *Ways with words: Language, life and work in communities and classrooms*. New York: Cambridge University Press.

Hill, C., & Parry, K. (1989). Autonomous and pragmatic models of literacy: Reading assessment in adult education. *Linguistics and Education, 1*(3), 233–284.

Irvine, P., & Elsasser, N. (1988). The ecology of literacy: Negotiating writing standards in a Caribbean setting. In B.A. Rafoth & D.L. Rubin (Eds.), *The social construction of written communication* (pp. 304–320). Norwood, NJ: Ablex.

Jaggar, A., & Burke-Smith, T. (Eds.). (1985). *Observing the language learner*. Newark, DE: International Reading Association; and Urbana, IL: National Council of Teachers of English.

Labov, W. (1976). Systematically misleading data from test questions. *Urban Review, 9*(3), 146–171.

Lemke, J. (1988). Genres, semantics, and classroom education. *Linguistics and Education, 1*(1), 81–100.

Lytle, S., & Schultz, K. (1990). Assessing literacy learning with adults: An ideological approach. In R. Beach & S. Hynds (Eds.), *Developing discourse practices in adolescence and adulthood* (pp. 359–385). Norwood, NJ: Ablex.

McDermott, R., & Hood, L. (1982). Institutionalized psychology and the ethnography of schooling. In P. Gilmore & A.A. Glatthorn (Eds.), *Children in and out of school: Ethnography and education* (pp. 232–249). Washington, DC: Center for Applied Linguistics.

Meier, D. (1972). What's wrong with reading tests? *Notes from City College Advisory Service to Open Corridors*, pp. 3–11.

Olson, R.A. (1980). *Evaluation as interaction in support of change*. Grand Forks, ND: University of North Dakota.

O'Neal, S. (1991). Student assessment: Present and future. *Language Arts, 68*(1), 67–73.

Pullin, D. (1985). *Educational testing: Impact on children at risk*. Boston, MA: National Coalition of Advocates for Students.

Rhodes, L., & Shanklin, N. (1993). *Windows into literacy: Assessing learners K–8*. Portsmouth, NH: Heinemann.

Scollon, R., & Scollon, S.B.K. (1984). Cooking it up and boiling it down: Abstracts in Athabaskan children's story retellings. In D. Tannen (Ed.), *Coherence in spoken and written discourse* (pp. 173–200). Norwood, NJ: Ablex.

Smitherman, G. (1981). "What go round come round": King's English in perspective. *Harvard Educational Review, 51*(1), 40–56.

Street, B.V. (1984). *Literacy in theory and practice*. Cambridge, UK: Cambridge University Press.

Street, B.V. (Ed.). (1993). *Cross-cultural approaches to literacy*. Cambridge, UK: Cambridge University Press.

Taylor, D. (1988). Ethnographic educational evaluation for children, families, and schools. *Theory Into Practice, 27*(1), 67–76.

Trueba, A.T. (1988). English literacy acquisition: From cultural trauma to learning disabilities in minority students. *Linguistics and Education, 1*(2), 125–152.

Valencia, S., & Pearson, P.D. (1987). Reading assessment: Time for a change. *The Reading Teacher, 40*(8), 726–733.

Wilkinson, L.C., & Silliman, E.R. (1990). Sociolinguistic analysis; Nonformal assessment of children's language. *Linguistics and Education, 2*(2), 109–126.

Wixson, K., Peters, C., Weber, E., & Roeber, E. (1987). New directions in statewide reading assessment. *The Reading Teacher, 40*(8), 749–755.

Part I
The Need For Alternative Perspectives

chapter 1
Language, Culture, and the Implications of Assessment

Karla F.C. Holloway

If assessment of an early elementary child's spoken language means a discovery of what this child does not know, it is not only a potentially misleading activity, it is also not a particularly important behavior. Such behavior is generally accompanied by the notion of *remediation*—identifying a wound, a weakness, and correcting it. Additionally, the pejorative and sometimes destructive nature of evaluative processes often does more harm than good in an early elementary classroom.

In terms of children's spoken language, there is actually little that needs remediation in terms of change and correction. The early elementary child's language is constantly shifting in terms of maturity and awareness, simply because of the child's constant exposure to new linguistic information. King (1985) notes that "children meet new demands for language use when they move into play groups, attend day care centers or nursery schools" and that "dialogue with a more skillful language user plays an important role in the process" of extending children's language, increasing their "range of competence" (pp. 24, 25). It is important to proceed cautiously here, for it is in the process of determining the nature of children's language that researchers and teachers may fall prey to a notion of a model of acceptable language that does not come from the language user, but extends from some notion of what kind of language will determine "success in school."

The language of the teacher, of other classmates, and of written and read language all affect the spoken corpus available to the young child. So rather than look at *evaluation* from a remediative model, the perspective that is critical for the early elementary teacher is that knowledge of children's language is information that they might use in developing classroom experiences that would add to the child's growing body of spoken, written, and read language. An important awareness for the teacher is that a child's spoken language reflects both what they know and *what they are in in the process of learning*.

This may be one of the most obvious aspects of an early elementary curriculum where *evaluation* need not have a problematic focus. There is very little useful information about competence or performance that comes from looking at what children's language does not do. Such a focus actually reveals more about a research perspective or bias than it does about the language user. The linguistic development of a healthy speaker invariably reflects universal stages of acquisition (Brown, 1973; deVilliers & deVilliers, 1978), regularities in learning strategies (Bever, 1970; Nelson, 1973) and underscores the biological nature of the acquisition process (Chomsky, 1975; Lenneberg, 1967). To suggest that the spoken language of any healthy child can reflect a lack of these biological endowments indicates an attitude that is uncomfortably close to a judgment of their humanity. Further, it imposes a model of language use that reflects a social hierarchy rather than information gleaned from a "natural" perspective of language use and development. This is a dangerous perspective in a public school system that is multicultural in population.

Smitherman (1985) cites Robert Pooley's 1969 and 1974 research that explores how "myths and misconceptions about language and negative attitudes toward language diversity are fostered in the school and perpetuated in the general populace of the public school experiences." Pooley's research, according to Smitherman, "powerfully demonstrates" how those who "depart from the idealized norm of standard English" are "condemned as immoral, ignorant and inferior." Smitherman's point clearly articulates the dangers of social/cultural biases in school systems that support one kind of language (dialect) over another.

With a perspective that supports and respects the natural development of a child's language capacity, the early elementary child's language is not language that requires remediation or a corrective. Instead, *assessment* of children's language in the early elementary school needs to reflect the broadest definition of this term that means an "assignation of value." Once we determine that a child's language has value, our classroom strategies reflect the clear advantage to that child's active participation in determining the language base of the classroom.

Obviously, there is a confusion of biological, social, and pedagogical information that is involved in a consideration of assessment. However, I believe that there are three rather basic understandings of children's language that classroom teachers can use as signals for instructional strategies without falling prey to the negativism often associated with evaluation and assessment.

In *Investigating Classroom Talk* (Edwards & Westgate, 1987), the authors include this statement in their chapter on their text's "rationale." They write:

> In the act of making statements about the world, or asking or answering questions, we also and simultaneously locate ourselves socially, indicate how we perceive others and announce, confirm or challenge how the situation is to be defined. As *observers* of the talk of others, we draw on this everyday knowledge in treating the words as evidence (p. 7; emphasis added)

I have intentionally truncated their last sentence, because the notion of "words as evidence" is so important to both the speaker and the hearer when we enter an evaluative mode. What is the evidence? If language users do, as Edwards and Westgate suggest, "locate [them]selves socially," may not this social evidence be self-condemnatory if society has relegated certain speakers to a second-class citizenship? If speech indicates perception, can it not also be evidence of a distinctiveness of perception—distinctions that ostracize and classify a way of thinking about the world that is not "standard?" I beg these questions because they underlie the first critical "understanding of language" I will discuss in this chapter.

CHILDREN'S SPOKEN LANGUAGE IS EVIDENCE OF PERCEPTION, ACUITY, MEMBERSHIP IN A CULTURAL COMMUNITY, AND AN EXISTING SENSE OF SELF-DEFINITION

What a wonderful and rich corpus available for classroom activities! Note that I have *not* said that children's language will tell what a child perceives, how they are keen and sharp individuals, or what cultural community is indicated. Such information is usually much more subtle than spoken language can reveal. Neither have I said that their spoken language will tell you how they define themselves. I have said, quite simply, that their spoken language is an indication that such judgment, definition, and membership have occurred. This is an important distinction, because it allows the teacher to understand that a relatively sophisticated language user stands before them, and that the potential to use this sophistication to enable curricular objectives depends on not ignoring this awareness.

Strickland (1985), who agrees that "evaluation is severely limited in its usefulness," suggests that "observation checklists and recordkeeping are two valuable evaluative methods that may supplement or substitute for standardized testing" (p. 94). Such lists and records are also important because they allow the teacher to enter categories that have been generated from a knowledge of the children in that particular classroom. These child-generated lists and records have greater potential for carrying with them a perspective that credits what that child is capable of as the basis for extending these capabilities than does a method of evaluation that begins with a deficit model, that is, what the child does not know. Instructional methodologies that extend from such records and lists become teaching practices that privilege the child over the curriculum. This privilege values what the child already knows and places that knowledge into a significant relationship with the learning that will occur in that classroom.

What can we learn to look for in terms of children's perception, their acuity, and their sense of identity and membership?

Comments such as "I think" or "I feel" from our children are verbal signals of their active perceptual capabilities. Learning to listen for such signals will allow us to pay a different kind of attention to the message that follows. We can be, as educators, more sensitive to the comments that follow such "sentence starters." We can use them as a basis for classroom interaction, allowing our children to participate in a forum that allows them the chance to understand and appreciate the value of different ways of thinking about the same issue, as well as the nature of differences themselves. Whether we talk about something as innocuous as a favorite season or something a bit more weighty, the opportunity to use thoughts and feelings acknowledges for us and them the significance of this kind of dialogue within a classroom setting.

"I noticed that he wasn't smiling."

Acuity is often associated with the visual realm rather than the spoken realm. But giving classroom opportunities to notice different aspects of an idea, a shared experience, a visualized object or picture without a "correct" perception governing the exercise is an opportunity for a subtle kind of interpretation on the teacher's part and on the student's. Who notices aspects of thoughtfulness? Who is attentive to shapes and colors? Who sees a "bigger" picture and who notices minutiae? Such information, perhaps a part of a checklist or record, can become a technique for instruction. "Today, we'll all notice shapes, tomorrow let's talk about things that are tiny." The potential for curricular involvement here is endless. It satisfies our goal of extending to children a variety of ways of attending to their environment and it builds on and shares attentive strategies that children themselves have refined through their linguistic sophistication.

"Who are they?" is similar enough, yet different from, "Who am I?"

I am not an advocate of what has been perhaps irreverently called the "touchy-feely" model of interactive behavior. I believe firmly in a student's right to privacy concerning their feelings about themselves and their attitudes towards others. This does not mean, however, that we cannot use a child's sense of self as a projection into exercises in characterization, guesses about nameless faces in magazines or newspapers and discussions that extend from such exercises and guesses. Such experience is another subtle use of a child's own, private awareness of family and community and an opportunity to extend that awareness, in a speculative sense, to others.

The second understanding of language and children's sense of their own language that I view as critical to assessment and to curriculum is discussed in the next section.

THE SPOKEN WORD IS CULTURALLY PRIVILEGED OVER THE WRITTEN AND READ WORD

Some may think that such a notion does not belong in text about assessment or a chapter concerning the evaluation of spoken language. I obviously disagree. Much of what we, as educators, assume about the teaching of language and literacy in early elementary classrooms depends upon a basic notion of using spoken language as a bridge to literacy. Although there is certainly nothing intrinsically damning about such a notion, there is certainly a danger in the practice of such a theoretical hierarchy.

In a rather interesting revisioning of history, the written word has supplanted the cultural affirmation of oral records as the primary record of experience and identity. Indeed, my first point of critical awareness is based on an understanding of spoken language as an indication that such judgment and thinking as relevant to culture and identity had occurred and is of value. In *"Race," Writing and Difference*, Henry Louis Gates, Jr., reminds us that, "after Rene Descartes, reason was privileged above all other human characteristics," and that "writing...was taken to be the visible sign of reason" (p. 8). The incorporation of this argument into the traditions of western education and thought has encouraged a schematic that devalues oracy and even uses writing as an indication and *measure* of one's "human characteristics." Gates notes that the consequence of such a structuration is that "without writing, no *repeatable* sign of the working of reason, of mind, could exist. Without memory or mind, no history could exist. Without history, no humanity, as defined [by Kant and Hegel, among other European philosophers]...could exist" (p. 11).

Prior to such philosophical racism as Rene Descartes', and as validated through even the slightest attention to children's interest in and use of language—orature had both value and validity. Not only does it manage to affirm one's cultural community and identity, but it represents that culture's value in the concept of the word. Sims (1982) begins her discussion of the Afro-American experience in children's fiction (*Shadow and Substance*) with this comment: "There is power in The Word. People in positions of power over others have historically understood, and often feared, the potential of The Word to influence the minds of people over whom they hold sway" (p. 1). Sims's historical word is *orate*; and although the thrust of her text is on literature, her appropriate opening sentences articulate her clear understanding that the historical word's power and creative energy were attached to its voicing.

My point is that children's sense of language also extends this creative power to spoken language and they do not intentionally turn that power into a mechanism to facilitate literacy. We, as educators, do that for them. When we do, we often also subtract from spoken language its individual energy and power—a message our children receive quite clearly from us.

In "Talking and Writing: Building Communication Competence," Rubin and Kantor (1984) discuss the usefulness of writing in "making meaning" for speech. Such direction is characteristic of what one may identify as a contemporary interest in a "bridge" between oracy and literacy. It is important to note that the implied equality of this bridge is misleading. Actually, contemporary thinking in the politics of education and educational philosophy privileges writing over speech and uses literacy to supplant the accuracy, intent, diversity, and *value* of our children's language.

Talking, telling stories, making creative worlds through the use of words, using language as a creative force are not merely skills that will enable literacy. We imply a culturally and historically inaccurate hierarchy if we see spoken language as a utilitarian bridge to the literature text. My concern is that our interest in the "functions" of language revises its culturally understood status and supplants it with a Westernized version of utilitarianism. The loss of position for orature is a critical loss in terms of the individual child and the speech community she represents. The school's culture and revisioned definition of language asserts itself into our interpretive frames. We are left looking at speech as signal for reading readiness.

To avoid relegating oracy to a literacy mechanism, or to a realm of "functions," I suggest that classroom practices that extend from understandings such as the two I list below privilege oracy in the way that our children naturally understand the power of the word:

- Children quite naturally use speech with great variety, shifting language and tone to reflect occasion and audience.

Have room in your records or checklists for recording certain kinds of language: poetic and reflective, detailed and factual, imaginative and argumentative, loud and assertive, and soft and diminutive. Noting the many ways children are using language increases our appreciation of their range and allows us to develop classroom experiences that utilize these capabilities in even more extensive ways.

- Children's oral language development is an increasing complex of categories and structures that both records what they have learned and extends cognitive networks making relationships between what they have learned.

Allow children to construct oral histories of their classroom experiences (field trips, lessons, special activities), that they practice retelling daily or weekly. These may be in the forms of patterned language, such as song or rhyme, but retain (and do not dilute) their oral status. Such a practice encourages children's natural categorizing of experiences and allows them to see that you too place value in their interest in organizing their world through language. As teacher, your direction of this activity under a specific heading is an indication of your instructional use of children's natural language strategies.

The final understanding of children's spoken language that I view as critical for the classroom teacher concerns the sometimes contradictory nature of the information that comes from research and the practices that come from our classrooms.

ANY PEDAGOGY, CONCEPTUAL FRAMEWORK OR
RESEARCH METHODOLOGY THAT SUPPORTS A
STANDARD OR MODEL OF *SUCCESSFUL*
CLASSROOM LANGUAGE BY NATURE DEVALUES
THE LANGUAGE BROUGHT INTO THE CLASSROOM
BY OUR STUDENTS. A *STUDENT-CENTERED
CURRICULUM*, IN FACE OF SUCH PEDAGOGY, IS A
CONTRADICTION IN TERMS.

Shuy (1984) notes quite accurately that, although "learning relies on language," learning is also often stymied because of "false information, incomplete knowledge, and stereotypes of language which educators inherit and pass along to future generations with discouraging faithfulness" (p. 167). I am quite convinced that it is no longer safe to rely on the research of linguists to pass on the notion of linguistic competence as a human characteristic. Perhaps we have relied too long on researchers to make these points without supporting a parallel emphasis on curriculum and classroom practices to reflect the research awareness. Curricular control and classroom practices have, for too long, been separate entities and separated from research discoveries. What we know about the competencies of the language user has continually, and even historically, been devalued in the face of the objective of a monocultural classroom in terms of language and literacy. Perhaps it will be the separation of these notions, the return of status and respect to spoken language and the clear understanding that literacy learning does not depend on the type, quantity, or style of spoken language that will finally disable the stereotypes we have become so "faithful" and proficient at passing from generation to generation.

The three issues of this chapter, (a) that language is evidence of knowledge and capability, (b) that oracy is culturally privileged, and (c) that linguistic 'standards' devalue the language of a culture and community, are critical to any model of assessment.

Alternatives to traditional measures of assessment are necessary because traditional evaluative measures are not designed to identify knowledge or to indicate the depth and cultural resonance of children's language, and they erroneously imply that certain language structures and use are prerequisites to learning. Strickland (1985) writes that tests are frequently not even administered or scored by the classroom teacher and are often returned in a "form of a list of overall scores of categories in which children have been placed," the consequence of which is that such tests "may not accurately reflect the educational goals and objectives of the program of the children being evaluated" (p. 95). This is the crux of the issue—the goals and objectives, not only of the program, but of the evaluative instruments as well.

If we assess in order to assist classroom practices, assessment needs to point out the strategies of the learner so that our practices might imitate these.

If we assess in order to know the individual child better, then assessments that stereotype, normalize, and standardize our class-rooms are of little assistance in our search for this kind of information.

If we assess in order to assure academic success, then our focus ought to be directed toward what the child has achieved, what naturally successful strategies have been utilized in language learn-ing, and how those strategies might be translated into classroom practices.

Such goals for assessment indicate that children's knowledge of the structures of language, their ability to generate and create new sentences for their increasingly varied experiences, their skill at networking and relating the previously known to the newly learned, their sense of both the repetitive nature of linguistic structures, and the generative nature of linguistic sense must form the bases of our assessment strategies. What links all of these is that they extend from what children know, what they do naturally, and from a basic affirma-tion of their capability and membership in a human community.

REFERENCES

Bever, T.G. (1970). The cognitive basis for linguistic structures. In J.R. Hayes (Ed.), *Cognition and the development of language*. New York: Wiley.

Brown, R. (1973). *A first language: The early stages*. Cambridge, MA: Harvard University Press.

Chomsky, N. (1975). *Reflections on Language*. New York: Pantheon.

deVilliers, J., & deVilliers, P.A. (1978). *Language acquisition*. Cambridge, MA: Harvard University Press.

Edwards, A.D., & Westgate, D. (1987). *Investigating classroom talk*. East Sussex, UK: The Falmer Press.

Gates, H.L., Jr. (1986). Writing 'race' and the difference it makes. In H.L. Gates (Ed.), *"Race," writing and difference*. Chicago: University of Chicago Press.

King, M.L. (1985). Language and language learning for child watchers. In A. Jaggar & M. Trika Smith-Burke (Eds.), *Observing the language learner*. Urbana, IL: National Council of Teachers of English.

Lenneberg, E. (1967). *Biological foundations of language*. New York: Wiley.

Nelson, K. (1973). Structure and strategy in learning to talk. *Monographs of the Society for Research in Child Development, 38*(149).

Rubin, D. & Kantor, K. (1984). Talking and writing: Building communication competence. In C. Thaiss & C. Suhov (Eds.), *Speaking and writing K-12*. Urbana, IL: National Council of Teachers of English.

Shuy, R. (1984). Language as a foundation for education: the school context. *Theory Into Practice, 23*(3), 167–74.

Sims, R. (1982). *Shadow and substance: Afro-American experience in contemporary children's fiction*. Urbana, IL: National Council of Teachers of English.

Smitherman, G. (1985). 'What Go Round Come Round': King's English in perspective." In C.K. Brooks (Ed.), *Tapping potential: English and language arts for the Black learner*. Urbana, IL: National Council of Teachers of English.

Strickland, D. (1985). Early childhood development and reading instruction. In C.K. Brooks (Ed.), *Tapping potential: English and language arts for the Black learner*. Urbana, IL: National Council of Teachers of English.

chapter 2
Toward an Alternative View of Writing Assessment

Loren S. Barritt

INTRODUCTION

Until recently a single ideal has dominated the conduct of educational inquiry and has had a significant impact on educational practice. The position is rooted in the philosophical movement called *positivism* developed by August Comte, who believed it possible to achieve irrefutable understanding with the application of scientific techniques in gathering information. This faith became the basis for the logical positivism of the Vienna Circle, whose views continue to have a significant impact on contemporary beliefs among educational researchers and practitioners. Perhaps most compelling among them: that it is only possible to achieve progress by using scientific methods.[1]

To the dominance of this philosophical position can be traced the rise of the educational research establishment with its use of "scientific" techniques to investigate learning, teaching, and student performance. These techniques differ in the degree to which they approach scientific respectability, yet they are similar because they

---

[1] This position carries many names. It has been called, *positivist, objectivist, empiricist, empirical-analytical*, and sometimes just *mainstream*. I am often at a loss to know what name to use, since each emphasizes one version of the faith and minimizes others. Because the views which support the position are so pervasive, it often escapes notice that there is an ideology here to be characterized. What is taken for granted doesn't have a name. It's just the way all of us do things around here.

rest on a common positivist faith that the laboratory experiment is the ideal way for getting to the bottom of things. Educational researchers have been driven to use other methods only because they cannot gain control of the situations in which they work. Because it is seldom possible to do a randomized, controlled experiment in a school, less rigorous techniques must be used, but always with the desire to come as close as possible to the ideal represented in the controlled experiment. This sustaining ideal is seductive, because it holds out the promise that the apparent uncertainties of daily life, which are believed to be rooted in individual subjectivity, can be swept away as the experimental evidence mounts.

The positivist view undercuts individual judgment for two reasons. First, because it privileges general understanding. Second, because individuals sometimes disagree and positivists equate consistency with accuracy. This places teachers at a disadvantage in any disagreement they might have with research understanding. The carefully worked out formulas for choosing samples and conducting research "permits" investigators to speak beyond their experience and do it with one voice. They can speak with some certainty about events that lie outside the field of their experience. In fact, positivist scientists are, in part, accorded the right to speak with authority *because* they are not personally involved. It is more likely that someone who has done a proper study of classrooms will be considered an expert about them than will an experienced teacher who only has had long experience in "one."

The positivist ideal, and the vision of knowledge and experience that sustains it, are nested in the heart of educational thought. The effects of these beliefs are to be seen everywhere, including wherever questions of judging student performance are considered.

AN ALTERNATIVE WAY

A fundamental change in the way educational research is understood is in progress. The positivist faith now has a challenger. The signs have been visible since the late 1950s. It has taken 30 years for those signs to make their way through university departments, to show up in changed faculty beliefs about the way research should be conducted and what the results of such work mean. The shift is far from over, but it is clear that the monolithic belief in the positivist vision is no more. The reasons for the change can be found in recent reinterpretations of the history and therefore the philosophy of science[2] and in dissatisfac-

---

[2] One excellent example of this work is Polanyi's book *Personal Knowledge* (1958).

tion with the results of the positivist program after more than 70 years of work. For some people the program just didn't seem to be going where it had promised. Positive understanding seemed to be unreachable.

The alternative viewpoint rests on a different set of assumptions about the nature of understanding and how we come to it. It is likely, in time, to have just as profound an effect on educational research and practice as did the positivist program. But for now the implications of this profound change of mind have yet to be worked throughout the system.[3]

At the heart of the alternative vision is the belief that human beings act creatively to make sense of experience. Languages are the powerful tools that invite us to activity and at the same time make interpretations possible. Stories are the vehicles for carrying these interpretations. Stories create "worlds" of meaning which provoke further interpretation. In this view, acts of interpretation are at the heart of being human. The study of experience, in this interpretive view, requires us to pay careful attention to forms of language, including nonlinguistic forms like body language.

In the interpretive view, language is not something that needs to be categorized or standardized in order to be understood. The particularity of the language is important, because it guides us in understanding the other person's point of view, knowledge is not assumed to be fixed and outside of human experience. It is part of that experience and is constantly making it and being remade by it. In this view human understanding is always necessarily in flux as interpretations grow in response to interpretations. Each of us is constantly making sense of the sense that others offer us.

People are not understood as separate digits in the interpretive view; they are part of a social world they helped to create and which in turn helps create them. The human world is a complex web of interacting meanings that shift and change. It is a world of dialogue in which each of us learns to see anew as we engage in acts of mutual understanding with other people. Think, as just one example, of the different roles each of us plays from earliest childhood to adulthood,

---

[3] The movement I am sketching has different names and different emphases. Some call it *human science*, others *hermeneutics*, from the Greek term meaning "interpretation," which was used by theologians to refer to their search in the Bible for God's proper meaning. Some prefer the term *ethnographic* and others *phenomenological*, which means the study of experience as it appears to those living through it. The least descriptive but most used term is *qualitative*. Whatever the term, however, the focus in all these cases is on the meaning-making capabilities of human experience, and the goal of investigation is to reveal these meanings through careful observation of the way people themselves understand things.

and how we are redefined in each. Each of us is in dialectical tension between our own understanding and that of other people. As one shifts, so does the other.

If this vision of self and world, of knowledge and being, is correct then understanding of the other is always an act of interpretation in which one person comes to know herself as she comes to know another. From an interpretive perspective it is not surprising that two "independent" observers of a common event—say the reading of a student's essay—could come to different interpretations, since there is so much at play in the writing and the reading of an essay. From an interpretive perspective it is essential that these differences be preserved so we can learn from them. In fact, from this perspective the absolute prohibition on disagreement as a means to assure scientific accuracy looks like the introduction of prejudice and hence inaccuracy into the situation.

I would be surprised if you did not have some concern for the direction in which such views take us. We seem to be moving away from the rock solid foundation of objectivity based on consistency, on which positivist science has been promising to build, in favor of the sandy subjectivity of disagreement. And you would be right. One way of characterizing the difference between the "positivists" and the "interpreters" is by reference to this concern. The positivists believe that the world is held together by the facts, which only the methods of "science" can reveal. Any other perspective they view with alarm because it seems to encourage subjectivity, opinion, irrationality, and in the end chaos. They counsel us all to have patience and perseverance for the long haul, as well as faith in the future of science.

The interpreters reply to these concerns was well stated by Gadamer, a philosopher of the interpretive tradition, in his book *Truth and Method*: "The only scientific thing is *to recognize what is* instead of starting from what ought to be or could be" (p. 466). In the interpretive view human experience "is," and so too is language, in which experience swims. In the interpretive view it is wiser to study what seems to be the case, to follow investigation wherever it may lead, and let the degree of certainty achieved take care of itself. The same sort of certainty found in physics may not result from the study of human events, but at least human events will have been studied not rarefied experimental forms which only occur in laboratories.

To those in the interpretive tradition experience takes place in an intersubjective world of connected consciousness, not one of disconnected isolation in which people are radically separate from one another. In this world, ordinary life is not so very full of uncertainty. In daily life we expect regularity, and we usually get it. In daily life we expect other people to be a part of the same world we inhabit, for them to understand us, and usually they do. There is no denying that misunderstandings also occur, but misunderstandings only make sense against the broad background of understanding.

The immediate impact that interpretive approaches have had on educational research has been the removal of constraints placed by methodological dogmas. The experiment is no longer the ideal case. Measurement is no longer essential to an investigation. Measuring and experimenting are in the interpretive view themselves interesting examples of creative interpretation by a community of language users. They are not the final arbiters of interpretive acts.

The interpretive approach grows out of the hermeneutic tradition, which has been influential in the study of published texts but has had little influence on the way student writing is considered. It is as though writing teachers forgot their own traditions and took up unfamiliar ones when student texts came before them. Writing teachers who were trained in the study of literature were lead to expect differences of interpretation. Dialogue and debate about the meaning of texts was important and expected. It is a measure of the power of science that when these same people were asked to judge students' writing, they abandoned their own training in favor of new criteria which were said to be scientific, criteria which assured there would appear to be agreement in readings given to a single text. Instead of the dialogue they were taught to expect as a result of different interpretations, they were now expected to "reach agreement" despite their misgivings. Instead of recognizing the necessary role of a reader's response in creating a meaningful text they were told to read as though they were one person. And they agreed to do it. I can only assume that this acquiescence came because their seemed to be a unanimous view among experts in the social sciences that it had to be done that way. Now that that seeming unanimity is no more, it is up to each of us to decide which view of science and knowledge will guide our practice.

AN INTERPRETIVE VIEW OF
JUDGING STUDENT ESSAYS

In the interpretive view the reading of a student paper involves both student writer and reader in an act of mutual reinterpretation. The writer must write for an audience he or she does not know and so must create one, and so too must the reader learn to know the writer from the text he or she has before him or her. There is no better way to illustrate this than to try to write an essay of the sort often assigned to students for assessment purposes, on "abortion" or "gun control" or "nuclear energy" or some other "meaningful" topic and directed to an "audience" like the one the students are asked to write to a U.S. Senate committee or the student newspaper. I urge you to try it. Write an essay either for or against "gun control" to send to a Senate committee. At least go through the preliminary steps to get started. As you reflect on your actions and reactions, you will be conducting an interpretive investigation. You will become aware of thoughts and actions which usually pass without notice. You will also have a better idea of what students go through to write an essay. I think you will see that it is not only a "writing" process. Writing an essay draws the writer and reader into a transaction that makes a context that influences the reading as well as the writing of the essay.

In my own reflections on trying to write a student assessment essay I find I have an immediate problem with the audience, because my "real" audience, the ones who wrote the question and will read the answer, have tried to help me with the problem of audience. I now have two audiences to keep in mind not one, the "real" audience and the fictive one. I raise for myself the question: How seriously should I take this requirement that I write to a Senate committee? What does the "real" audience know about Senate committees? Since I conclude the "real" audience probably doesn't know very much about Senate committees, I need to consider my "real" audience in this light. It is not them directly I must write to, but their idea of a Senate committee. I know they are all likely to be writing teachers, which probably means English teachers, so to start I need to consider what English teachers would like to believe about the sort of arguments that would convince a Senate committee. It all gets pretty complex, once you begin to take the experience seriously. And it gets worse if you consider that each of these young writers is likely to handle this interpretive problem differently. Some will miss the audience distinction I am making; others won't. What is a reader to do with this interpretive problem when there is a text before him or her?

I don't mean to claim by this example that every student writer will think through the problem of audience in this way. I do mean to suggest that they will have made some sort of audience to which they must write, and for many this act of interpretation will lead to inhibition that is likely to alter writing performance. I also mean to argue that judgments like these cannot help but play a role in understanding the text produced and therefore should not be ignored in evaluation.

If we recognize that students are acting meaningfully, expecting dialogue with a particular sort of audience, then we ought also to recognize that we are already caught in a web of meaning with them which is also a set of obligations. We are obligated to read seriously and thoughtfully, to recognize the mastery of required forms and of creative solutions, to be appropriately lenient in cases where time limits have been imposed, in other words, to become something like the audience the essay was written to please. In writing to us the student is making of us a particular sort of reader. Sometimes we can see that we are trusted, and sometimes we realize we are not. In the former case we may even be asked to judge, without prejudice, harsh words about the essay exam itself, or we may be expected to recognize irony. If the writer views us with suspicion, we are likely to have a safe, five-paragraph essay with topic sentences at the lead of each paragraph, using only the words this student knows he or she can spell.

From an interpretive point of view, an examination of the experience of reading and judging student essays reveals that writers become part of the readers problem in deciding about an essay. It does no good to counsel that only the text should be judged. The existence of the text depends on the readers' understanding of the writers' intentions.[4] If irony can be read then the question arises whether it was intended. Could a student be so clever? Would he or she try something like that in these circumstances?

In the transaction between writer and created audience and reader and created writer, there is a lot of room for interpretation. This is also true for published texts. With so much in play between writer and reader, it is not surprising that readers sometimes disagree. These disagreements are often of sufficient size statistically to raise questions about the accuracy of the final judgments. In the positivist view the answer to this problem is training for judges to make discrepancies go away.

In the interpretive view it is a contradiction to invoke the idea of "science" in order to suppress disagreement. If readers disagree accuracy demands that we acknowledge it, not hide it. In considering disagreement, we have an opportunity to learn about ourselves as readers, students as writers, and what they have understood from our teaching.

---

[4] These ideas were first developed in collaboration with my colleagues, Patti Stock, Francelia Clark, and Grace Dunn at the English Composition Board at the University of Michigan. That work was reported in a paper in *College Composition and Communication* in 1986. The ideas presented here are my effort to say what I believe are the implications of what we found there.

From an interpretive perspective, procedures designed to produce a common reading look terribly unscientific, like "cooking" the data.[5] The question that needs to be answered is, what do these reader judges, whom we trust because they are experienced in teaching writing, think of this text? Particularly, why have they reached different judgments about it? Disagreements present an opportunity to learn. They are not the sign that someone has made a mistake. They are the result of the different interpretations that readers and writers make in creating a language that intends to say something.

When students who write assessment essays write as expected, like students, and readers read as they have been taught, disagreements can be reduced significantly. But the price is high, because writers and readers often have to suppress what they want to say to achieve commonality. In the interpretive view disagreement is welcomed because it arises where unconsidered viewpoints occur. It arises when student writers become other than expected in the eyes of the reader. It arises when readers see something different in a text.

Reading is after all a complex process. Reading to make a judgment is no less complicated. I doubt any judge has been able to go through very many essays without shifting his or her sense of the task and the strength of this or that conviction. In a single essay so much "dialogue" takes place as the reader tries to nail down this writer: "Is he or she clever or not? Was that a subtle joke that I just read, or was it unintentional? If it happens again I will assume it was intended." But then something else happens: The essay collapses. "Which part represents what this student can do?" And so it goes, as the sands of the discussion shift and the text goes by. It is unfair, because it is inaccurate to put a single score on so complex a transaction between two people who meet on a piece of paper. With published texts we of course don't do it. With published texts we discuss our readings so everyone can follow our interpretation. But with student texts we are willing to compromise, a lot.

The requirement that there be a single reading of student texts is at the core of psychometric theory from which educational measurements derive their justification. It is contrary to that theory to expect validity in the absence of reliability. In the world of psychometrics, consistency is a necessary condition for accuracy. The positivist

---

[5] I am always struck by the suggestion that positive science is accurate and interpretive science inaccurate. My own dissatisfaction with positive programs applied to the human world developed from the conviction that the prescription of positivist methods distorts the case. I think interpretive views are actually more accurate, because they reflect our understandings instead of prettying them up.

position also has certain "practical" advantages over the interpretive view. It serves the needs of educational institutions if there is a single correct answer for placement, admission, or a grade. In the bureaucratic world it is inconvenient to have to acknowledge that in some cases disagreements accurately reflect what is the case.

I've made no attempt here to deal with the politics of these alternative views. In this chapter I have only tried to show that it can no longer be claimed that there is no alternative to lock-step ways of reading student texts. There is now, for those who wish to claim it, an alternative view of students, readers, and the texts which come between them.

REFERENCES

Barritt, L.S., Stock, P., Clark, F., & Dunne, G. (1986). Researching practice; Evaluating assessment essays. *College Composition and Communication, 37*(3), 315–327.
Gadamer, H.G. (1975). *Truth and method.* New York: Seabury Press.
Polanyi, M. (1958). *Personal knowledge.* New York: Harper.

Part II
Anthropological Perspectives on Assessing Children's Language and Literacy

The chapters in this section take an anthropological perspective on the assessment of children's language and literacy. Of primary concern to an anthropological perspective is the concept of culture. In 1871, Tylor defined *culture* as "that complex whole which includes knowledge, belief, art, morals, law, custom, and any other capabilities and habits acquired by man as member of society" (in Peacock, 1986, p. 3). More recently, cultural anthropologists have focuses less on the surface features of culture and more on underlying processes. For example, Goodenough (1981) defines *culture* as the shared set of standards or expectations for feeling, believing, thinking, and acting that people in a group hold for each other. Geertz (1973) defines *culture* as a system of meanings and significances within which people interact. Regardless of how one defines culture, the focus of attention is less on individual behavior and more on what people together do, the context in which they do it, and what meaning and significance it has.

In taking an anthropological perspective, *assessment* is redefined. That's an important insight for at least two reasons. First, what we take to be a common-sense definition of *assessment* is only its definition from one perspective—generally speaking, the perspective of experimental psychology. Secondly, whenever a new perspective of assessment is employed, a new definition of *assessment* is needed. There is no such thing as having a new or alternative perspective with an old definition.

Emihovich, in her chapter on the language of assessment, makes clear how bound the traditional definition of *assessment* is to experimental psychology. Putting assessment into another perspective raises questions about assessment not otherwise visible. Emihovich recognizes that for many teachers, traditional assessments of children's language and literacy are a current reality and are likely to be around at least in the near future if not the distant future, too. If teachers are to be advocates for children and themselves, they need to understand traditional assessment both from the perspective of experimental psychology and anthropology. Bloome challenges us to redefine assessment. In so doing, he asks us to question the basic assumptions traditionally held about children's language and literacy in school. He lists a series of questions derived from looking at children's language and literacy from an anthropological perspective that can be used to redefine assessment and to better understand what children do. But he warns that it is not the questions that matter but the perspective in which the questions are formulated and the contexts in which they are used. Watrous and Willett note that traditional assessment is primarily used to exclude children; in part, that is inherent in its definition. They ask us to redefine assessment by setting the agenda of assessment as greater inclusion of children in the classroom community. They see anthropology as providing a perspective for helping us redefine assessment as inclusion rather than exclusion. Jennings, responding to the chapters, considers how such challenges might be possible in her classroom and school. Traditional assessment is part of how schools exercise control over students and teachers. To challenge traditional assessment is to challenge the power and control relationships between schools, teachers and students. She reminds us how far some schools have come and how far some have to go to move beyond schooling as the exercise of power and control.

Anthropological perspectives on the assessment of children's language and literacy do not provide an immediate technology that can be bought today and used tomorrow. They don't even provide a checklist. Instead, they challenge us to see children's language and literacy differently, and then to redefine assessment.

REFERENCES

Geertz, C. (1973). *The interpretation of cultures*. New York: Basic Books.
Goodenough, W. (1981). *Culture, language, and society*. Menlo Park, CA: The Benjamin/Cummings Publishing Company.
Peacock, J.L. (1986). *The anthropological lens: Harsh light, soft focus*. New York: Cambridge University Press.

chapter 3
The Language of Testing: An Ethnographic-Sociolinguistic Perspective on Standardized Tests

Catherine Emihovich

Every professional field of study develops its own specialized language and set of practices to enable its practitioners to maintain an aura of expertise and to exclude those outside the field who haven't learned the "codes" by which ideas and intentions are transmitted. Phillips (1983), a sociolinguist who studied the language of lawyers and how new practitioners were socialized into learning the new forms of talk expected of them, referred to this socialization process as "acquiring the cant." Her choice of words lends a religious overtone, like the cant of true believers, suggesting that the new adherents are indoctrinated through professional training into a society that both mystifies those on the outside looking in, and supports its members by providing them with a language where the meaning is inaccessible to all except a chosen few.

Like other professionals, psychometricians, people who construct the *standardized tests*[1] upon which every important academic decision for children's futures is based, and educational psychologists, those

---

[1] I use this term to refer to "tests which have been constructed by test specialists, and which have been administered and scored under standard and uniform testing conditions so that results from different classes and different schools may be compared" (Sax, 1980, p. 17). These tests are commonly used to measure subject area achievement, or

primarily charged with the task of assessing children's performance, have their own highly specialized, arcane language. And teachers who do not understand this language, and how it is used to explain a child's performance, which often results in practices that are detrimental to the child's well-being (especially so in the case of minority children and nonnative speakers of English), cannot persuasively argue that their own assessment of the child's competence, based on countless observations of the child in multiple contexts, should be given credence.

The contrast between what might be called the *natural* language of the teacher in describing a child's competence (e.g., "Johnny has a hard time staying focused on the lesson") and the cold, technical jargon produced by the use of tests (e.g., "Johnny can be characterized as having attention deficit disorder") is striking. In the first case, the teacher makes use of contextual information to judge Johnny's behavior; he or she may recognize that his attention is not captured by the lesson, but that he can spend hours working by himself on the computer. In the second case, the psychologist judges the child with reference to performance on achievement tests that may have no intrinsic meaning to the child, and consequently, he has no reason to perform well. The psychologist may also use terms like *two standard deviations below the mean* or *a recorded stanine score of 1*, and, if the teacher does not understand the concept of norm-referenced testing, he or she is unable to argue in the child's behalf, in that what is observed represents the norm for that child, and that children's performance should not be based on artificially derived standards.

In this chapter I intend to broaden teachers' knowledge of standardized tests by examining them from an ethnographic-sociolinguistic perspective. My argument will be presented in four sections: first, I will contrast the difference between a decontextualized vs. contextualized testing procedure, and illustrate the importance of this difference using several examples from sociolinguistic research; second, I will discuss some of the linguistic assumptions underlying the construction of test items; third, I will reexamine the meanings of specific psychometric terms, especially with reference to the concept of validity; and fourth, I will close by suggesting what actions teachers can take to ensure that their children are not unnecessarily penalized by poor performance on standardized tests.

---

aptitudes like intelligence. In the text, I will specify which type of standardized test I am using to illustrate my points. I would like to thank Janet Pilcher for calling my attention to this distinction.

THE TESTING CONTEXT

When children are asked by "strange people to perform strange actions or answer strange questions in strange rooms or situations,"[2] they are being asked to perform in a decontextualized test situation. In other words, their performance is being assessed in a context quite different from the one in which they would normally perform similar kinds of actions. The assumption made by the test constructors is that, if all extraneous variation (degrees of differences) is removed from the testing situation by having all children complete the same items, and hear the same directions from the same test giver (this is the reason why all standardized tests emphasize that the directions must be followed exactly), then any remaining differences in performance can be explained by underlying differences in ability. I find this assumption very questionable for the simple reason that the test makers have overlooked the fact that the testing situation is an *interactive context* in its own right, a context in which all the participants need to share an understanding of the appropriate norms and expectations of behavior in order to participate fully (Emihovich, 1990). Considerable evidence has been amassed to suggest that this shared understanding does not exist for many young children, minorities, nonnative speakers of English, and/or members outside the mainstream middle class.

A few examples will clarify this point. Margaret Donaldson (1978), a British psychologist, noted that the idea that young children do not acquire the Piagetian principle of conservation before the age of 7 was based on a misinterpretation of children's performance on standard tasks used to determine the child's level of cognitive development. In one such task, the adult shows the child a row of buttons, asks the child "how many buttons are there?" and then, after having moved the buttons further apart, asks the child if there are now more buttons. A typical 5-year-old usually responds that there are "more" buttons. However, when a teddy bear is used to move the buttons apart, the same child will now say that the number of buttons are the same. Donaldson suggested that the difference lies in the fact that a child may assume that the adult was dissatisfied with the child's original answer and consequently moved the buttons, while the child understands perfectly that "a teddy bear can't mess things up." Donaldson provided numerous other examples to illustrate the fact that the

---

[2] This comment was made by Patrick Dickson in his role as discussant of a paper I presented on testing children's behavior at the 1987 annual AERA meeting.

context of the testing situation has a tremendous effect on young children's performance, and that it cannot be taken for granted that they perceive the situation in the same way as do the adults. In order for them to perform well, Donaldson suggested that children need to have tasks make "human sense."

Early childhood and elementary teachers should be the most concerned with this issue regarding the testing of young children for either aptitude or achievement, since it is in the early grades (K–2) when initial decisions about the child's placement in reading and math groups are being made. In fact, it is not uncommon for a child who is experiencing what psychologists call "developmental lags" (meaning the child is not performing as well as classmates of a similar age in relation to an artificially derived norm) to have his or her entire academic placement decided by the end of first grade. Although a child's understanding of what is expected in the test situation may develop over time (many children do acquire "test-wise" skills), by then it may be too late to change the damaging effects upon the child's self-esteem of having been treated as "deficient" in a specific area.

A second example is taken from the work of Labov (1973), a sociolinguist well known for his work on the language patterns of inner-city minority youth. Although Labov spent considerable time in the field to become familiar with the community under study, he still recognized that, as a Caucasian, academic researcher, he would have difficulty in acquiring accurate, naturally occurring forms of talk from adolescents. To compensate for this problem, he enlisted the services of a trusted African American man from the same community. However, in a famous interview situation, even this adult was unsuccessful in getting individual boys to describe the linguistic game, "playing the dozens," until the situation was changed to resemble that of a party, complete with several people and potato chips and soft drinks. Labov persuasively argued that assumptions made by several researchers (Bereiter & Englemann, 1966; Jensen, 1969) concerning the "impoverished" language of inner-city minority students was based on these same students' performance on standardized tests where the students may have been reluctant to reveal themselves to strangers, or where they were simply playing a game with the researchers. From their perspective, "jiving" with the researcher would have been an appropriate act, and they may not have realized (or cared) that this behavior was read quite differently by the tester. Many teachers have undoubtedly had the experience of attempting to convince their minority students to take classrooms tests seriously; how much more difficult is the task when the students see nationally distributed standardized tests as even more removed from the context of their daily lives.

A third point with reference to the testing situation as an interactive context is that human dynamics take precedence over the antiseptic delivery of directions that test makers assume will occur. By providing standardized directions that every teacher is expected to follow to the letter, the test makers hope to reduce random sources of error arising from some children receiving more help than others. However, what the test makers have failed to consider is that information can be carried on nonverbal channels as well as verbal ones. I have watched videotapes of people conducting oral language assessment, and have seen the testers provide unconscious behavioral cues as to the correct answer. For example, when a tester was asking a child to place an object "under the table," to determine if the child understood the concept of *under*, at the same time she was speaking she was also moving her hand under the table. Furthermore, an extensive analysis of these videotapes by Hugh Mehan and his associates at the teacher education program at the University of California at San Diego revealed that the transmission of this kind of information was not random, but patterned in relation to the child's status. Testers were more likely to provide this assistance when the child was from a Caucasian, middle-class background than from a minority, low-income background.

The likelihood that children will benefit from receiving this indirect assistance, or that they will recognize certain aspects of the test situation as congruent with their experiences in other settings, is a direct function of their sociocultural background. Generally speaking, Caucasian, middle-class children (I say *Caucasian*, although I agree with LeCompte's [1985, p. 114] assertion that the term *educational mainstream* has more to do with culture and class-induced congruity with school-imposed attitudes and behaviors than with ethnicity per se) find most school experiences, including test situations, to be culturally congruent with the experiences they have had at home. A good example is found in the work of noted educational ethnographer Heath (1983), who studied the home–school discontinuity in the lives of minority and Caucasian children in the rural and urban South. She discovered that even a simple task like asking questions was overlaid with cultural significance. Caucasian, middle-class children are accustomed to having their mothers read to them and ask questions about the story, questions which the child is expected to answer even though he or she knows quite clearly that the mother already "knows" the answer. This same pattern of interaction is duplicated in the classroom, where the teacher asks questions to which he or she too knows the answers. In contrast, many low-income minority children only hear adults ask questions to which the adult does not know the answer, as a legitimate request for information, and consequently, they fail to answer teacher-generated questions because they perceive them as superfluous. Other test behaviors, such as asking follow-up questions to confirm a child's response, may be read by minority children as unnecessary, since they have already answered the first time.

All of the above examples illustrate the point made earlier that the test context is interactive in nature, and that the behaviors are negotiated within a given framework. The same linguistic constructs that Green (1983) suggested apply to teaching as a linguistic process can be applied equally well to testing situations: (a) face-to-face interaction is rule governed, (b) meaning is constructed and signalled during interaction, and (c) classrooms [or test situations—insert mine] are communicative environments. The fact that these constructs apply does not preclude the use of tests, but it does mean that ethnographers are more reluctant to accept test results on their face value without asking substantive questions about who is being tested, under what conditions, and how the results should be interpreted.

A contextualized assessment process offers a sharp contrast to decontextualized testing procedures. Here I draw upon the excellent work conducted by Taylor (1988), who has developed the concept of ethnographic evaluation of children's performance, particularly with reference to literacy acquisition. As she noted,

> In adopting the ethnographic perspective of the social construction of behavior, the oversimplified pronouncements based on traditional evaluative procedures have to be rejected or redefined. Instead of analyzing "in-the-head" knowledge of children we have to examine the environments in which that knowledge is applied.... Essentially it means taking the ascribed "problems" out of their heads and relocating them within the socially constructed frameworks of their daily lives. (p. 68)

In this model, the children and their parents become "interpreters" of their experiences to help the evaluator understand the child's behavior in context. The same perspective can be applied to the classroom situation, where it is now apparent through extensive studies (Cook-Gumperz, 1986; Erickson, 1982; Green, 1983; Mehan, 1979) that academic performance is a joint construction involving both the teacher's and students' efforts, and not just simply the result of what abilities rest within the child's head. Through extensive documentation produced by ethnographic observations and interviews, the complexity of a child's behavior can be captured in ways that no single test score can ever hope to match. This knowledge can then successfully be used to provide the child with an optimal learning environment, rather than making recommendations based on decontextualized testing procedures that often devalue what the child can be expected to accomplish.

One objection that many school personnel (especially administrators) are likely to raise with the approach suggested by Taylor (1988) centers on the time-consuming nature of ethnographic assessment, compared to the ease of using standardized test batteries. While acknowledging that this is not a trivial problem, I would argue in turn that this objection has both a manifest and hidden agenda to it. The manifest agenda focuses on the issue of time management, and I believe that, as the use of computers become increasingly widespread, with powerful database tools that can record both qualitative and quantitative forms of information, teachers will be able to maintain extensive records on children's progress, and to print reports that utilize narrative descriptions as well as test scores.

However, the hidden agenda centers on the metaphor used to define education in most schools. Lakoff and Johnson (1980) noted that metaphors are deep seated in nature and are used to structure the way we think about the world. The guiding metaphor for schools in our society is the idea of education as industrial production; as Marshall (1988) perceptively noted, much of the research on academic work in classrooms and classroom "management" is based on the concept of school as "work." In this model, what students do is considered "output," and their learning is treated as a "product" which can be measured using large-scale testing programs that are both efficient and cost effective. As an alternative to this metaphor, Marshall (1988) proposed substituting the concept of school as a "learning place." This conceptualization would entail several dramatic changes, such as setting goals that focus on the acquisition of knowledge and skills by the learner for intrinsic benefits rather than extrinsic rewards, and changes in authority relations between teachers and students that are based on "expertise and knowledge *to be shared or developed* and on the *desire to help individuals acquire or construct knowledge* (Marshall, 1988, p. 14; emphasis in original). More importantly, this model would also entail changes in assessment, in that narrative descriptions would be needed to demonstrate that a process oriented approach to learning results in complex and multifaceted outcomes, which are achieved slowly over time, not in incremental bits that are easily broken down and measured.

Even if the testing situation were approached from a contextualized perspective, it would not be sufficient from an ethnographic standpoint to ensure that the meaning of the test items was understood in the same way by both the tester and the child being tested. In the next section, I examine some of the linguistic assumptions that need to be considered in interpreting test item responses, and contrast them to the psychometric assumptions underlying test item construction.

LINGUISTIC ASSUMPTIONS UNDERLYING TEST ITEMS

In constructing a well-designed standardized test, one which is intended to be given to a nationwide sample of children, the test makers need to be certain that the test items are not biased against any one cultural group. If it can be proven that a group of children are unlikely to have had experience or knowledge of a particular concept because of their background, then it can be argued that their poor performance on that item reflects this lack of knowledge, and not a lack of ability in understanding the concept. A good example is the question "What is a ruby?" which appeared on the original Wechsler Intelligence Scale for Children (WISC), and which was later dropped on the revised version (WISC-R). An analysis of group differences on this item demonstrated that low-income children were far more likely to answer incorrectly because they lacked familiarity with this concept, either because their parents did not own jewelry of this type, or because they had not read fairy tales of princesses who wore diamonds and rubies. To their credit, many test companies have become more sensitive to the issue of cultural bias and have revised tests to take into account cultural differences in experience.

However, the problem becomes more complex when the items involve not just knowledge of cultural objects, but also a reasoning process that requires the student to accept underlying assumptions about the meaning of the item in question. To examine this issue in detail, I will analyze people who will make good classroom teachers. This item was selected because it is one which many minority students tend to answer incorrectly.

Item: Of the following behavior management techniques, which is likely to be the most effective in maintaining goal-directed behavior in students?

A.   Student receive negative consequences for any off-task behavior.

B.   A major reward is given to the entire class once all have reached the goal.

C.   Reinforcement is given periodically regardless of work progress.

D.   Increments of progress toward the goal by each student are reinforced.

E.   Students are encouraged to work at their own pace.

What are the major assumptions made in this question? First, it assumes that students will have been exposed to behavioristic learning theory principles proposed by Skinner. While this assumption is not too difficult to satisfy, because the majority of educational psychology texts used in major colleges of education include a chapter on behaviorism, it still could be argued that some students, notably minority students in small colleges, may lack exposure to these theories. However, that argument is less important than the next one, which is that students not only need to have been exposed to this type of learning theory, they also need to accept without question the tacit value premise of behaviorism, that principles of learning derived from studies of animals (primarily rats and pigeons) can be applied to human behavior. In Skinner's theory, the optimal way to encourage an animal to reach a target goal (set by the researcher, of course) is to reinforce successive approximations of the behavior that will result in achieving the goal. This principle is known as *shaping*, and it was very successfully used by Skinner to teach pigeons to dance. He would wait until the pigeon performed an action that was close to the target behavior, reinforce it, wait for another similar action, reinforce that, and so forth. Naturally, it never occurred to the pigeons to wonder why they should want to do this, nor did it occur to them to engage in off-task behavior once the connection had been made between "dancing" and reinforcement. If the reader has been following the argument up to this point, he or she will have realized by now that the correct answer to the above item is "D."

The problem with Skinner's theory is that the parallel to human behavior cannot be clearly drawn, because as every teacher knows, students do often wonder why they are being asked to perform certain tasks, and they often have their own behavioral agendas that conflict with the teacher's agenda. In the case of minority students, there is persuasive evidence that they bring a completely different interpretation to this item. This evidence was obtained from the work carried out by a distinguished group of sociolinguists who were asked by the Educational Testing Service to review items to determine if they were biased against minority group members. The researchers asked several minority students to answer the questions and to discuss their reasoning process used to arrive at the answers.

The response of an African American male teacher is typical; he noted that he would have selected "B" because he liked the idea of a "major reward" being given to everybody because they all worked on-task, a response which emphasizes the value of cooperation. He also stated that "A" appealed to him because he felt that students need to be aware that getting off-task has negative consequences. Although he recognized that students need to be given positive feedback for their performance, he felt it more important in the type of classrooms he taught in that students knew the consequences for bad behavior. Interestingly, this teacher did have enough meta awareness of the implications of the question to state that he thought the answer the testers probably wanted was "D," but he disagreed with the idea that the most effective way to obtain students' goal-directed behavior was to use only positive reinforcement. He acknowledged that he felt somewhat frustrated that the question required an either/or choice; he would have preferred most of all to have had available an answer that combined both positive and negative consequences.

The point to be stressed is that this student was unwilling to accept the major value premise of the theory, particularly since his cultural experience led him to believe that students don't necessarily behave the way the theory predicts, that positive reinforcement is always better than negative consequences. Another perspective on this issue is that he wanted to use personal experience as a gauge by which to judge the issue of 'effective behavior-management techniques,' and not abstract theory. As an added commentary, when he had to answer questions dealing with issues of interpersonal behavior, where personal knowledge would be more relevant, he was able to identify the correct answer. I suspect that many minority students who fail to perform well on entry-level teacher tests share his perspective; they are simply unwilling to accept the primacy of abstract theorizing about behavior derived from the ideas of academicians in lieu of their own judgments about what works in classrooms. The fact that he was aware of the answer the testers wanted suggests another interpretation; perhaps other students like him are unwilling (or not cynical enough) to play the game of "guess the answer," a game students need to learn to become successful in taking tests.

The issue being debated is the concept of validity, which has quite a different meaning from a psychometric viewpoint as contrasted to an ethnographic viewpoint. This difference is discussed in more detail in the next section.

PSYCHOMETRIC VS. ETHNOGRAPHIC VALIDITY

The above example was presented to illustrate the point that the construction of test items is a far more complex process than typical measurement textbooks describe. Instead of holding test makers accountable to meeting linguistic assumptions about how different groups approach the meaning of items, based on their cultural experiences, we allow them to hold the items accountable to psychometric assumptions as to whether the item is an adequate sampling from a pool of items representing the domain, or construct, under study. All too often, the technical discussion of issues related to item analysis (the process of determining whether an item correlates well to the total score has good discriminant value, and is neither too easy nor too hard) takes on a surrealist air, in that the items themselves become "real," and not the attitudes, beliefs, and cognitive processes of the people who responded to them. In other words, the items are seen as having an "objective reality" in that people will either respond to them correctly or incorrectly, and the question of validity in the psychometric sense (do the items measure or correspond in some way, to the construct they are intended to measure) is assessed in relation to how the items perform in a complex statistical procedure known as *factor analysis.*

In the case of a very basic skill that is being evaluated (e.g., math computation, $2 + 2 = 4$)[3] this argument works, because it would be difficult to argue in opposition that children, depending on their cultural background, could interpret that item differently. But in the case of items purporting to measure more complex skills ("effective classroom management"), the "objective reality" doesn't exist; there is no definitive standard (or right or wrong answer) as to what constitutes *effective classroom management,* and what we are left with is a subjective construction of what that item means within the framework of specific cultural experiences.

Test makers would offer two defenses to the argument I just presented. First, they would claim that the population of students used to construct the norms for all standardized tests are carefully selected to ensure that all types of cultural and ethnic groups are represented. In this respect, they are correct; no reputable test maker today would

---

[3] In speaking to several math educators who take a social constructivist view of mathematics learning, I realized this assumption was incorrect. Sandra Atkins helped me understand how students could construct the relationship that $2 + 2 = 6$, depending on the mode of presentation.

publish a test that had not met this requirement. However, sampling from a broad population base does not ensure that biased tests items will be detected. To understand why, teachers need to know how biased test items are identified. The typical procedure is to divide the scores of all those persons who have taken the test into two distributions: those who scored above the 50th percentile or better, and those who scored below the 50th percentile. If, on any particular item, the persons scoring in the top half were predominately Caucasian, while the persons scoring in the bottom half were predominately minority, then that item could be identified as culturally biased. If the two distributions were statistically equivalent in terms of ethnicity (I say *statistically equivalent* since adjustments have to be made for the fact that minority students proportionally account for about 20% of the testing population), then the item would not be flagged as being biased, because each distribution would have contained a balanced proportion of each ethnic group. This procedure works quite well if the assumption is met that the persons within each distribution are essentially similar in performance.

However, in the example I previously used of the minority teacher responding to a test item, it is clear this assumption is not necessarily true. Let us say for the sake of argument that this minority teacher's overall score put him in the top half of the distribution. But on this particular item, had he given the answer he wanted to choose, he would have been scored wrong. What can easily happen (and generally does), is that his overall performance relative to Caucasian teachers taking the test might have been about 20 points lower. Another perspective on this issue is that, if we take just the top half of the distribution and examine the ethnic composition of students at each percentile point, what we are likely to find is that, at the 99th percentile, virtually all students are Caucasian; at the 98th percentile, perhaps a few minority students are included, and it may not be until about the 85th percentile (approximately 1 standard deviation below) that we find included a substantial number of minority students who comprise a proportional part of the top half of the distribution. For text makers, the lack of minority students in the extreme upper percentiles does not necessarily reflect cultural bias in items; it simply reflects underlying differences in ability.

In fact, the test makers would use this information as their second defense: that one way of establishing psychometric validity is to determine concurrent validity (the correlation between performance on one measure with that on another) and predictive validity (how well one test score predicts performance on another). The fact that minority students' scores may be represented in the top half of the distribution but clustered around the 85th percentile (1 standard deviation below) parallels their performance on standard IQ tests, where they also score approximately one standard deviation below Caucasian. Thus, performance on one artificially constructed measure, and the resulting correlation is used as evidence that the first test is a valid or "true" measure of the trait or ability in question. Yet, as I previously demonstrated, the minority teacher would have scored wrong on that item, not because he didn't understand, but because he understood too well; he simply disagreed with the reasoning underlying the question. But none of the complex reasoning strategies he used are counted as part of the "right" answer, and if his final score puts him at the 85th percentile, the items he got wrong are treated as differences in ability, not differences in cultural perceptions. If some Caucasian teachers in the top half of the distribution got this item wrong too (as some undoubtedly did), then the item would not be flagged as biased, because the statistical procedure is based only on differences in total scores, and cannot be used to identify differences in reasoning on individual items.

In contrast, an ethnographer puts an entirely different emphasis on the meaning of validity. As Hammersley and Atkinson (1983) have indicated, there are at least two ways in which ethnographers approach the problem of construct validity. First, "what is involved is not simply finding indicators for a concept. Rather, there is an interplay between finding indicators and conceptualizing the analytic categories" (p. 185). In other words, an ethnographer interested in measuring or assessing some form of learning would not simply ask the question, "What behaviors are associated with this concept?" Instead, he or she would also be interested in asking, "Under what conditions can I expect to see these behaviors?" and more importantly, "What do the participants describe as learning behaviors?" Responses to these questions would be used to reshape and modify the instrument as it was being developed.

A second difference Hammersley and Atkinson noted lay in the difference between quantitative researchers' desire to identify standard indicators for concepts, and the ethnographer's unwillingness to do so. For example, if the concept is reading comprehension, a standard indicator on a standardized test is that children should be able to read passages and answer questions, all within a specified time frame. Again we see the pervasive influence of behavioristic learning theory, which states that, if all children receive the same stimulus (the test item) and are tested under the same conditions, any differences in performance can be explained by differences in ability. As I noted earlier, this assumption works quite well for pigeons, which are incapable of conceiving of alternative possibilities, but not for children (or humans), who bring their own social construction of what "reading" means into the test situation. An ethnographer would also be concerned with a much broader definition of reading comprehension, and would seek other sources of information to probe students' understanding of text. They would not be content to accept a student's score on a reading comprehension test as the sole indicator of "reading comprehension."

What the above discussion demonstrated is that from an ethnographic-sociolinguistic perspective, the meanings derived from the testing situation are of paramount concern. As Hymes (1977) pointed out:

> It is in the nature of meanings to be subject to change, reinterpretation, re-creation. One has to think of people, not as the intersection of vectors of age, sex, race, class, income, and occupation alone, but also as beings making sense out of disparate experience, using reason to maintain a sphere of integrity in an immediate world. (p. 26)

When test makers stop thinking of children and begin thinking of item responses, when they stop thinking of learning and begin thinking of scores, their language is a reflection of this behavior. It is the ethnographer's task to "deconstruct" the meanings the test makers have created to restore the notion of human potential inherent in every child. But teachers, too, have a special role to play in this process, and some of the actions they can take are detailed in the last section of this chapter.

RECOMMENDATIONS FOR TEACHERS

In making these recommendations, teachers need to be aware that, for the time being, standardized tests are a cultural and political reality. They are a cultural reality in the sense that American society is test oriented; we want to have a tangible measure of what it is our children are expected to know *in comparison with their peers*. I emphasize the last part, because, as McDermott and Hood (1977) have noted, "American concern for documenting what children know appears as much organized by the pressures to sort out achievers from nonachievers as the desire to equip every citizen with a necessary stock of knowledge at hand" (p. 233). Tests are also a political reality in the sense that state legislators view them as a means of legitimating the educational system, of attracting new businesses to areas with high test scores, and of justifying the need for more funding to troubled districts.

However, these facts should not lead teachers to believe that they are powerless when confronted with standardized testing programs in their district. At issue is the question of what information about a child's achievement is valid, and how can it be obtained from other sources besides standardized tests. In fact, teachers can adopt a wide variety of strategies to deemphasize the power of tests in children's lives, with the strongest weapon being the teacher's professional judgment. These strategies are described in greater detail in the next section.

Use of Teacher Judgments

The first step teachers can make is to refrain from reviewing standardized test data in a child's folder until the child has been observed in multiple contexts within the classroom over time, at least for the first few months. Given the intense pressure to slot children into instructional groups as early as possible, a realistic course of action would be for teachers to use their own assessment instruments to gain a sense of the child's level of development, but they should not look at standardized test scores until they have made their own observations. Not only would this practice prevent children from being unfairly labeled as "slow" learners, it would also help establish the primacy of teacher judgments in contextualized settings over the test score observations in decontextualized situations.

In some cases, additional, hidden advantages can exist for children beyond not placing labels on their performance. As a former high school English teacher, where I routinely waited 2 months into the semester before examining folders, I recall a situation where I realized that one of my students, a ninth grader in a basic English class, was having greater difficulty in reading than the other students. When I went to the guidance office to look up his record, I saw that his IQ score placed him in the severely retarded category. After having observed this student for several weeks, I knew this score could not possibly be valid, and I pointed out the discrepancy to one of the counselors. He arranged to have the student retested, and it was learned that the first score was a score from another test which had been entered into the wrong column. Imagine the consequences if I had accepted the score at face value before ever meeting him, and insisted that he be transferred into a special education class. Instead, I was able to give him more appropriate instruction, and he finished a successful year with his classmates. One student, one small victory for the teacher, but one with a giant impact in a student's life.

In keeping with the emphasis on teacher judgments, teachers can also acquire the skills to become more systematic in their observations and documentation of student progress. This aspect is part of the movement known as the "teacher as researcher," where teachers utilize ethnographic techniques to determine patterns in children's behaviors and to analyze these patterns in relation to the social context of the classroom (Goswami & Stillman, 1987). As Strahan (1983) noted, "ethnographic procedures have the potential to help teachers discover more about their intuitive insights" (p. 203). The point to keep in mind is that teachers can discuss other aspects of a child's performance that are not revealed by test scores. By becoming more skilled as ethnographic observers themselves, teachers can conceptualize and document alternative perspectives on children's learning that may offset negative information acquired through standardized tests.

As teachers systematize their process for collecting information, they can take advantage of powerful microcomputers and more user friendly software to develop teacher generated databases which contain learning profiles on individual children. These profiles can be shared among teachers, and could also include detailed information on what instructional strategies are most appropriate for a particular child. In one sense, technology can incorporate features of the informal network teachers already have in place in most schools, that of sharing information in the teachers' lounge. While there would be an initial learning curve to become familiar with the hardware and software, teachers will find that this new technology can greatly reduce the amount of time they spend on paperwork, and that it makes possible the kind of careful documentation that provides a more comprehensive assessment of a child's performance.

A fourth step teachers can take is to follow a procedure Wolcott (1988) described as "destandardizing" the tests. He was referring to a case where a teacher on an Indian reservation would use old copies of standardized tests to teach the students how to answer questions of this type. Every teacher without much trouble should be able to get copies of old achievement tests to help students to become more familiar with the item format, and to acquaint students with test-wise strategies such as not spending too much time on a single answer, answering all the questions they know first, and so on. While following these procedures may not raise scores to any significant extent, it will help reduce some of the anxiety students feel, especially in the younger grades.

In addition to focusing on testing strategies, teachers can also use test items as a teaching tool. In this case, the emphasis is not so much on teaching students to identify the "right" answer as it is on getting them to think more critically about what skills or information the items are testing. I can illustrate this point with a sample item taken from a fourth-grade language arts workbook commonly used in most schools. In this item, the children were asked to identify the sentence in which the word *cauldron* has been used incorrectly:

1. The cauldron has been cooking for an hour;
2. I hung the heavy cauldron over the fire;
3. William Shakespeare's play *Macbeth* begins with three witches dancing around a huge cauldron; and
4. Drop in a few carrots when the stew in the cauldron starts to boil.

The problem with this item is that all the sentences are semantically correct; each one conveys meaning that is easily understood. The teacher in this instance should look over sentences like this in advance and teach children to recognize how meaning is conveyed, and not look just for the "right" answer that exists in some test constructor's head.[4]

What I have just described are steps teachers can take in exercising their professional judgment to determine the kinds of information useful for assessing children's performance, in documenting information to construct longitudinal databases which can be shared, and in helping children become more familiar with existing test forms. However, I believe it is also imperative that teachers develop a knowledge base in the area of tests and measurement, for reasons explained below.

Knowledge Base on Tests and Measurements

The first suggestion I have is one that many teachers are not likely to find appealing, but it's one I believe is necessary, both for understanding the language of testing as well as for improving classroom tests. As part of their coursework, either at the undergraduate or graduate level, teachers should take a basic measurement class that covers the use of standardized tests and helps teachers construct their own assessment measures. Most teachers tend to avoid a course like this, because of the mathematics involved (although there are very few calculations to be performed), but it places them at a real disadvantage

---

[4] I saw this item when helping my son with his homework, and I wrote a note to the teacher saying that he couldn't select the "right" answer because we couldn't figure out which one it was. He didn't get marked off for the item, but I still don't know what the correct answer is.

when speaking to guidance counselors, district evaluators, or school psychologists. The best analogy here is visiting a foreign country without knowing the language; you can get by if you find someone to translate, but you never communicate your ideas as well as if you spoke the language, too. Mastery of the discourse of measurement would also empower teachers to speak more assertively on their students' behalf.

There are two other advantages of taking a course in this area. One is that teachers will learn how to construct their own tests, a feat that is more difficult to do well than most teachers think. The most important aspect of test construction is to identify a domain of knowledge, and then to consider what items or task are the best way to assess whether that knowledge has been acquired by the child. This process is known as *establishing construct validity*, which Messick defined as:

> An integrated evaluative judgment of the degree to which empirical evidence and theoretical rationales support the *adequacy* and *appropriateness* of *inferences* and *actions* based on test scores or other modes of assessment. (1989, p. 5)

In other words, a teacher must consider whether his or her test measures the child's knowledge or ability in ways that permits others to assume that the measure is an accurate reflection of underlying competencies, and that they can use this information for diagnostic and instructional purposes. If teachers acquired knowledge of psychometric procedures for establishing construct validity while maintaining an ethnographic perspective on validity in terms of the *meaningfulness* of test items to both the child's cultural and social background and the situated context of instruction, then perhaps classroom assessment could become the primary evaluative tool rather than standardized tests.

A second advantage of teachers taking a measurement course is that they will be able to understand better the information provided about the test items, and to use them for teaching purposes. Very few teachers are aware that they can request a detailed item profile from the testing company that gives a comprehensive breakdown of each item on the test in terms of the skill that is being tested, and how well children are doing on any particular item in relation to children within that age group. To give an example, I requested this information to help teachers at a local school evaluate their language arts program. We discovered that reading comprehension was assessed through eight items, and that, on three of these items, the performance of first graders was below national norms. By having this type of information available, teachers can pinpoint specific weaknesses in their program and consider alternative strategies for instruction.

However, there is another side to this story. A second use of this detailed item profile is that teachers can decide whether these items are the most appropriate way to assess reading. I emphasize this last point, since several teachers were surprised to learn that, on this particular reading test, only eight items dealt with comprehension of text; the rest of the items focused on discrete skills like letter recognition (15 items), auditory word rhymes (9 items), sound-letter relations (9 items), adding sounds (9 items), taking sounds away (9 items), blending (9 items), and recognizing words in sentences (9 items). Thus, on a 77-item test, approximately 10% was devoted to reading for meaning; the rest was testing the presumed skills needed to learn to read. Since these teachers were using a whole language approach, they realized immediately that their children would be at a disadvantage in taking this test, since they did not emphasize the breakdown of skills. But by becoming more aware of what skills were being tested, they were in a better position to challenge some of the assumptions underlying the construction of these items, and to argue (successfully, I might add) that their program needed an alternative means of assessment to demonstrate how well their students read.

This last point leads to another suggestion for teachers in that they should attempt to acquire information on new tests and assessment procedures which are being developed to accommodate the changing nature of learning and instruction. In the area of early childhood education, for example, the researchers involved in Project Spectrum have developed an innovative set of procedures to assess young children's competencies in a naturally occurring school setting, rather than an artificially constructed testing situation (Wexler-Sherman, Gardner, & Feldman, 1988). Exciting work is also being conducted in the area of dynamic assessment (Lidz, 1987), which builds on Vygotsky's (1978) concept of the *zone of proximal development* to assess the child's potential for learning in collaboration with others. In the models currently being developed, learning is viewed as occurring within a dynamic interaction process rather than as being a static product of direct instruction alone (Minick, 1987). Although the field is relatively new, not only has a burgeoning literature developed, but also a schism among researchers in terms of how Vygotsky's concepts are to be realized in assessment practices. The arguments on both sides are too long to be summarized here; the reader is encouraged to pursue them elsewhere (see Brown & Ferrara, 1985; Campione, Brown, Ferrara, & Bryant, 1984; Feuerstein, 1980; Rogoff & Wertsch, 1984; Wertsch, 1985).

Another encouraging development is that new tests are being developed in conjunction with the whole language approach to reading and writing. For example, a new reading test developed by researchers at the Center for the Study of Reading and the University of Illinois at Chicago for the Illinois State Board of Education is currently being piloted in Grades 3, 8, and 11 (Valencia, Pearson, Reeve, & Shanahan, 1988). In one sense, it represents a compromise solution, because the test still requires that children identify several "correct" answers from the testers' perspective, and it is still norm referenced in terms of performance. However, by its use of a more "natural" language and the possibility of multiple answers, it may help drive the curriculum in terms of teachers constructing their own tests like this.[5] As we work toward the goal of becoming less fixated on norm-referenced tests to inform us of what children know and can be expected to do, the movement away from a single "correct" answer is a good beginning, but certainly not the end of what still needs to be done.

CONCLUSION

As noted earlier in this chapter, historically the dominant metaphor for schooling was derived from industrial production and emphasized the idea that learning is a quantifiable product that is easily measured. In more recent views, learning is conceived as a socially mediated process where children construct their knowledge of the world with the help of teachers who provide the necessary scaffolding to assist children in mastering more complex ideas. As both researchers and practitioners collaborate in developing this new concept of learning that better utilizes principles of children's development, alternative models for assessment that are not product oriented will be needed as well. The movement toward using alternative assessments that rely heavily on teacher judgments is already in force (Maeroff, 1991). What I hope this chapter has demonstrated is that teachers today have the opportunity to influence the next direction classroom assessment will take, and that an ethnographic sociolinguistic perspective provides teachers with ways to challenge the conventional testing methods currently in effect.

---

[5] I want to thank one of my graduate students, Pam Engler, for this insight into beneficial aspects of the test.

REFERENCES

Bereiter, C., & Englemann, S. (1966). *Teaching disadvantaged children in the preschool.* Englewood Cliffs, NJ: Prentice-Hall.

Brown, A.L., & Ferrara, R.A. (1985). Diagnosing zones of proximal development. In J.V. Wertsch (Ed.), *Culture, communication, and cognition: Vygotskian perspectives* (pp. 273–305). New York: Cambridge University Press.

Campione, J.C., Brown, A.L., Ferrara, R.A., & Bryant, N.R. (1984). The zone of proximal development: Implications for individual differences and learning. In B. Rogoff & J.V. Wertsch (Eds.), *Children's learning in the "zone of proximal development"* (pp. 77–92). San Francisco: Jossey-Bass.

Cook-Gumperz, J. (1986). *The social construction of literacy.* New York: Cambridge University Press.

Donaldson, M. (1978). *Children's minds.* New York: Norton.

Emihovich, C. (1990). Ask no questions: Sociolinguistic variations in experimental and testing contexts. *Linguistics in Education, 2,* 165–183.

Erickson, F. (1982). Taught cognitive learning in its immediate environments: A neglected topic in the anthropology of education. *Anthropology & Education Quarterly, 13,* 149–180.

Feuerstein, R. (1980). *Instrumental enrichment: An intervention program for cognitive modifiability.* Baltimore: University Park Press.

Goswami, D., & Stillman, P.R. (Eds.). (1987). *Reclaiming the classroom: Teacher research as an agency for change.* Upper Montclair, NJ: Boynton Cook.

Green, J.L. (1983). Research on teaching as a linguistic process: A state of the art. In E. Gordon (Ed.), *Review of research in education* (pp. 151–252). Washington, DC: American Educational Research Association.

Hammersley, M., & Atkinson, P. (1983). *Ethnography: Principles in practice.* London: Tavistock.

Heath, S. (1983). *Ways with words: Language, life and work in communities and classrooms.* New York: Cambridge University Press.

Hymes, D. (1977). What is ethnography? In P. Gilmore & A.A. Glatthorn (Eds.), *Children in and out of school* (pp. 21–32). Washington, DC: Center for Applied Linguistics.

Jensen, A. (1969). How much can we boost academic achievement and IQ? *Harvard Educational Review, 39,* 1–123.

Labov, W. (1973). *Language in the inner city.* Philadelphia: University of Pennsylvania Press.

Lakoff, G., & Johnson, M. (1980). *Metaphors we live by.* Chicago: University of Chicago Press.

LeCompte, M.D. (1985). Defining the differences: Cultural subgroups within the educational mainstream. *The Urban Review, 17,* 111–127.

Lidz, C.S. (Ed.). (1987). *Dynamic assessment: An interactional approach to evaluating learning potential.* New York: Guilford Press.

Maeroff, G.B. (1991). Assessing alternative assessment. *Phi Delta Kappan, 73*(4), 272–281.

Marshall, H. (1988). Work or learning: Implications of classroom metaphors. *Educational Researcher, 17*, 9–16.

McDermott, R.P., & Hood, L. (1977). Institutionalized psychology and the ethnography of schooling. In P. Gilmore & A.A. Glatthorn (Eds.), *Children in and out of school* (pp. 232–249). Washington, DC: Center for Applied Linguistics.

Mehan, H. (1979). *Learning lessons.* Cambridge, MA: Harvard University Press.

Messick, S. (1989). Meaning and values of test validation: The science and ethics of assessment. *Educational Researcher, 18*(2), 5–11.

Minick, N. (1987). Implications of Vygotsky's theories. In C.S. Lidz (Ed.), *Dynamic assessment: An interactional approach to evaluating learning potential* (pp. 116–140). New York: Guilford Press.

Phillips, S. (1983). The language socialization of lawyers: Acquiring the "cant." In G. Spindler (Ed.), *Doing the ethnography of schooling* (pp. 176–211). New York: Holt, Rinehart & Winston.

Rogoff, B., & Wertsch, J.V. (Eds.). (1984). *Children's learning in the "zone of proximal development."* San Francisco: Jossey-Bass.

Sax, G. (1980). *Principles of educational and psychological measurement and evaluation.* Belmont, CA: Wadsworth Publishing.

Steffenson, M.S., & Gutherie, L.F. (1984). The effect of situation on the verbalization: A study of black inner-city children. *Discourse Processes, 7*, 1–10.

Strahan, D.B. (1983). The teacher and ethnography: Observational sources of information for educators. *The Elementary School Journal, 83*(3), 195–203.

Taylor, D. (1988). Ethnographic educational evaluation for children, families, and schools. *Theory Into Practice, 27*, 67–76.

Valencia, S.W., Pearson, P.D., Reeve, R., & Shanahan, T. (1988). *Illinois goal assessment program* (Grade 3). Illinois State Board of Education (unpublished sample).

Vygotsky, L.S. (1978). *Mind in society.* (Edited by M. Cole, V. John-Steiner, S. Scribner, & E. Souberman). Cambridge, MA: Harvard University Press.

Wertsch, J.V. (Ed.). (1985). *Culture, communication and cognition: Vygotskian perspectives.* Cambridge: Cambridge University Press.

Wexler-Sherman, C., Gardner, H., & Feldman, D.H. (1988). A pluralistic view of early assessment: The Project Spectrum approach. *Theory Into Practice, 27*(1), 77–83.

Wolcott, H.F. (1988). Ethnographic research in education. In R.M. Jaeger (Ed.), *Complementary methods for research in education* (pp. 187–216). Washington, DC: American Educational Research Association.

chapter 4
You Can't Get There From Here

David Bloome

As I see things, it is not possible to have an anthropological approach to the assessment of language and literacy if assessment is defined as measurement of individuals' language and literacy performance or competency. To assess an individual is to ask questions about the psychological states (e.g., cognitive, affective) of an individual, usually in comparison to other individuals. Such questions are, in my opinion, antithetical to an anthropological perspective of human behavior (see also McDermott & Hood, 1982). Rather than asking about individual performance, questions are asked about how the group (community, school, classroom, instructional group, peer group, family, etc.) functions, structures its social relationships, the "world view" it holds, how it defines what it is doing, the rationale the group gives to what it is doing, the ways or standards for acting, thinking, feeling, believing, and valuing held by the group—in brief, questions are asked about the culture(s) of various kinds of groups and subgroups and their activities. In part, the questions generated from an anthropological perspective derive from a view of human behavior that holds as fundamental an inseparability of an individual from cultural activity, cultural interpretation, and cultural context (see Bloome, 1991; Green & Bloome, 1983; Guthrie & Hall, 1984; Heath, 1982; Hymes, 1980; Schieffelin & Gilmore, 1986; among others, for the application of anthropological perspectives to language and literacy in educational settings).

Recent books and articles by educational anthropologists have raised serious questions about current language and literacy assessment practices (e.g., Emihorich, 1990; Trueba, 1988). They have highlighted the cultural biases inherent in the assessment tools educators use, and they have shown the subtle, ethnocentric assessments often made during teacher–student interaction (e.g., Collins, 1987; Cook-Gumperz, Gumperz, & Simons, 1981; Gilmore, 1987; Hymes, 1981). Perhaps most importantly, they have raised important philosophical and political questions about the nature and role of assessment within classrooms and schools. They have argued for broader definitions of assessment that focus attention on the various social and cultural contexts of students activities (e.g., the classroom context, school context, community context, etc.) rather than on students themselves.

Unfortunately, it is exactly the kinds of questions that focus attention on individuals, questions that separate students from the cultural contexts of their lives both in school and out, that educators all too often ask in assessing language and literacy. Regardless of any benevolence in our intention, to ask questions about how well individuals are doing is to conceive of education, achievement, and assessment in ways that are essentially incompatible with an anthropological view of educational processes, because it is to view people as acting outside of culture—as if that were possible.

To make matters worse, when culture is considered in educational assessment, it is usually treated as if it were a character trait, cognitive structure, or background information. But culture is not an attribute of individuals and is not reducible to cognitive structure or background information, any more than a dance is reducible to someone's knowledge about how the steps go. A dance is in the doing, in the broad, tangled complexity of meanings involved in dancing. While there is no dance without people, there can be knowledge about dance steps, knowledge about music, even previous experience in dancing, without there being a dance. To try to understand a dance (one that is ongoing) by asking how much the dancers know about the dance steps, or how much they are learning, is not only absurd, but it is to miss the dance and the dancers altogether. Nonetheless, in schools the central assessment question is the assessment of individuals, usually in comparison with each other.

What, if anything, can an anthropological approach contribute to that question? As the farmer said to the lost traveler, "You can't get there from here. You first have to go down the road a bit."

In this chapter, a series of questions are listed that address the assessment of language and literacy in classrooms. These questions came from a 3-year study I conducted with teachers at an urban K–8 school that served an economically, ethnically, and racially diverse student population. As we explored what was happening in classrooms and in community, a series of questions were raised about the role that schooling played in the development of reading and writing. Some of the broader questions were:

- What is the nature of academic reading and writing in our classrooms?
- What kinds of readers and writers are our students becoming?
- How do we define achievement? Do we equate achievement with assessment? with school learning?
- What is the role of schooling in how students define themselves and reading and writing?
- What is the relationship of schooling and the communities from which the students come?

Any question can be taken out of the framework within which it was intended to be used. One can take one or more of the questions above and ask them in ways that transform them to the same old set of questions that have traditionally been asked in educational assessment. The result will be a set of assessment questions with the appearance of an anthropological approach without its substance or insight. Thus, the question above cannot be presented in isolation from the circumstances in which they arose or in isolation of the framework in which they are intended to be asked. In brief, in order to ask the questions above and generate other questions worth asking, it is important to first "go down the road a bit."

REDEFINING ASSESSMENT AND ACHIEVEMENT

Before asking questions that can be used to assess student language and literacy, three issues must be briefly discussed: the equation of achievement with assessment, text reproduction and text production, and the relationship of community and school. Each issue concerns social relationships and cultural dimensions of using language and literacy in the classroom.

EQUATING ACHIEVEMENT AND ASSESSMENT

In typical educational practice, *achievement* and *assessment* are nearly synonymous terms. To achieve, a student must not only know what we want the student to know, but also show it in a specific way. For example, it is not enough to read and understand a story; a student must show in a specific way (e.g., answering test questions, writing an essay) that he or she has read and understood a story in the way we want the student to read and understand it. If achievement cannot be appropriately demonstrated, it has not occurred.

The equation of achievement with assessment is understood by students. It is something they learn as part of learning what school is about. And, as students progress through the grades, the importance of equating achievement with assessment becomes more obvious and profound. By the time students reach the upper elementary, junior high and senior high grades, they are likely to orient their academic behavior to assessment rather than to learning, inquiry, curiosity, or academic substance.

But whose rule is it that achievement and assessment are equated? To answer that question, we must first realize that the equation of achievement with assessment is a social and cultural issue. The equation of achievement with assessment structures social relationships between teachers and students and among students themselves. Teachers are assigned the role of determining how language and literacy are to be used; it becomes part of their social identity. Children react to how we enact the role of teacher and to how we define their role as student. For example, consider below the very brief encounter from a reading group discussion of a basal story.

Teacher: What did Bill do?
Student: He went to get Sally.
Teacher: Very good. Bill went to get Sally.

The teacher has the responsibility for posing the questions, for determining what is and what is not important to know from the story, for determining what is an appropriate response and what isn't, and what forms of response are and are not appropriate. Implicit in the way in which the question and interaction take place is the assumption that a response to text is made by an individual and that one answers questions by oneself, without the help of others. Also implicit is that the response should be made at that time, at that place, and in public. The student responds to the question and, in so doing, continues to learn about the role of the student as reader in the classroom. From previous experience, the student has learned not to say "to get Sally" even though that is factually correct, because that form of response is not appropriate—a complete sentence is needed. The teacher validates that a correct response in both form and substance has been given by giving the student a positive evaluation. By repeating the response, the teacher gives the response authority.

It is important to note that the equation of achievement with assessment is not necessarily an explicit act of teachers. Indeed, many teachers have attempted to remove assessment altogether from children's classroom experiences. In part, this has come from the increasing developmental orientation of elementary teachers, especially those in the lower grades. In some cases, they have been successful in changing report cards so that students are not graded or compared with other students. In upper grades, teachers often want to focus student attention on more sophisticated and complex interpretations of texts and academic content. However, they often find themselves frustrated by students who demand to know, "How many pages does the essay have to be?" "Does spelling count?" "How many points towards my grade does this assignment give me?" and "What do you want us to write?" Through their classroom experiences, students have learned that achievement and assessment are synonymous in school.

Text reproduction is, as its name suggests, the reproduction of an extant text, for example, copying out of an encyclopedia. Text reproduction can involve both oral and written language; responding to a teacher's question by stating the information in the textbook, writing down an answer taken from the teacher's lecture. Text production is the creation of an original text, either oral or written. Text production is often associated with creativity, such as the writing of an original story or essay. However, text production does not always involve exciting or aesthetically intriguing texts—text production can be boring and mundane. What defines text reproduction and text production is not the end text, but the social process in which people are engaged.

For example, consider a classroom situation in which the teacher has assigned students the task of writing a report on a foreign country. Students find the information in encyclopedias and textbooks, and reproduce it. The teacher evaluates the content of the reports on their fidelity to extant texts on that foreign country, and the form of the reports on their fidelity to extant forms for making reports. What is most prominent in this example of text reproduction is the social relationship between the students and the teacher. They define their social relationship, their social identities and their activities, through how they use written language.

Text production involves a different set of social relationships between teacher and students. The teacher cannot evaluate based on extant texts. As such, the role and identity of the teacher changes. Similarly, the role and identity of the student changes. The social roles of teacher and student are negotiated in terms of the function(s) of the text(s) produced. Achievement—the production of a text—is not equated with evaluation but with the social and communicative functions the text accomplishes, such as raising a political issue, entertainment, expression of personal feelings, communication of information, development of imaginary "worlds," and exploration of new areas, among others. Inherently, text production is not possible when achievement is equated with assessment.

It is important not to view text reproduction and text production in terms of cognitive processes. Both text reproduction and text production can involve complex or simple sets of cognitive processes. What is key about text production and text reproduction is what students learn about what oral and written language is for in academic settings. With both text reproduction and text production, a set of social relationships is established through the use of language. Students learn how language is used to establish these social relationships and how the social relationships between teacher and student influence how language will be used. Over time, students learn that, in academic settings, social relationships are organized in a particular way and that language is used in particular ways. Simply put, they become enculturated to school uses of language, which in many cases are characterizable as text reproduction.

COMMUNITY, SCHOOL, AND LITERACY

Scholars have argued about whether schools really do lead to economic mobility. Whether they do or not, most people believe that failing to do well in school will hurt someone's chances of getting a good job and diminish opportunities for a successful life. For some families, doing well in school can be taken for granted. They know their children will learn to read and write, get good grades and go to college. Although children may be occasionally bored in school, schools work for their children. For other families, doing well in school cannot be taken for granted. Nor can they take for granted that schools are supportive of their children. In order to do well, children will have to work very hard and show that they know all that the teacher and school want them to know. And for some families, school is viewed as overtly antagonistic towards their children, defining their children as deserving of the lowest status in society (for example, placing children in the lowest reading groups, assigning failing grades, suspending them from school, or referring them to special education classes). All of these relationships get worked out and displayed through reading, writing, and oral language.

In general, families are not ignorant of the role of reading, writing, and oral language in the success their children have in school. Based on their own experiences in school or from the popular wisdom in their community, they may provide their children with early reading and writing activities designed to give their children an advantage. What is important to note is that the orientation families take with regard to literacy development in many cases is primarily directed to school success, which may not be the same as fostering reading, writing, and language development.

In brief, reading, writing, and language use in school is different than it is in home and community settings. That difference is not an issue. What is an issue is how schools and families understand those differences and deal with them. How they do so is essentially a cultural and cross-cultural issue with important economic and political consequences.

QUESTIONS FOR EVALUATING
READING AND WRITING

The issues that have been raised above—the equation of achievement with assessment, text reproduction and text production, and home, school, and literacy relationships—are typically invisible issues. We do not see what we do as equating achievement with assessment, fostering text reproduction, or emphasizing school success over reading, writing, and language development. We do not see these issues, because the school culture within which we work does not highlight them and fails to give us a language to describe them. What we do seems natural and rationale, we are not prompted to question it. What we need are questions, ways of looking at students' reading, writing, and language, that will make visible what is happening in our classrooms and schools.

In the rest of this chapter, I list a series of questions that help make visible the issues discussed earlier. In asking any set of questions, a series of values are displayed. In the questions below, importance is placed on reading and writing development as text production. The value placed on text production is inherently related to a definition of education that is broader than schooling and that shifts schooling and academic achievement away from the dominant center of education (see Willett & Bloome, 1993).

In presenting the questions, I describe one or more events taken from the study described earlier in order to illustrate and frame the questions.

"AND THE SUN GOT SUCKED UP"

Researchers and educators have often used children's drawings as a way to evaluate their literacy development. Drawings become more complex and representational, involve symbols approximating words, and then include strings of letters, often representing the story line. But from an anthropological perspective, what children do with drawing and early literacy activities is more than a developmental issue, it is a cultural issue. It is a cultural issue, because various cultural values and interpretations are given to how students use language, including drawing.

In the kindergarten classroom, students were grouped at tables, making pictures. They had previously been talking in a learning circle about Spring. The teacher had told them to draw a picture about Spring on one side of their paper. They could draw whatever they wanted on the other side.

Jay (all names are fictitious) first drew a picture of a boy flying a kite (see Drawing 1). When asked about his picture he said:

I'm flying a kite on a breezy day.

Drawing 1

His picture is representational; facial features include eyes, nose, and mouth; and the kite is drawn in great detail and color. On the other side he drew a picture of the Easter Bunny (see Drawing 2).

> And this is the Easter Bunny carrying Easter Eggs A Basket. It has four colors, yellow, purple, a red and blue.

His pictures, and his descriptions of them, look much like the pages in many of the books he shared with parents and teachers. His description of them involves naming behaviors similar to those prompted by his teacher and parents. Through his picture and description, Jay is showing that he is learning the language of the classroom.

Compare Jay's pictures and description to Andy's. Andy's first picture has a person flying a kite, with a sun and a cloud. There is a face representing the wind blowing the kite, similar to what was shown in the teacher group. Stylistically, the picture meets cultural expectations for what kindergarteners' pictures should look like (see Drawing 3).

Drawing 2

Drawing 3

But now examine Andy's second picture. At first glance it looks like scribbles—a nonrepresentational, meaningless display of lines and colors. But when Andy describes his pictures, what he has done takes on new meaning (see Drawing 4).

> [Referring to Drawing 3] This is me flying my kite, the wind came along and blow my kite that's a little [flipping over the sheet, referring to Drawing 4] that's when the storm started to come, when the bad, the tree caught on fire, the wall busted down and let's see the plane caught on fire and started round in a whirlpool. The sun got sucked up like the tree and let's see, and a, the water came up and made it worse. The sun got sucked up and that's about it.

When asked if there was anything else he wanted to say about his picture, he replied,

> It had red and different colors, cause I thought it would look pretty the grass was supposed to be on fire so I colored it nice. The tree bark caught on fire.

What appears to be scribbles and nonrepresentational is, in fact, a narrative. It is a 2-page book. Although Andy's second drawing does

Drawing 4

not look like what we expect (perhaps want) kindergarten drawing to look like, he does indeed show sophisticated language use. He has learned to use language to create narratives, integrating academic topics (information about Spring from the previous teacher led discussion) with his own thoughts and imagination. His language use does not mirror that of the classroom as does Jay's.

Interestingly, Andy was not the only child to produce a "scribble"-like drawing. Andy was working next to Richard. Richard also drew a fairly standard looking picture of a person flying a kite, but on the other side of the paper, he drew a narrative (see Drawing 5).

> This tornado drains the sun's power. Qualifier has made a hurricane cause it knocked the door down and the sun's power knocked the door down and it caught the house on fire.

Side by side, Andy and Richard, along with two other boys, had constructed a shared way of doing narrative.

There are a series of questions generated by the kindergarten students' drawings:

- Where are students producing narratives? What are the narratives they produce like? How do they display their narratives?

Drawing 5

- To what extent do students' narratives integrate personal, community and school knowledge?
- To what extent do students' narratives reflect forms associated with school texts? community texts? peer texts?
- Over time, what have students learned about the relationship of narrative and narrative form to achievement and success in school?

FROM THE WORLD BOOK ENCYCLOPEDIA

As mentioned earlier, the students at the K–8 school came from diverse cultures. Indeed, many families had immigrated recently. In order to celebrate and support cultural diversity, teachers often had students investigate various parts of the world from which students came.

In the seventh-grade class, the teacher designed one unit to focus on Southern Asia. Students were randomly assigned countries on which they were to report. Since several students had been born in Southern Asia, students were encouraged to use each other and parents as sources of information. Reports could focus on any aspect of the country assigned, from geography to politics to myths and literature to daily life. The teacher arranged library time and class time so that students could work with each other and get the information they needed for their reports.

In following what the students did, one student typifies the general approach. He was born in India, attended school there, and learned three languages there; Punjabi, Hindi, and English. By chance, he was assigned to report on India. He knew a lot about India. I had been to his house to interview his family about their views on school and learning to read and write. He had participated freely in that interview, describing at length differences between India and the United States. I had accompanied the family as they went to the Sikh temple, and spent the day with them in stores that specialized in Indian food and other specialty items. Yet, when he went to write his report he copied nearly word for word from an outdated and inaccurate *World Book Encyclopedia*.

Copying from the *World Book Encyclopedia* was probably more difficult and time-consuming than writing from his own knowledge. And in copying, he violated the teacher's direction to use what students in the class knew about the South Asia countries.

Such events raise a series of questions:

- To what extent does text reproduction characterize students' written language activity?
- To what extent do students view school tasks as text reproduction activities?
- To what extent do students view school texts (textbooks, encyclopedias, lectures) as authoritative over personal and community knowledge?
- To what extent do students view personal, peer, and community knowledge as valid for school tasks?
- Over time, what have students learned about the relationship of text reproduction and text production to achievement and success in school?

"WE DON'T KNOW NOTHING"

In the seventh-grade English/Social Studies classroom, the teacher wanted students to generate and explore their own questions. The teacher would begin a unit, for example a unit on the Civil War, by having students brainstorm what they knew, or thought they knew, about the topic, and then list questions they wanted to pursue. She provided a broad range of information sources, including historical fiction.

For some students it was easy to brainstorm information and generate questions, but others had problems. For example, one group of students had much difficulty brainstorming what they knew about the Civil War. This group consisted of four students: one had immigrated from the Phillipines during the conflict surrounding Marcos, one was from the People's Republic of China via Hong Kong, another had immigrated from Nicaragua before Samoza was overthrown, and the fourth was an African-American student born in the city. They began to discuss what they knew about the Civil War by sitting in silence. They occasionally exchanged nervous giggles, rewrote their names on their notebooks, and looked at what each other had not written. One student offered that the Civil War was Vietnam, but the other students did not support that; they remained silent, rejecting the suggestion.

It is important to note that the teacher had made it clear that they could brainstorm information even if they were not sure it was correct. Yet the students continued to sit in silence until one of them surreptitiously took a textbook from a bookshelf and began to write information from the book. The other students looked on and then copied from what the student wrote and read. When the teacher came by the group, she admonished them for using the textbook, making clear that they would have time to use textbooks later but that she wanted what the students already knew. The textbook was reluctantly put away, and when the teacher left, they copied from what each other had copied from the textbook.

Near the end of the time allotted, the teacher asked students to raise their hands if they were done. One of the students in the group raised his hand. Misunderstanding what the handraising signaled, another student rhetorically asked, "Why you raising your hand? We don't know nothing." And the hand was lowered.

- To what extent do students view their own knowledge and that of their community as valid for school learning?
- To what extent do students view knowledge as something produced as opposed to something revealed?
- To what extent are student self-definitions and definitions of self by peers and teachers based on the accumulation of textbook knowledge? community knowledge?
- How do students define ignorance and competence with regard to text reproduction and text production and school and community knowledge?

"I'M GONNA WEAR SHORTS"

As often happens when students are assigned seatwork, they do something else instead. Carl, Mark, and Samuel sat near each other in the seventh grade classroom. During a lesson in which I sat with them, they were supposed to be working on their social studies reports but instead spent time talking about the change in the weather, the dance, and the new student code of conduct.

About 2 months earlier, the school district had passed a new get-tough-but-stay-within-the-law student code of conduct. Students had to read the code in homeroom and sign a sheet saying that they had read the code. Mark still had his copy of the code in his notebook. He had been told that he could not wear shorts to school. The weather was getting hot, and it was hot inside the school and even hotter in their classroom. Mark wanted to wear shorts. But the student code read that students had to dress appropriately. Unusual clothing was not allowed. No clothing could be worn that would distract from the academic atmosphere of the school. Shorts, according to the principal, were not appropriate; they distracted from the academic atmosphere. However, the student code also said that students could wear clothing consistent with their cultural and religious backgrounds. Mark argued with Carol and Samuel that shorts were part of his cultural and religious background. He wore shorts at home and in his community. And, when his church sponsored summer picnics and other summer events, he often wore shorts. Samuel kept pointing out that the code said that clothing could not be distracting, and that the principal would say that shorts were distracting and not appropriate. Mark argued back that shorts were not distracting, sweating and being hot were distracting, and that even if they were distracting, the rule didn't apply if the clothing was part of a student's cultural and religious heritage.

- To what extent are the reading and writing behaviors displayed by students in formal academic activities similar to those employed in informal activities?
- To what extent do students engage in academic reading and writing activities primarily to get them done? And to what extent do they define *academic reading and writing* as "getting done" or "getting through"?
- What definitions of reading and writing are displayed by students in informal activities?

THE QUESTIONS IN THE QUESTIONS

Each of the questions above, generated by carefully looking at students and what they are doing, requires educators to ask a broader set of questions.

* What is the nature of academic reading and writing in our classrooms? What are the underlying cultural and ideological assumptions of academic reading and writing?
* What kinds of readers and writers are our students becoming? What cultural assumptions about personhood are being played out in our definitions of reader and writer?
* How do we define achievement? Do we equate it with assessment? Do we view achievement as located solely in school learning? does achievement necessarily mean isolation from one's home community? Is achievement linked to text reproduction?
* How much do we actually see? How much remains invisible to us?

The evaluation of student language, whether oral or written, is never divorced from the evaluation of the language of our classrooms. The readers and writers students become are in large part creations of what happens in our classrooms.

The questions listed throughout this chapter have focused on narratives, text reproduction and text production, and the relationship of school to home and community. Implied in those questions is the assumption that students often learn uses, forms, and values for written language based on what's valued in the classroom. However, what's valued in the classroom is not necessarily what we say we value. The value of things depends on our actions and on our students' action. Also implied in the questions is an importance placed on native narrative production, narrative content, and forms generated by students themselves or from their own community knowledge. An importance is placed on these items because they are linked with empowering students and supporting the diverse communities from which they come to school.

The questions in this chapter are just a small subset of questions that might be asked from an anthropological perspective. These questions can be used by individual teachers evaluating oral and written language within their own classroom. These questions can form the basis of a discussion among a small group of teachers across grade levels concerned with student oral and written language. Or the questions can be used by a school or school district interested in linking its evaluation of students' oral and written language to a discussion of empowering students as language users and supporting students' home communities. The format in which the questions are used is less important than an understanding of what the questions can and cannot do. The questions cannot assess the psychological states of individual students, cannot measure cognitive competency, and cannot compare one student's achievement with another's or with a cohort's. However, if asked within the framework from which they were derived, the questions can tell us about the kinds of readers, writers, and language users our students are becoming, and how our classrooms are contributing to what they are becoming.

REFERENCES

Bloome, D. (1991). Anthropology and research on teaching the English language arts. In J. Flood, J. Jensen, D. Lapp, & J. Squire (Eds.), *Handbook of research on teaching the English language arts* (pp. 46–56). New York: MacMillan.

Collins, J. (1987). Using cohesion to understand access to knowledge. In D. Bloome (Ed.), *Literacy and schooling* (pp. 67–97). Norwood, NJ: Ablex.

Cook-Gumperz, J., Gumperz, J., & Simons, H. (1981). *School–home ethnography project* (Final report submitted to the National Institute of Education). Washington, DC: U.S. Department of Education.

Gilmore, P. (1987). Sulking and steppin'. In D. Bloome (Ed.), *Literacy and schooling* (pp. 98–120). Norwood, NJ: Ablex.

Emihovich, C. (1990). Ask no questions: Socialinguistic isues in experimental and testing contests. *Linguistics and Education, 2*, (2), 165–183.

Goodenough, W. (1981). *Culture, language, and society*. Menlo Park, CA: Benjamin/Cummings Publishing Co.

Green, J., & Bloome, D. (1983). Ethnography and reading: Issues, approaches, criteria and findings. In J. Niles & L. Harris (Eds.), *Searches for meaning in reading/language processing and instruction: Thirty-second yearbook of the National Reading Conference* (pp. 6–30). Chicago: National Reading Conference.

Guthrie, L., & Hall, W. (1984). Ethnographic approaches to reading research. In P. Pearson, R. Barr, M. Kamil, & P. Rosenthal (Eds.), *Handbook of reading research* (pp. 91–110). New York: Longman.

Heath, S.B. (1982). Ethnography in education: Defining the essentials. In P. Gilmore & A. Glatthorm (Eds.), *Children in and out of school: Ethnography and education* (pp. 33–57). Washington, DC: Center for Applied Linguistics.

Hymes, D. (1980). *Language in education: Ethnolinguistic essays*. Washington, DC: Center for Applied Linguistics.

Hymes, D. (Project director). (1981). *Ethnographic monitoring project*. Final report submitted to the National Institute of Education. Washington, DC: U.S. Department of Education.

McDermott, R.P., & Hood, L. (1982). Institutionalized psychology and the ethnography of schooling. In P. Gilmore & A. Glatthorn (Eds.), *Children in and out of school: Ethnography and education* (pp. 232–249). Washington, DC: Center for Applied Linguistics.

Schieffelin, B., & Gilmore, P. (Eds.). (1986). *The acquisition of literacy: Ethnographic perspectives.* Norwood, NJ: Ablex.

Trueba, H. (1988). English literacy acquisition: From cultural trauma to learning disabilities for minority students. *Linguistics and Education, 1*(2), 125–152.

Willett, J., & Bloome, D. (1993). In A. Carrasquillo & C. Hedley (Eds.), *Whole language and the bilingual learner* (pp. 35–57). Norwood, NJ: Ablex.

chapter 5
Assessing Students As Members of a Literate Community

Beth Gildin Watrous and Jerri Willett

INTRODUCTION

As educators, we are accustomed to thinking about literacy assessment as an act in which individual progress is measured against specific criteria. Our criteria for language learning provide a concrete and frequently unquestioned vision of the skills and abilities children need to participate in literate society. Because we fail to use flexible literacy criteria, we often fail to recognize growth. Because we are accustomed to thinking about individual performance, we often fail to recognize the factors beyond academic competence that may affect student growth. Specifically, we fail to recognize that literacy is not a concrete set of skills but a social process within which students develop their identities as readers. We fail to take into account the powerful influence of the classroom social environment upon students as learners.

An anthropological perspective is concerned with the process of group formation and maintenance, and with ways individuals learn to identify with the group. It can help us "try to grasp the larger configuration of society, nature, and meaning in which that element which we call 'the individual' has a place" (Peacock, 1986, p. 18). With respect to literacy, an anthropological perspective can help us look at what children need to do to become members of a literate society, at the criteria used to evaluate success within the group, and at literacy as a social process. It can assist us in making conscious the norms, values, and routine understandings that guide assessment in our classrooms. In the process, it may illuminate ways our daily actions contribute to exclusionary practices, rather than facilitating membership in the literate community.

This chapter takes an anthropological perspective to better understand how social context affects the interaction and assessment of individuals as members of a literate community. It explores ways educators may gain valuable insights into a frequently executed but rarely analyzed task, assessment. It takes the position that assessment is often used to separate children from peers, to label students as successes or failures. It examines the possibility that the educator-as-anthropologist can gather and analyze data in a manner that promotes inclusion rather than exclusion and is thus consistent with the goals of education in a democratic society.

We first consider what it means to be a member of a literate community and how one attains membership. We then explore the process of forming an identity as a group member. Next we consider the classroom as a small community and examine the role of assessment in identity formation. The concept is made concrete through a case study detailing one aspect of assessment in a first-grade classroom. Finally, the question of how an anthropological perspective might inform educational decisions is considered.

THE LITERATE COMMUNITY IN A DEMOCRATIC SOCIETY: EQUAL PRIVILEGES FOR ALL MEMBERS

What does it really mean to be part of a literate community? Membership implies more than the mechanics of reading and writing. It implies the ability to interpret texts, to have access to community symbols and accumulated knowledge, and to enter into discussion, interpretation, evaluation, and reflection with others in the community. According to the ideals of a democratic society, all members should have equal access to the literacy system. All should be able to participate as contributing members of the literate culture, to decide what is in and what is out in terms of content, styles, and meaning. All should be permitted to participate in changing and enriching the literacy system (Kress, 1989). The role of the teacher is to help students become members by modeling behaviors that facilitate the formation of a literate identity recognizable to self and others. It is to help students more effectively participate in the literacy system, to both understand and constructively question literacy norms. In short, one role of the teacher is to foster identity formation, and consequently full participation, in literate society.

IDENTITY FORMATION

A literate identity is both ascribed (created by birth and socialization) and achieved through negotiation (Royce, 1982). Ascription yields only minimum competency in the identity. Individuals must consciously affirm and reaffirm identity for it to remain a valid and recognized part of their being. They must demonstrate competence during ongoing assessment in order to remain an recognized member of the group.

Identity formation as a reader is tied to the reality individuals experience and accept as their own. Reality may be experienced through role playing, through participating in the social world. Roles have been defined as types of activities performed by types of actors (Berger & Luckmann, 1966). Hence each role has an identity attached to it. As individuals take on the variety of roles played out in everyday life, they take on the world those roles define. As they play the roles, they learn and practice the skills needed to accurately enact them. By taking on socially acceptable roles, players gain the competencies needed to internalize them and, in the process, are socialized, or inducted, into society. The ability to define oneself as a reader thus requires experience with, and participation in, a variety of socially acceptable reading roles.

"Roles and therefore identity are socially bestowed in acts of social recognition" (Wuthnow, Hunter, Bergesen, & Kurzweil, 1984, p. 45). Accordingly, reading identity is a social product that may only be understood within the particular context in which it is shaped and maintained. Identity formation as a reader depends, not only on the existence of shared definitions of reading, but also upon the existence of effective ways to establish oneself as a reader.

Periodic displays, or signals, communicate an individual's knowledge of literacy norms. These are often assessed stringently by the group, for they serve both to maintain bonds between members and strengthen the boundaries separating them from nonmembers. Members engage in cultural labeling; they "assign labels to others in response to cues they have learned as diagnostic" (Royce, 1982, p. 200). Those engaged in identity formation as readers need access to group members and to occasions when key behaviors occur in order to absorb the language and rituals of reading. They need practice ascertaining culturally acceptable meanings in order to emerge as one whose interpretations and assessments count. Identity as a member of a literate culture and specifically as a member of a community of readers may be achieved and maintained in this fashion. Students may assume literacy as a birthright. Despite this assumption, many must work extremely hard to acquire and maintain literacy, and few have the opportunity to help define it.

THE CLASSROOM AS A SMALL COMMUNITY

Identity formation and maintenance occurs within social groups embedded in a community. Each element of the group is a small community of its own as well as part of the larger whole. In this light, classrooms are both embedded in their school and local communities and communities unto themselves. They have leaders and followers, language, shared symbols and traditions, values, explicit and implicit laws, social organization—in short, their own culture. Children form aspects of their cultural identity not only at home and in the community-at-large, but also within the classroom community. The process of literate identity formation begins in the home and is extended in the classroom where it becomes a central focus. For example, in classrooms where books and environmental print are plentiful, literacy achievements are broadly defined and highly praised, home cultures are reflected, and student reading and writing are prominently displayed, children tend to experience reading as a valued activity. They may internalize that value as they take on the tasks, roles, and identities that define literacy within the classroom and prepare to enter the larger community of which it is a part.

LITERACY ASSESSMENT WITHIN THE SCHOOL COMMUNITY

Ideally, literacy assessment provides information to guide the formation of a literate identity. However, assessment has too often been used as a means to select out rather than recruit in. Literacy assessment within the classroom is often conceived as a narrowly defined process that puts evaluation into the hands of one all-powerful individual. It is often based on an inflexible set of criteria indicating what one must know to be considered a reader. This picture only represents a small part of assessment. In fact, literacy assessment is carried out continually by educators and peers alike. Negotiation and evaluation occur within ongoing face-to-face interaction as students and teachers enact socially prescribed, routine classroom events. Assessment is a powerful force which can include or exclude students from community membership.

Teachers can help students acquire a reading identity by using assessment in a different way, as a tool to illuminate student development, to document success and growth in language learning. Assessment can recruit students into the literate community if it illuminates success; it selectively excludes if it simply highlights failure. Through assessment teachers can grasp the configuration of the literate classroom in which the child-as-language-learner has a place. They can gather, interpret, and evaluate data reflecting all aspects of language learning. They can assess how student, parent, teacher, and institutional perceptions of what constitutes reading and writing affect opportunities for participation.

Literacy assessment that is informed by an anthropological perspective can help teachers approach readers as participants in a social process. It can help them first understand students as members of a literate community and then use these understandings to further student growth. Ideally, such assessment will answer questions such as:

* How does the individual fit into the classroom community?
* Are the frames of reference used by teacher and students mutually understood or do they clash?
* What other factors might be affecting access to literacy?
* What might change if the environment (literacy supports/hindrances) changed?

ASSESSMENT IN ONE CLASSROOM COMMUNITY: A CASE STUDY

The case study that follows is an example of how an educator's openness to an anthropological perspective helped her better understand the nature of assessment in her first-grade classroom. An anthropological lens enhanced her perception of particular individuals as members of a literate classroom community. It enhanced her understanding of the role educators can play in extending literacy rights and opportunities to all community members. These insights would have been impossible to achieve without a clear sense of the interaction between community and individual, of the role this community played in both fostering and hindering the reading identity of a particular first grader.

The case study focuses on one aspect of emerging literacy in this first-grade classroom. It examines ways in which children's assessment of what counts as literacy, and thus who counts as literate, may be shaped within the daily routine. More specifically, the study focuses upon identity formation, illustrating ways identity as a reader may be created through constant negotiation and evaluation during face-to-face interaction with teacher and peers.

SETTING

The research was conducted in a rural New England elementary school serving approximately 150 students in heterogeneously grouped classes, grades K–6. Many students were from families affiliated with the nearby state university. The study was a collaborative effort between the school's first-grade teacher and an outside researcher.

The year the study was conducted, the classroom teacher, hereafter known as Mary, was implementing a two-pronged effort to eliminate ability-based reading groups. She wished to replace them with a combination of individualized reading and collaborative learning structures such as reading conferences, shared reading and reading partners. A related initiative involved substituting predictable books, poems, and songs for the traditional basal texts. Mary's conscious questioning of values and goals was transforming both material and structural features of the classroom culture.

Examining the setting from a broader sociocultural context, it is apparent that administration, parents, and other teachers supported Mary's work. Their excitement and interest was enhanced by Mary's efforts to communicate the changes in her program (and the reasons behind them) via parent newsletters, the school newsletter, staff meetings, and informal conversation. In addition, a shared set of values had been slowly building among staff for about 15 years concerning the nature of the school as a community and the importance of literature and student writing within that community. Literacy was a symbol of mainstream identity here as it was in the community-at-large.

Monitoring Change

As time passed, Mary became increasingly conscious of her classroom as a community and of reading as a social process within that community (Bloome, 1985, 1987). These new understandings affected not only her thinking about reading and writing in school, but also her views on assessment (who assesses and for what purposes).

Research questions asked during the fall examined the degree to which students identified by Mary as high, average, and lower functioning readers and writers were appropriately challenged and reinforced within shared reading activities. Data suggested that readers with varying skills could interact as literate community members within the context of shared reading experiences.

As a result of these findings a new focus was established. Both researchers wished to look further at John, one of the least mature readers in the class. They wished to determine the degree to which an emerging reader might experience success not only in large groups, but also in small group, and independent literacy activities.

JOHN: A MEMBER OF THE FIRST GRADE COMMUNITY

Data from the fall study highlight John's ability to successfully interact with people and text during shared reading when (a) making contributions to class discussion based on out-of-school experiences, (b) asking questions concerning the text or a related experience, (c) defining words, (d) recognizing a small number of familiar words, and (e) guessing the letters needed to complete various gamelike tasks (i.e., minimal cue messages, Hangman). Success was indicated by the fact that John's responses resembled those of peers. He did not stand out as different in the eyes of teacher or classmates. Rather, his responses illustrated many of the shared values that characterize this classroom community.

John's independent reading and writing skills developed more slowly than those of his peers. Mary and the special needs teacher attributed this fact, at least in part, to visual-motor and visual-memory difficulties. They noticed he was far more passive during small group activities than during shared reading, letting students he perceived as more capable readers and writers take the lead. On the other hand, he behaved in a manner that indicated the desire to own and take pride in his achievements as a member of the classroom community. For example, after reading "The Three Little Pigs" during shared reading, he volunteered to construct the Third Little Pig's house out of legos with a friend. Although he only watched and commented rather than collaborating in the actual construction, he volunteered to share about the project during a follow-up group meeting. He stated, "We built that brick house from legos and it took a lot of time, about an hour. It's not quite finished. Glen and I will finish it tomorrow." This presentation of self (Goffman, 1959) was acceptable to his partner because of the value placed upon *we* rather than *I* in the classroom community. The partner was as capable of egocentric behavior as any typical first grader; Mary actually found him more egocentric than most. The fact that he allowed John to claim membership highlights the way collaborative values smoothed over boundaries that might be raised in more individualistically oriented classrooms. It highlights values that enabled John to form an identity as an emerging member of this literate classroom community.

IDENTITY FORMATION: JOHN NEGOTIATES HIS RELATIONSHIP TO THE COMMUNITY OF READERS

By mid-year, John's behavior indicated his growing awareness of the ways independent readers are expected to behave in classrooms that place a high value on *literacy* (as understood within a broad definition of the term). In the examples that follow, his language and interactions reflect a need to be recognized as an independent reader by both adults and peers. They also highlight the social issues involved in establishing oneself as a reader and the interactional language (language used to establish and define social relationships) that may be used in reading-related negotiations. John had internalized the value placed upon literacy (especially reading) within the school and classroom cultures.

Successful Identity Formation: Teacher and Peers Jointly Assess

Social authority may be equated with reading ability both in and out of the classroom (Johnston, 1984). Data from this study reveal many cogent examples of John's efforts to use reading-related strengths to establish a reading identity and rights to the privileges accorded all readers. His strong verbal and metacognitive skills were frequently used to this end.

John's most successful verbal interactions often occurred during shared reading sessions as he related personal experiences and interests to text. In doing so, he created an association between himself and the literature in culturally appropriate ways. A discussion of the phrase *British rule* followed the reading of a Shel Silverstein poem about George Washington. John's contribution reflected a recent trip to Boston taken with his family:

This poem is about George Washington. Before the Revolutionary War there was the Boston Tea Party. England wanted America to pay taxes, but America said no. There was a boat called the Beaver. The people who wanted to rule themselves dumped the tea into Boston Harbor. We went to Boston to see the Beaver and heard about the Tea Party.

John's success was reflected in the interested expressions on the faces of peers and in the confirmation he received from Mary that he had helped everyone understand the concept of British rule.

Another successful identity formation strategy involved John's ability to retell familiar, well-loved stories. On one occasion, he taped a retelling of "The Three Little Pigs." His use of detail was remarkable, as was his ability to use voice changes to mark different characters and shifts from dialogue to narration. John asked to hear the tape of the retelling; his facial expressions indicated great pleasure as he listened. He shared the tape with peers on his own initiative. Their sustained interest and request to hear the tape again attested to his success in establishing a literate association between himself and the story.

A third successful verbal strategy involved John's response to literature during story time. He was frequently the only child to ask questions or offer other verbal responses within this context. For example, following a description of the city in *The Caboose Who Got Loose* (Peet, 1971), John remarked, "I'd like to live in that city because I'd live near the train station!" The nods of several classmates attested to the value they placed upon his contribution. Shortly afterward, the teacher initiated a discussion about the black smoke in one of the illustrations and asked what differences it might indicate between the way trains operated then and the way they do now. John was the only child to offer a response and to receive praise for his insights. He stated, "They don't use coal now; they use diesel." Moments later he asked, "Will you take us there someday?" [referring to the Deerfield Freight Yard]. His comment initiated a spirited discussion about a possible field trip to that site. John was an active participant in story time, able to signal community membership in culturally appropriate and acceptable ways.

John's confidence in his identity as a student with strong metacognitive skills helped him take the risks needed to form a new identity, that of independent reader. He made good use of his ability to think and talk about reading strategies; he built positive associations between himself and literacy in the eyes of teacher and peers.

John's use of rehearsal provides a powerful example of his ability to use a reading strategy to assert a new identity and have it accepted within the classroom community. The following statement was John's response to a situation in which he paused for a moment before beginning to read a sentence out loud and then realized that several classmates were about to jump in and read it for him: "It's my sentence. I'd like to read it first in my mind, please." He successfully bought himself some additional time by verbalizing his strategy to peers.

The following exchange occurred when John was asked about his participation in shared reading (he sometimes joined in and sometimes did not):

B: This morning when Mrs. F. was reading the chart with the group, were you reading in your head or were you reading out loud?
J: In my head.
B: How do you choose which things you'll read out loud? Do you have a way of deciding or choosing?
J: I say [begins using a dramatic reading voice], "I don't know that very well; I think I'll read in my head." Or I'll say [begins dramatic voice], "I know that one well; I'll read that out loud."

John was able to use this strategy to enhance successful identity formation because it was an acceptable option in his classroom community. Both teacher and peers defined the beginning stages of reading development as legitimate forms of reading. Rehearsing a sentence in ones mind before reading it aloud might not be labeled reading in some first-grade classrooms. However, it was a culturally acceptable reading strategy in Mary's classroom and in the surrounding school community. Process was considered as important as product by teachers and students alike. The fact that John needed to process before reading aloud was taken neither as a weakness nor as an indication that he engaged in a "babyish" way of reading. Rather, rehearsal was respected as one of the tools John used to make meaning from print.

Time, which often serves as a constraint to identity formation (i.e., "That's not really reading for someone your age."), appeared to play a relatively minor role in this classroom community. Because developmental stages and milestones (such as reading aloud without previous processing) were not preset at specific grades or ages, success was not tied to a time clock. John used metacognitive strengths to defend his ability/right to use a variety of reading strategies; age did not hinder his efforts at impression management.

Impression management is a technique used by individuals seeking to establish cultural membership. John's culturally appropriate interactive skills may have helped him successfully manipulate cultural clues. He accomplished impression management in the preceding examples through his ability to know himself and to make quick and accurate assessments of peers and setting. A related interpretation suggests the successful use of alter casting, the manipulation of an interaction to ones advantage. John chose to emphasize his memory, storytelling, and metacognitive skills; classmates with different strengths might have chosen to emphasize direct interaction with text. The fact that a broad range of skills was valued within this classroom community gave him the opportunity to make this choice.

One of the important roles teachers play is to reinforce alternative values that help increasing numbers of students form identities as readers. For example, Mary reinforced both storytelling and reading as highly valued forms of communication within the classroom community. She continually modeled the concept that all students must have the time they need to successfully read aloud to the group. She praised children for respectful listening behaviors. These factors contributed to the situational consensus that existed during classroom events involving both teachers and peers. Such consensus reinforced the predictable expectations that help students feel safe taking risks. The expectation that he would be supported in using any language system (reading, writing, listening, or speaking) to signal membership helped John affirm his reading identity as teacher and students jointly assessed.

Constraints On the Use of Identity Formation Strategies: Peer Assessment

As individuals negotiate and evaluate membership, they may face constraints on the use of identity formation strategies. Constraints may be physical, sociological (such as time, mentioned earlier), psychological, or structural (Royce, 1982). John consistently struggled to establish his reading identity when activities centered around use of text. He found it more difficult to engage in the manipulation-of-situation (alter casting) used so successfully during many of the previously described group sessions. John's struggles were particularly apparent during peer–peer activities, that is, when the teacher was not part of the interaction. A sociological constraint, social stratification, might have contributed to this situation.

In Western societies, written language skills are often valued more highly than oral language skills. In general, the reader/writer is more highly valued than the storyteller. When Mary was not around to reinforce alternative values, students may have reverted back to mainstream values that undercut identity formation for some aspiring readers. They may have assessed membership on the basis of "master status" (word-for-word reading) rather than on characteristics relevant to the particular environment (the ability to make meaning from print using a variety of strategies).

Mainstream values sometimes hindered indentity formation when children practiced reading familiar literature with partners. In the examples that follow, children were establishing authority in terms of who would offer to read, whose offer would be accepted, who would determine what would be read, and what choices would be legitimized. They were negotiating and establishing exactly whose interpretations count. John struggled to assert his own voice but was unable to create a strong association between himself and reading in the minds of peers. He thus failed to engage in shared decision making with his reading partners.

Immediately preceding the first example, John had read *Ten Apples Up On Top* (Lesieg, 1961) with help from his partner and had listened to her read *Frog and Toad Are Friends* (Lobel, 1970). He was about to take his second turn as reader:

J: Oh, now it's my turn to read. Want me to read a picture book?
L: I think we're supposed to read a real book.
J: Okay, *Ten Apples Up On Top.*
L: I think you've already read that one.
J: I'm going to read the beginning.
L: I don't want to hear it again.
J: Oh, yes you do! [He reads three lines.]
J: I don't really want to read this. [They begin to discuss book marks; John then asks Linda to read him a book.]

Children could choose the book they wished to share with their partner. It is significant that John was unable to persist in establishing his choice of either a wordless book (first choice) or a repeated reading (second choice). Also of note is his retreat into a passive nonreader role after giving in to Linda's demand.

What constraints were acting on this situation? One psychological constraint may have involved John's degree of willingness to risk embarrassment or ostracism should Linda tire of his persistence. Do the advantages (control of book choice) outweigh the disadvantages (Linda's scorn or anger)? High visibility made the psychological constraint even more powerful. John and Linda were surrounded by other reading partners quietly going about their business. Loud complaints from Linda would have created a highly visible display likely to draw negative attention to John and his plight. An alternative response to the risks inherent in high visibility was to maintain a low profile. John's acquiescence helped him maintain a low profile. The price he paid was the loss of a membership right, a second turn at demonstrating reading with the book of his choice.

Immediately preceding the next example, Ben had invited John to share a private space with him during silent reading. At first they read separately and then John invited a reading association with Ben:

J: Will you read this to me? [Ben reads a few pages. They begin turning the pages together, using the pictures as cues for a discussion of the plot.]
J: I'll read this book to you now, Ben. [He reads a few lines and then stumbles upon one or two words.]
B: You don't have to read anymore, John. Do you want to hear this book [holds up a wordless book]?

They talk the book through together. Ben exerts control over the process by holding the book and turning the pages. At one point, John offers to show Ben his favorite page. Ben agrees, but takes the book back immediately afterward. He turns his body so he is only partially facing John:

J: Turn around so you're facing me, Ben. I want to try reading this book to you. This one's gonna be easy!

Ben pays no attention and begins to show John a different book. John again offers to read but Ben distracts him with a hand held number game he has in his pocket.

Constraints from the mainstream abound when comparing this example to the first. Linda played a nurturing and supportive role until she rebelled against John's attempts to read *Ten Apples Up On Top* a second time. In contrast, Ben dominated the relationship throughout the interaction. Essentially he said, "I can read and won't give you a chance to try." As a member of a dominant or elite group (the readers), he exaggerated aspects of his culture in order to heighten boundaries between himself and an aspiring member. Such actions relegated John to spectator rather than participant status (Britton, 1970).

Literacy Assessment From An Anthropological Perspective: What Can We Learn?

Literacy assessment in this case study was approached from an anthropological perspective. It looked at the process of group formation and maintenance and at the individual as an aspiring member of the classroom community. It did not highlight John as a failure, as a nonmember with little chance of gaining group acceptance. It did not measure his progress against predetermined criteria indicating success or failure as a reader. Instead, it looked at the strategies John employed to establish membership and the degree to which he was successful in his efforts. It also examined the ways the community both hindered and facilitated these efforts.

The description of identity formation strategies that emerged from this case study was shaped by a questioning process similar to ones employed by anthropologists during field studies. In fact, asking questions about sociocultural life is the primary work of an anthropologist. Because one's assumptions shape which questions are asked, anthropologists begin their exploration by asking very broad questions. The most important task of an anthropologist is to find out which questions are the most important to ask within a particular community. For example, in Mary's classroom community, two important questions included: (a) How is reading defined? and (b) What are the socially acceptable ways of demonstrating community membership?

From such questioning and reflection, anthropologists begin to notice patterns and discover the meanings those patterns hold within the community. For example, in Mary's classroom community, retelling familiar stories, asking questions about stories, sharing personal experiences that relate to stories, reading books with familiar stories supported by pictures, expressing opinions about stories, engaging in physical activities that relate to stories, and reading independently were all ways to demonstrate literacy. This wide range of behaviors allowed students with diverse skills to participate as literate community members. A second pattern that emerged from the data suggested that relating personal experiences and interests to text was a way for a child to create an association between himself and literature. A third pattern suggested that alternative values and definitions of literacy were reflected in student behaviors to a greater extent when the teacher was present than when students interacted on their own. Asking questions and finding patterns can lead to an integrated description of how a classroom community works.

Recognizing and describing significant patterns of classroom life is only the first step. Recognition must lead to action to improve student learning. What insights might an educator gain by looking at his or her school or classroom through an anthropological lens? How might this approach to assessment help him or her engage in productive decision making about the school/classroom community?

It is impossible to assess the individual student without assessing the social context within which he or she is involved. In Mary's case, she was pleased to realize that her new learning environment provided many opportunities for children with developmental profiles like John's to successfully negotiate a literate identity. She also realized that she needed new ways to help some children broaden their definitions of what constitutes reading and thus become more equitable in their reading partnerships.

The patterns uncovered in other classrooms may be very different from those uncovered in Mary's. Regardless of specific patterns, with conscious awareness comes the possibility of changing, accepting, or celebrating the often unnoticed aspects of classroom life.

Knowing this, what can be done to change literacy assessment and, as a result, environments for language learning? How can the goal of equitable access for aspiring readers be furthered? It is possible to:

- Examine and become highly conscious of ways that values effect classroom life.
- Examine and become highly conscious of ways that definitions of reading affect classroom life.
- Approach observation, interpretation, and evaluation in ways that reflect an understanding of reading as a social and ethical process.
- Examine the information obtained through standardized assessments and interpret it from an anthropological perspective. What values, beliefs, knowledge, and social structure does the instrument represent? How do these impact upon data collection and interpretation?
- Combine data gathered during reading events with interpretations of standardized data when reporting to parents and administrators; do not allow standardized data to be presented out of context.
- Be aware of constraints on efforts to create equitable classrooms.
- Develop strategies for resolving possible discontinuities between classroom and mainstream/home values, between some students' weak reading identities and the strong identities necessary for full community membership.

Whether in the classroom or in the school as a whole, teachers can make a difference in ensuring that all students consider themselves active members of a literate community.

REFERENCES

Berger, P., & Luckmann, T. (1966). *The social construction of reality*. Garden City, NY: Doubleday.

Bloome, D. (1985). Reading as a social process. *Language Arts, 62*(2), 134–142.

Bloome, D. (1987). Reading as a social process in a middle school classroom. In D. Bloome (Ed.), *Literacy and schooling* (pp. 124–149). Norwood, NJ: Ablex.

Britton, J. (1970). *Language and learning: The importance of speech in children's development*. London: Penguin.

Goffman, E. (1959). *The presentation of self in everyday life*. Philadelphia: University of Pennsylvania Press.

Johnston, P. (1984). Assessment in reading. In P.D. Pearson (Ed.), *Handbook of reading research* (pp. 147–182). New York: Longman.

Kress, G. (1989). *Linguistic processes in sociocultural practice*. New York: Oxford University Press.

Lesieg, T. (1961). *Ten apples up on top*. New York: Random House.

Lobel, A. (1970). *Frog and toad are friends*. New York: Harper & Row.

Peacock, J.L. (1986). *The anthropological lens: Harsh light, soft focus*. Cambridge, UK: Cambridge University Press.

Peet, B. (1971). *The caboose who got loose*. Boston: Houghton Mifflin.

Royce, A. (1982). *Ethnic identity: Strategies of diversity*. Bloomington: Indiana University Press.

Wuthnow, R., Hunter, J., Bergesen, A., & Kurzweil, E. (1984). *Cultural analysis: The work of Peter L. Berger, Mary Douglas, Michel Foucault, & Jurgen Habermas*. London: Routledge & Kegan Paul.

Discussion: Assessment in My World

Maryann Jennings

"This is a trick," said Leon, age 12.

Leon was right, but that didn't keep him from failing the test. Leon knew the teacher was using the test to find out what he didn't know. And he knew the teacher and everyone like her couldn't care less about what he did know.

I am a teacher. I was not Leon's teacher, or anyone like her. I am, however, blunt on occasion.

The whole "assessment" part of my job mostly makes my stomach hurt.

The three chapters in this section forcast optimistic changes in the uses of assessment in education. They excite me. I can't wait for educators to gain new knowledge about and find new perspectives on assessment; the nurturance that can result with changed attitudes is the bright promise education has always been for me. However, those chapters' heady descriptions of life in other classrooms feels a bit remote from the realities I face every day. It's hard to get genuinely enthused about positive changes in assessment when, in my school for example, the tracking system renders "high" classes lily-white and overloads the "lows" with children of color.

I appreciate that the authors question the sacrosanct reputation of assessment; it cannot be questioned loudly enough for me. Yet their call for assessment to be nurturing and the creation of community in the classroom seems to neglect a few important considerations.

Simply put, I would like to have seen the authors get closer to the bone than they did, because before such change in assessment can begin, we need to examine some underlying issues.

For example, take Leon and his twin sister Lenora, who speak English as a second language. They live in the Hispanic section of our city and ride the bus for an hour to get to school. They both work. There's not a lot of time to do homework, and never a quiet place to study for a test. Lenora failed the test, too.

Everyone knows the How of assessment. It is in schools and our experiences of schooling that the essence of evaluation is clearest. It is quantification. That is, according to some "standard," how well do I measure?

For most of us that has really meant: Where am I lacking? or What don't I know?

The deeper questions I wished to see addressed are: Why are we compelled to evaluate students? For whom? To what end?

Control.

Power.

It seems to me that the deeper issues of management, control, and power-over drive the assessment machines. And this is a particularly ugly reality we choose to ignore.

Look around. Broad varieties of assessment/evaluation have been used throughout history as management tools: marketing surveys, newspaper editorials, sales figures, public opinion polls, radar speed traps, customer response cards, egg-laying production numbers, and batting averages. All manner of assessment is not necessarily bad, but those forms that work to maintain control and power-over are spitefully incapacitating and demoralizing.

As I see it, power-over is the signature of authoritarian and competitive relationships. They exist in fundamentally unbalanced settings, such as schools, in which an individual or group exercises their capacity to control the experiences, behavior, and thoughts of others.

Traditional evaluation in school is mostly about maintaining power-over. The test Leon was struggling with was a "standardized placement" exam, only what was standard on the test certainly didn't relate to what was standard in Leon's life. And the predictable results placed him on the "low" track in school with no real opportunities for future advancement.

From my experience, assessment is used to control everybody: teachers and administrators as well as students.

Examples abound:

Teachers use a familiar battery of weapons, including innuendo and sarcasm in class discussion, surprise quizzes, and trick questions, to test students: find out what they don't know in order to label and reward or humiliate them.

Administrators keep track of teachers' grade distributions: those who "give" too many As or Fs are called in to explain their deviance from the norm, the curve.

Supervisors and superintendents keep track of school administrators: principals who suspend too many or too few students are suspected of tyranny or leniency.

It is a system that has built an institutionalized behemoth of assessment that legitimizes itself and the maintenance of difference and competition: a beast breathing down everybody's neck. With such a well-established tradition in education as well as in the rest of society of using assessment as a tool to control or punish, is it realistic to think it can be used to nurture?

Watrous and Willett's idealistic call for educators to "gather and analyze data in a manner that promotes inclusion rather than exclusion and is thus consistent with the goals of education in a democratic society" makes my old 1960s heart swell. It is the honorable challenge of teaching I choose every day.

It is also the reason I have my seventh graders sit right next to each other in a circle on the worn carpet to discuss their scary stories. They must read their own stories aloud as the rest of us listen and prepare to ask questions or make suggestions. After reading, the author calls on the listeners one at a time, and they talk with each other about the story. I keep out of it as much as I can. Every student has something to add. Later on, I find they are still talking with each other about the stories on the way to another class.

But, once there, they will not be allowed to speak or move from their seats.

My day-to-day work as a teacher shows me that one of the goals of education in our society is exclusion, not inclusion. The lofty tones of our textbooks and commencement speeches, the principal's peptalks and teachers' lectures, are lies for the majority of students we serve. No matter how hard they work, they have the wrong answers, the wrong cultural background, or the wrong expectations. They are assigned a slot and kept on that track until they "get" it: until their lives mirror what the assessment tools expected and predicted.

Current assessment practices guarantee the status quo, that those with knowledge, money, and power will keep, and those without will never get.

There was Orlando, who rarely came to school, and when he did, more often than not he would simply walk right out the door whenever he felt like it. When he managed to get to my class. Orlando made noises, tipped his chair back, cracked on all the other students (all of whom were younger than he), and liked to draw cartoons instead of write. Because of his absences, he was always so far behind that it would have taken mature, dedicated effort to catch up. Even though that class was small, I could not give him the attention he desperately needed in order to succeed. One day they suspended him for skipping, and he never returned. I hate it that I couldn't make a difference in his life.

Sometimes I wonder what I'm doing. Am I perpetuating the status quo, or actually restructuring it stick by stick, student by student, as I imagine?

No matter how supportive and inclusive my classroom may be, my junior high students face dangerous front lines elsewhere in the building. In too many classrooms, the only legitimate activities are veiled power struggles between teacher and students in which assessment is a weapon to keep students in place, labeled as successes or failures. Like the teachers in those classrooms, many educators loudly define schools and classrooms as "battlefields" or "front lines" and proclaim their superiority over the children there, as if such superiority was more than sophomoric.

As long as a classroom is a battlefield, and as long as schools are for control, no true community can grow.

At the beginning of every class, students come through my door, reacting to events in the last class or in the corridor. There is a lot of noise. I wait because they are not ready to be in the present yet. They need time to ventilate and acclimate. Soon enough, they become aware of where they are and what's next. We may have lost some foolish minutes in order to gain important feelings of comfort and respect.

Even before we can worry about "the literate community" that Bloome and Watrous and Willett mention, we first need to have, and take seriously, the simple idea of community inside the classroom: the accepting place where it is safe to be vulnerable, to share, to take risks, to fail, succeed, and grow.

I always figured Frost had it right enough when he said, "Home is where, when you have to go there, they have to take you in." Public school classrooms are the same: we have to let in every student coming to the door. However, as in Frost's "home," there is not necessarily any warmth or acceptance implied.

It is chilling to observe that if students have been assessed and assigned to a "low" class, like Leon, they are likely to find that classroom a battlefield, not a community. These classes, the ones who need our best talents, our most supportive challenges, and our best love, are routinely given the most inexperienced, insecure teachers. I've seen teacher and student call each other names and insult each other's families in order to get on top and stay there. It is beyond all reason to expect a true community of safety, personal knowledge, growth, and dignity to develop there.

I believe that in too many classrooms, the control and power functions of assessment are driven by the even more subterranean human fuels of fear and insecurity. My own struggles around changing how I am in the classroom tell me that those of us whose confidence is informed by our fears and insecurities are able to work graciously in nurturing ways with our students, while those of us with tortured self-esteem can only operate in fear, waging endless wars of self-preservation on the front lines in our classrooms.

The faces I see in my seventh- or eighth-grade classes every September can't help but express variations of deep distrust. They know my job is to find out how much they do not know and humiliate them if I can in the process. That is what they know and expect, because that is what schools and society have taught them.

It takes a long time before any students can believe that they can value what they know and that they can learn from each other. Some of them never believe it.

We need to start asking questions of ourselves. We must question our intentions: What am I doing? Why am I doing it? Am I enabling students or disabling them?

Get the assessors to assess themselves. Perhaps we even need the assessed to asses the assessors.

That's how we can begin to use assessment better.

To answer Watrous and Willett's call to use assessment to nurture, we must exorcise the notion of assessment that expects, predicts, and ensures the failure of our students. We must abandon the competitive model where only one can be on top. We must question our fears and insecurities, if we are ever to accept difference and value it, to take an alternative perspective on assessment.

The two most informative texts for me when I began teaching nearly 20 years ago were *Teaching as a Subversive Activity* by Postman and Weingartner and *Catch-22* by Heller. From them I learned about the intransigence of bureaucracies. From them I learned how not to kill myself fighting against immoveable monoliths like assessment: Don't use force, don't try to break the rules, bend them. Use judo to make a "soft revolution."

I may have gotten a perspective from Heller, Postman, and Weingartner. I got the rationale from my own experiences in the crucible of public schooling.

Grades.

They still make my stomach hurt because I remember how they feel.

In my satchel at school I carry around my seventh-grade collection of horse essays with the uninspiring grades written across the front. I always show my students. I guess I do that so I won't forget.

I was a smart enough kid, but I never understood why I got certain grades. It didn't matter if they were good grades or bad ones. I just never knew why I got them.

What I experienced as a student, I see students today enduring: Teacher makes the assignment. Write an essay. Due Friday. Students write and turn in what they think might be what the teacher wants. Teacher hands back marked-up, graded papers. No discussion or explanation. No understanding. No learning.

It doesn't have to be this way.

To subvert traditional writing assessment, my students and I use the following strategies:

Before students hand me any work to be evaluated, they help each other go through several steps:

* Know the criteria for that specific work (which has been established by the class)
* Team up with other students to get and give content and editing suggestions
* Ask questions, use the teacher as a resource
* Complete the checklist of criteria
* Give yourself grades
* Do it over if you feel you can achieve greater success

When I give grades for work, and I am required to do so, every piece gets four separate grades:

* Revision Work. Original work, revisions, and editing are all attached. Basically, this grade reflects the effort expended in trying to write a successful piece.
* Content. In the criteria list, there are several items such as logical development or description. This grade assesses what has been written.
* Mechanics. Also in the criteria list are such things as spelling, sentence structure, and so on. This grade tells the form.
* New Skills or Strategies. During the writing of a piece, new skills or strategies are introduced and practiced. They are included in the criteria list. This grade is based on at least an attempt to use the new skill or try the new strategy and the amount of success achieved.

In addition, we use discarded tests from different departments and old copies of "standardized" tests for my students to teach each other the tricks of answering questions.

That's the way I have to do it. With practice and refinement, I work judo on the system so my students can't be taken down.

I don't much like looking at the big picture of public school education, because I see such desperate need for incredible change deep inside educators themselves, and such slim hope for any. Assessment will forever be used to control and oppress as long as it arises out of the dominant mindset, which knows not of different classes or cultures, and cares not.

Despite the cumulative negative weight of day-to-day frustration, I cannot conceive of ever abandoning my role in the classroom. I have always felt my students are the new humans on this planet, trying to figure out how it's done. My function is to help demystify as much of it as possible.

The descriptions in Bloome, and in Watrous and Willett, of what is happening right now with students elsewhere sent me through a charged loop of emotions. First they made me envious; then I got mad. If such things can happen there, why not in my city's public schools too?

Then I got back to work because those descriptions are also my hopes for the future. I have always wanted to make that kind of difference in the world.

Send me Leon...every day and in a small class.

So we could demystify the tricks together.

Part III
Socio-psycholinguistic Perspectives on Assessing Children's Language and Literacy

What is language? Every approach to assessment contains an implicit answer to this question. What is measured, and how it is measured, depend upon how language is defined, and different definitions lead to different approaches to assessment. The most influential definitions of language for assessment in recent years have come from the fields of linguistics and psycholinguistics. The alternative perspectives represented by the chapters in this section both build upon and challenge linguistic and psycholinguistic definitions of language and the approaches to assessment that are based on them. By drawing on sociopsycholinguistic perspectives, the authors in this section urge us to reconsider and expand our definitions of language in ways that have important consequences for assessment.

Over the last three decades the fields of linguistics and psycholinguistics have had an enormous impact on the assessment of children's language and literacy. By defining and studying language as an object in itself, linguists made important discoveries about the abstract and complex rules that govern its structures. The linguists' descriptions of language structures provided tools for analyzing children's oral and written language as a product and assessing it against adult standards. Assessment strategies involved securing samples of children's language, often using formal and standardized procedures, and examining these language samples for such features as the length and complexity of sentences and the use of particular grammatical structures like passives or embedded clauses (e.g., Hunt, 1965; Loban, 1976). Children's oral reading miscues were assessed for their similarity to the linguistic properties of the text (e.g., Goodman, 1969; Weber, 1970).

Psycholinguists borrowed the linguists' tools and began to study language as a cognitive process, looking at the ways the human mind learns and manipulates language structures. The psycholinguists' studies of children's language offered both practical methods and developmental standards for assessing children's progress toward adult language. New strategies were developed for assessing children's production and comprehension of language forms and structures, and the results led to new expectations about the order in which children learned linguistic patterns (e.g., Brown, 1973; Menyuk, 1969). In addition, the psycholinguists helped shift the focus from language as product to language as process, leading to a search for the logic underlying children's language learning and the assessment of cognitive operations such as overgeneralization and comprehension strategies (e.g., Ferreiro & Teberosky, 1982; Slobin, 1978).

On the one hand, the influence of linguistic and psycholinguistic perspectives has led to increasingly elaborate analyses of children's language and literacy that remain largely in the province of researchers and those trained to diagnose language disabilities. These approaches to assessment are often based on the use of standardized tasks designed to isolate what are believed to be very specific aspects of language processing that may be underdeveloped or deficient in individual children (e.g., Wiig & Semel, 1980). These diagnostic approaches, which emphasize the search for disability, often convince teachers that much of children's language is pathological in ways that can only be remedied by experts.

On the other hand, teachers who strive to build on children's strengths have also been influenced by linguistic and psycholinguistic perspectives in the way they view children's language in the classroom. They have learned from linguists and psycholinguists to appreciate the complexity of children's language and the resources children bring to learning it, and they have come to reevaluate the children's linguistic "errors" as reflections of their learning. These teachers have developed strategies for assessing children's language based on naturalistic observation in the classroom, just as child language researchers observe children's language in the home (e.g., Genishi & Dyson, 1984; Goodman, Goodman, & Hood, 1988; Jaggar & Burke-Smith, 1985).

So why in recent years a new perspective—a socio-psycholinguistic approach (Harste, Woodward, & Burke, 1984)? What does it offer that linguistic and psycholinguistic approaches to assessment do not? To answer that question, we need to look at what has been left out of linguistic and psycholinguistic definitions of language. For language is not only a complex structural system which is learned and manipulated by human minds, it is also a functional communication system used by people to serve social purposes. As Slaughter points out in the first chapter of this section, "all language occurs in a social context of some sort," and it is social context that is left out of linguistic and psycholinguistic definitions of language. All three chapters in this section ask us, in different ways, to consider the social context of children's language and the social context in which we assess it.

Slaughter's chapter establishes the sociolinguistic base for the assessment of oral language, but the principles she outlines are equally applicable to the assessment of written language in the two chapters which follow. The effect of these principles is not only to broaden the criteria for assessing language, but also to alter the procedures by which it is done. In both cases, the focus shifts from language as structure to language as communication, and assessment itself is viewed as a communicative act. From this perspective, we see that the evaluator is inescapably a part of the social context of assessment, and the way he or she interacts with the student has a great deal to do with the kind of language displayed. Slaughter argues for "supportive assessment contexts" which both elicit and model authentic communication, and she shows us ways to achieve such supportive contexts by attending to both the evaluator's ways of using language and the students' culturally based ways of using language.

Keenan's chapter extends the notion of supportive contexts to the assessment of young children's knowledge of written language. She argues that we need to create contexts that reduce the constraints on children's displays of written language so that they will show us more of what they know than what they can write conventionally. Her descriptions of three children's writing demonstrate that an unstructured situation with an open-ended prompt may not have the effect of reducing constraints. Based on her work with a diverse urban population, she recommends two ways of creating more supportive assessment contexts—by formulating requests for writing that put the focus on content and by interacting with children in ways that encourage risk taking and nonconventional representations.

In the final chapter of this section, Benedict reminds us that authentic communication is a two-way street. She argues that since evaluation is an integral part of the writing process, assessment is always going on in classrooms and students are doing it as much as teachers. By talking with students about their own criteria for evaluating their writing, teachers not only gain insight into what students know and value about writing but also encourage them to become more aware of their evaluation criteria, as well as those of peers and teachers. Benedict also shows us that the social context of students' writing plays an important role in their evaluation of their own writing and suggests ways to create supportive classroom contexts for meeting students' different needs in evaluating their writing.

In their discussion of the chapters in this section, Tepper and Costa, two elementary teachers from a multicultural urban school system, address additional issues in the use of socio-psycholinguistic perspectives on assessment. They suggest the need to consider multiple language samples collected over time from different social contexts and the importance of the child's sense of security and confidence within the context of instruction and assessment. They also discuss the role of assessment in supporting the social process of change toward holistic language and literacy instruction in schools.

Together the chapters in this section explore new directions for thinking about social context in the assessment of children's language and make important practical suggestions for broadening assessment criteria and changing assessment procedures. These alternative approaches to assessment are based on an expanded answer to the question: What is language? They represent a paradigmatic shift away from defining language as only product or cognitive process and toward defining it as social interaction and communication.

REFERENCES

Brown, R. (1973). *A first language: The early stages*. Cambridge, MA: Harvard University Press.

Ferreiro, E., & Teberosky, A. (1982). *Literacy before schooling*. Exeter, NH: Heinemann.

Genishi, C., & Dyson, A.H. (1984). *Language assessment in the early years*. Norwood, NJ: Ablex.

Goodman, K.S. (1969). Analysis of oral reading miscues: Applied psycholinguistics. *Reading Research Quarterly, 1*, 9–30.

Goodman, K.S., Goodman, Y.S., & Hood, W.J. (Eds.). (1988). *The whole language evaluation book*. Portsmouth, NH: Heinemann.

Harste, J.C., Woodward, V.A., & Burke, C.L. (1984). *Language stories and literacy lessons*. Portsmouth, NH: Heinemann.

Hunt, K.W. (1965). *Grammatical structures written at three grade levels* (Research Rep. No. 3). Champaign, IL: National Council of Teachers of English.

Jaggar, A., & Burke-Smith, A.T. (Eds.). (1985). *Observing the language learner.* Newark, DE: International Reading Association & Urbana, IL: National Council of Teachers of English.

Loban, W. (1976). *Language development: Kindergarten through grade twelve* (Research Rep. No. 18). Urbana, IL: National Council of Teachers of English.

Menyuk, P. (1969). *Sentences children use.* Cambridge: MIT Press.

Slobin, D.I. (1978). Cognitive prerequisites for the development of grammar. In L. Bloom (Ed.), *Readings in language development.* New York: Wiley.

Weber, R. (1970). A linguistic analysis of first grade reading errors. *Reading Research Quarterly, 5,* 427–451.

Wiig, E., & Semel, E. (1980). *Language assessment and intervention for the learning disabled.* Columbus, OH: Charles E. Merrill.

chapter 6
Alternative Language Assessment: Communicating Naturally With Students in Assessment Contexts

Helen B. Slaughter

University of Hawaii at Manoa

Oral language is ubiquitous in teaching and learning, and yet often goes unnoticed in discourse about instruction and assessment. While much lip service has been given to the importance of oral language development, until recently very little actual study of oral language interaction and learning had been done by teachers and educational researchers in real life and classroom settings. However, this is changing with recent work in sociolinguistics and ethnography in the study of language and communication in the classroom (Cazden, 1988; Green & Harker, 1988; Edwards & Westgate, 1987).

This chapter will present a conceptual framework for assessing and evaluating oral language based upon, and compatible with, research on language as it functions in various formal and informal social contexts. The chapter will focus upon establishing a natural context for assessment, especially as related to eliciting language from young children in kindergarten and the primary grades, and from children from second language backgrounds. Knowledge about assessment features, and things that teacher-examiners can do to elicit speech samples to provide a more valid picture of students' communicative competencies, is especially important in the assessment of younger children, who are less likely to be aware of testing games, the outcomes of which may greatly affect their futures.

Assessment concerns a disciplined and systematic attempt to take the measure of something, or to estimate the merit and worth of something. Guba and Lincoln (1981) explain that both *merit* and *worth* are questions of value. *Merit* addresses the question, "Is it good in and of itself?" while *worth* refers to such questions as "Who and what is it good for?" *Worth* refers to relevance in a particular context. In more traditional methods of language assessment, language has usually been assessed as a thing in itself, apart from the context of its purpose and function, while in alternative language assessment, an attempt is made to assess and evaluate language as it functions naturally within various communicative contexts.

In education, assessment has traditionally taken the form of psychometrically developed instruments or tests that are administered in a standardized and context-reduced manner. Testing and comparing test results among individuals or groups has been one of the armaments or features of quantitative research approaches. Often student response modes are limited to a narrow range of correct answers predetermined by the test developer. For instance, the Peabody Picture Vocabulary Test (PPVT) (Dunn & Dunn, 1981), a well-known test of receptive vocabulary, assesses vocabulary as separate from discourse, or the stream of language in which the words are used. In this test, the examiner is instructed to name an object and ask a student to point to a picture representing the object, or a gerund or adjective, but the examiner's request is not supposed to include an article. In other words, the examiner mustn't use an *a* or *the,* since to do so might give away the answer if one picture shows more than one of something. But because the article is excluded, the examiner's resulting discourse is ungrammatical. This is a case where the rules of the testing game actually override any concern for using valid or natural language in assessment. In contrast, in alternative assessment a primary concern is with validity, that is, that the assessment measures what it purports to measure, of both the language used within the assessment process and the language that is assessed.

Assessment is often distinguished from evaluation in that assessment provides one part of the database upon which a subsequent interpretation, or evaluation, may be based, either in entirety or partially. Evaluators are careful to distinguish testing from evaluation, since so much more is involved in evaluating a program than simply looking at test results (Cronback et al., 1980). More recently, evaluators have moved away from exclusive reliance on quantitative or experimental research paradigms and have begun to recognize the contribution to our understanding of teaching, learning, and schooling that may be provided through qualitative, naturalistic, and ethnographic approaches to research and assessment (Bogdan & Biklen, 1986; Goetz & LeCompte, 1984; Guba, 1987; Guba & Lincoln, 1981; Hammersley & Atkinson, 1983). In like manner, language educators are wise to distinguish between testing and assessment. In technical terms, testing presents a set of assumptions and limitations that may preclude a valid assessment of language. On the other hand, the term *assessment* can suggest a wider range of alternatives for appraising language than testing.

A SOCIOLINGUISTIC BASE
FOR LANGUAGE ASSESSMENT

A major tenet of sociolinguistics is that all language occurs in a social context of some sort, bounded by past experiences of the interactants' social norms, intentions, and purpose. As Hymes (1974) showed, the sociolinguistic context determines who can speak, what can be said, how long one can speak, when one can speak, and to whom messages may be addressed.

Teachers and students, especially second language or minority students, may have varying conceptions of the sociolinguistic context of an assessment situation (Slaughter, 1988). In this perspective, context is not a given in a situation, since the people involved, called the *interactants,* may to a greater or lessor degree influence or change the context of the interaction (Cazden, 1988). Therefore, paying attention to the social context in which the assessment of language occurs is of paramount importance in constructing alternatives to the conventional testing methods currently used in schools. However, it is not only the context in which language data is collected that must be reconceptualized. Sociolinguists view language itself, especially the flow of discourse as it occurs in natural settings, as indistinguishable from the social context. Therefore, rather than assessing only *language,* from a sociolinguistic perspective we should be assessing students' *communicative competency,* or a speaker's ability to get the meaning across in a way that meets his or her intended purposes.

Oral discourse is complex and multileveled, consisting in varying degrees of overlapping and orchestrated systems of phonology and prosody (sound, intonation, rhythm, and expression), syntax (grammar), semantics (meaning), lexicon (vocabulary), nonverbal communication, and pragmatics (purpose). To communicate meaning, all of these systems must work together. To separate out any part from the rest for testing or assessment purposes may not only destroy the meaning of the language being assessed, and hence seriously impair the validity of the assessment results, but may place severe limitations upon a student's ability to perform at an optimal level during the assessment session.

Thus, the way language is perceived, the units in which it is recorded, and the methods employed in its analysis will also differ from the conventional view in an alternative language assessment model. Finally, as alternative and competing models of language assessment are developed, new directions for language instruction and practice in classrooms may become apparent. Ultimately, sociolinguistic models allow the possibility of debate about questions of language and power, shared dominance among teachers and students, and the empowerment of less privileged groups, such as low achievers and/or language minority students, through more open and egalitarian forms of assessment and classroom discourse.

ECOLOGICAL VALIDITY
IN LANGUAGE ASSESSMENT

The principle of *ecological validity* (a concept derived from Brim, 1975; Bronfenbrenner, 1976; and more recently described in Ashton & Webb, 1986) is that the broader and immediate physical, social, and psychological enviornment in which research, evaluation, or assessment is taking place greatly impacts upon the behavior of the persons being studied. If the purpose of language assessment is to determine the strengths and needs of students' language competencies in a variety of naturally occurring situations, then educators must attempt to design assessment procedures that allow students to use the language strengths that they would use in more natural environments. In other words, in assessing speaking and listening, students must be observed or placed in situations that will engage them in speaking and listening in meaningful contexts.

Assessment Must Occur Under Ecologically Valid Conditions

This position is easier to state than to obtain, as we shall see in the remainder of this chapter. For instance, much of the knowledge base about children's language development during the school years is problematic because of the artificial experimental conditions under which studies were conducted. Children may often be able to speak more competently under spontaneous and natural conditions than under experimental, or test-like conditions. Conversely, certain experimental conditions may elicit behaviors that cause a student to appear to be a more competent language user than he or she would be under the press of ordinary oral language interaction in natural situations. As stated by Karmiloff-Smith, "What the child *can* do is not necessarily equivalent to what the child *does* do" (1979, p. 313). In language assessment, it is what a person can do with the language, how well he or she functions as a language user, that is at issue (Jones & Spolsky, 1975).

Another problem with the attempt to develop ecologically valid conditions for language assessment has to do with the nature of classroom discourse and the teacher register. With the exception of certain programs that promote child-initiated inquiry and a learner-based curriculum, classrooms have been seen as sterile environments for language development because teachers dominate most of the talk (Cazden, 1988; Edwards & Westgate, 1987; Goodlad, 1983). Cazden (1988) describes the teacher register as one where teachers talk most of the time, "initiate almost all interactions...and interrupt but are not interrupted" (p. 160). In addition, Brown and Levinson (1978) say that teachers engage in face-threatening acts, which may sometimes, but not always, be softened by various politeness strategies. While the teacher, or evaluator, may attempt to create a more egalitarian context for assessment, students may nevertheless be reacting to past experiences of embarrassment in their interactions with adults in formal situations where their language was deemed unacceptable. It is insufficient to attempt to define a natural language environment in terms of the language observed by nonparticipant researchers in classrooms, since many classrooms are notoriously poor language interaction environments for children, especially for linguistic minority students. Instead, it is important to search out those existing contexts or establish new contexts that support students' natural language competencies and facilitate communication.

Keeping Oral Language Natural in Assessment

Despite the countervailing forces listed above, there are important reasons for attempting to design naturalistic contexts for assessment. In addition to validity, mentioned above, the most important of these are those of empowerment and fairness. In naturalistic contexts that are designed to facilitate oral language expression, the language sample elicited is more likely to be at a higher level and seen as proficient (Donaldson, 1978). As children engage in extended talk on topics they know well, and about which an adult may be able to show genuine interest, more complex structures and meanings are likely to appear. In natural contexts, children usually know the purpose of a communicative exchange, but in testlike, decontextualized contexts, students may not know the purpose of the assessment. Similarly, in alternative assessment the teacher or evaluator is free to make the purpose of the assessment clear during his or her interaction with the students. This may be done in a variety of ways. For example, during a conversational interview the examiner may engage in a "give-and-take" kind of talk with the student, thereby modeling the kind of discourse that is expected and permitted within the assessment situation (Bennett & Slaughter, 1983; Slaughter, 1988). This kind of giving-and-getting information, or symmetry in adult–child conversations, elicits a wider variety of types of discourse from children than the usual teacher questioning strategies. This is fairer in terms of assessment, because, when students know what is expected of them, through teacher modeling as well as telling, students are more likely to be able to display the language skills that they may already command in nonassessment contexts.

In naturalistic assessment, as well as in naturalistic evaluation and research (Bogdan & Biklin, 1986; Guba & Lincoln, 1981), the researcher or evaluator is inescapably a part of the context. This view presents a clear alternative to that of conventional testing, where the evaluator attempts to standardize the assessment by remaining impersonal and presenting an identical task to everyone. In the latter view, interacting with students during assessment jeopardizes the interpretation of results. For example, Edwards and Westgate state that "neutral, standardized and 'scientific' assessment of language skills is impossible wherever the child's relationship with the test, and insight into the test-situation are in fact part of the task" (1987, p. 21). On the other hand, from the viewpoint of naturalistic assessment, a student's relationship with the testor is always part of every test situation, with an unfairness or lack of validity resulting from our failure to recognize this fact in conventional assessment. As noted by Edwards and Westgate (1987), in all language assessment it is necessary to recognize that the researcher affects the speech that is elicited, and to make allowances for this fact in evaluation. "Those allowances may well include recognizing that speakers from different social backgrounds are unlikely to perceive the 'same' situation, however carefully the researcher has tried to standardize the questions, prompts and cues, and may feel very differently challenged or threatened by it" (Edwards & Westgate, 1987, p. 21). Naturalistic or alternative assessment may go further than recognition of this fact, in making needed adaptations to assessment procedures to improve the communication context of the assessment system.

ELICITING ORAL LANGUAGE SAMPLES

Linguists have long held the view that spontaneous speech provides the best data sample about how well children can talk. Conversation and narrative discourse (storytelling and other forms of narration) are often more coherent, fluent, and complex when occurring within naturally occurring speech events that serve some particular purpose for the speaker. However, different people have differing opportunities and reasons to speak in public situations, such as the classroom, and collecting data about an individual's oral language proficiencies from spontaneous speech may be impractical for assessment purposes. Also there are some students who, for one reason or another, for example, perhaps reluctance to use a nonstandard dialect in the classroom, rarely speak in the classroom. Therefore, direct elicitation of oral language from students is often necessary in a systematic approach to assessment.

A few years ago the bilingual educators in a large school district in Arizona decided that they wanted to develop an alternative assessment method for determining the bilingual proficiency of Hispanic and other linguistic minority students. These teachers and bilingual specialists had found that the conventional tests used for measuring the language abilities of children in English and Spanish often resulted in scores or ratings that were widely discrepant from the linguistic abilities that the students' own teachers had observed in daily interaction in the classroom. They wanted something different, something that was not a test; they wanted more, not less, information than an ordinary test could provide. Through several years of the combined efforts of school district evaluators, bilingual resource teachers, language researchers, and classroom teachers, the Language Proficiency Measure (LPM) was developed (Bennett & Slaughter, 1983; Powers, Johnson, Slaughter, Crowder, & Jones, 1985; Slaughter, 1988; Slaughter et al., 1982).

The LPM assessed students' communicative competence in two major language areas: (a) the ability to participate actively in conversation, and (b) the ability to produce a narrative text in oral discourse. According to Wells (1981), conversation is the bedrock of communication. Through conversation we can assess a student's ability to produce (speak) and respond to (listen) language, and to initiate, respond to, and extend talk on a variety of topics. Slaughter et al. (1982) found criteria relating to linguistic fluency developed by Filmore (1979) was appropriate in defining language proficiency:

1. The ability to talk at length;
2. The ability to talk in coherent, reasoned 'sematically' dense sentences;
3. The ability to have appropriate things to say in a wide range of contexts;
4. The ability...to be creative and imaginative in...language use (Filmore, 1979).

To this Slaughter and Bennett added:

5. The ability to contribute actively to and influence the course of the development of an interactional situation (1982, p. 22).

Eliciting Conversational Discourse. Using the LPM procedures, an adult examiner attempts to strike up a casual conversation with a student so that he or she is free to talk on topics where the cognitive background of the information is well known to that individual student. The purpose of this kind of assessment procedure is to assess listening and speaking abilities needed for normal communicative interaction, not to test a student's knowledge of various subject matter contents.

Research conducted during the developmental phase of the LPM indicated that the way a teacher–examiner interacted with students during the conversational interview greatly influenced a student's ability to engage in sustained and proficient conversational interaction. The more testlike the interview became, in terms of a teacher's direct questioning and rapid changing of topics, the less likely it was for a student to produce extended discourse on a topic. Conversely, when a teacher assumed a more egalitarian stance and actively listened to and built upon topics initiated by students, the more likely it was for students to exhibit conversational proficiency.

A testlike pattern is easily recognized in that it shows long pieces of discourse and questions by the teacher, with one word or very brief responses by the student. For example, a teacher pursued the following topic only until the child, a bilingual kindergarten student, provided an answer to the initial question.

T: O.K. Tell me about your family. How many people are there?
C: Mm. Two.

T: Two? Your mom, your daddy and you?
C: My sister.
T: And your sister?
C: And my baby brother. [Notice that the child is beginning to follow the teacher's lead in terms of syntax, indicating the student's natural proficiency once the conversational context is made clear.]
T: So how much is that?
C: A bunch.
T: A bunch? Yeah a whole bunch. [The teacher then changed the topic.]

Topic development between teacher and student involves more than the teacher modeling of a give and take conversational context. It also involves background knowledge on the examiner's part of a child's view of the kind of thing being talked about. Often when teachers questioned children about their play or toys, children began a conversation that would have triggered talk between themselves and another child, but about which the adult had little to say. Hence, the adult changed the topic, further distorting the conversational context of the assessment process. For example, in the following dialogue (translated from the Spanish) a bilingual kindergarten student was asked "what do you like to play?"

C: My teddy bear.
T: And how do you play with your teddy bear?
C: Uh, I throw it up and then I catch it.
T: Mm. Do you play with it as if it was a ball? Okay, and what are you going to do today after school?

On the other hand, topics such as cooking and favorite television shows seemed to work better as conversational topics between adults and children.

T: Do you help your mother cook?
C: I don't know how to cook.
T: But do you help her?
C: Yeah.
T: Yeah? What do you help her make?
C: I help her do la pizza. We're gonno do, me and Nina, are going to do la pizza, and Nina does the salad, and I do the cheese.
T: And how do you do the cheese? What is your job when you do the cheese?
C: I get the thing and I go like that.

In another example about a student's birthday celebration, the teacher–examiner knew through personal experience just the kind of question to ask a Hispanic bilingual student. Then when the child responded to the topic, the teacher–examiner could authentically respond to the topic and help the student to expand on it.

T: What do you do on your birthday?
C: Um, my parents take me out to eat.
T: They take you out to eat? Do you have pinatas?
C: Yes.
T: You do. Oh.
C: Me and, me and my mom make um. They cost too much at the store.
T: You make them? What, how do you make them?
C: Take a balloon and we paper mache it. Then leave it for a few days and when it gets dry we, um pop the balloon inside. We then, then we decorate the outside.

The original LPM elicitation procedure was designed to assess one student at a time, but a recent application of this assessment procedure to assessing the language proficiency of kindergarten and first-grade students who are participating in a Hawaiian Language Immersion Program was changed to assess two students during the same session (Slaughter, Watson-Gegeo, Warner, & Bernardino, 1988). This was done to facilitate establishing rapport with students, and because other research on Hawaiian children had suggested that a "talk story" context would facilitate the elicitation of discourse from Hawaiian children (Boggs & Watson-Gegeo, 1977; Watson-Gegeo, 1975).

Assessing two students at a time provided a superior context for generating conversation, as students had the advantage of an audience that included another child as well as an adult. Often the second child would build upon a topic introduced by the first child, thus enriching the language sample and facilitating the elicitation procedure. Shy children were more likely to be drawn out by this method. The only weakness of the technique was when one child dominated the conversation, and in these cases the examiner would try to encourage the other child to participate by saying "And what do you think?" In some cases, the dominant child also adopted this approach, allowing entry into the conversation of the first child.

The following example shows how an adult examiner (E) (Slaughter) stimulated conversation between two kindergarten students in an assessment context, and then allowed the children to continue to converse between themselves.

E: Oh. so two different dogs had puppies? That must be an awful lot of puppies around there.
C1: But Trixie only had one and Tracie had more than one. She doesn't like people to look at her puppies, only people that she knows!

E: Oh, I can see that she doesn't trust the people if they're strangers then. Yeah, she wants to make sure that she can trust them. So do you [directed to the other child] have any pets in your house?

C2: Yeah! One dog, and one kitten, and one baby kitten, three baby kittens.

C1: I know them.

C2: Cute, yeah?

C1: Yeah, the kitten scratches!

C2: And (they sleep on your, yeah). [Both children laugh.]

E: So what do you feed the kittens?

C2: Baby food.

C1: And then, they only eat this mush, the babies, and eat this kind of food.

C2: No, they eat from their mother!

C1: They can eat, they can eat (stuff) catfood!

C2: Yeah?

C1: But, the you know the babies can eat from the mother, and the baby cat food, right?

C2: Yeah.

C1: From the mother, that's for drink, and from the cat food, that's for eat!

C2: hmm [laughs softly].

Eliciting Narrative Discourse. Narrative is another, perhaps *the* other essential kind of discourse used in communication. Rosen (1986) has said that it is in narrative that our most human and valued feelings and beliefs are expressed. Following the assessment of conversational proficiency, the examiner asked each student to tell a story from a wordless storybook in order to assess the student's ability to produce narrative discourse. The ability to produce narrative discourse, that is, a story, is believed to be important in early literacy development.

Narrative discourse was elicited by asking the students to first look through a wordless book, taking their time, and then tell the story, using the wordless book as a prop. There has been a great deal of research in studying narrative discourse using wordless books, one outcome of which is that, as students begin to read, or are read aloud to, their wordless storybook stories begin to resemble book-like language (Purcell-Gates, 1988). Sometimes their prosody, namely the "linguistic variation in pitch, loudness, speed and rhythm (including pause) of speaking" (Crystal, 1979, p. 33), resembles that of oral reading.

The method recommended for eliciting narrative discourse is quite different than that for eliciting conversational discourse. While it is important that the examiner show interest in, and actively listen to the story produced by the student, showing his or her interest through body language and possibly back channel feedback (i.e., *un-hum*), the examiner must refrain from interfering with the student's storytelling and allow the student to construct his or her own story. This is important, not only for obtaining a language sample that hopefully contains cohesive and extended speech, but also for maintaining a natural or ecologically valid context for storytelling. In natural situations, a storyteller gains and holds the floor, or the audience's attention, during the storytelling episode. Therefore, in asking students to tell a story, it is also necessary that we provide the communicative space that will permit them to do so without constant interruption.

In the example from the Hawaiian Language Immersion Program mentioned above, having two children take turns telling a story during the same assessment session generally worked well, although with the younger children (kindergarten level) the examiner sometimes had to remind the nonactive child not to interrupt the narrating child's story. Younger children, that is, kindergarteners, tended to look huriedly through the book and tell the story more simply, while older children, that is, first graders, took more time looking through the book and told longer, more detailed stories. Older children also tended to be more interested and responsive to each other's stories, laughing or showing interest in the pictures, while younger children mainly focused on their own book, although this wasn't always the case.

Analyzing and Evaluating Oral Language Samples. It is important to recognize that oral language contexts produce surface features in language different from those produced in written-language contexts. In brief, oral language must be analyzed and evaluated on the basis of criteria established for oral, not written, language. Criteria established for the LPM for analyzing conversational discourse involved assessing the student's ability to interact with and make sense when engaged in speaking and listening with a teacher–examiner. Specific categories used in conversational analysis included (a) the ability to produced elaborated talk on the topic (b) the ability to produce complex meaning relationships (c) the ability to produce complex grammatical relationships, (d) the ability to provide adequate background information when talking about a topic, (e) the ability to produce an explanation of how to make or do something, and (f) the ability to participate actively in the conversation by initiating, shifting or changing topics. The analysis of narrative discourse categories included (g) the ability to produce a complete story with a full plotline, (h) the ability to produce complex meaning relationships, (i) the ability to produce complex grammatical relationships, and (j) the appropriate use of verb-tense variation in storytelling. We also noted the use of quotative speech, that is, *he said, she said,* and sound effects in telling the story. (More information about this can be found in Slaughter, 1988.)

In summary, alternative assessment in sociolinguistically valid contexts frees both the teacher–examiner and students to explore topics more fully and engage in language performances, for example, telling a narrative, that support students' language strengths and enables the assessor or evaluator to identify the language strengths that students possess, before turning attention to students' language development needs. Supportive assessment contexts also provide models for the kind of genuine and authentic communicative contexts that are more truly educative, or facilitative of the human exchange of ideas.

REFERENCES

Ashton, P.T., & Webb, R.B. (1986). *Making a difference: Teachers' sense of efficacy and student achievement.* New York: Longman.

Bennett, A., & Slaughter, H. (1983). A sociolinguistic/discourse approach to the description of the communicate competence of linguistic minority children. In C. Rivera (Ed.), *Ethnographic and sociolinguistic approaches to language proficiency assessment* (pp. 2–28). Clevedon, UK: Multilingual Matters.

Bennett, A.T. (1983). Discourses of power, the dialectics of understanding, the power of literacy. *The Journal of Education, 165*(1), 53–74.

Bogdan, R.C., & Biklen, S.K. (1982). *Qualitative research for education: An introduction to theory and methods.* Boston: Allyn and Bacon.

Boggs, S., & Watson-Gegeo, K. (1977). From verbal play to talk story: The role of routines in speech events among Hawaiian children. In S. Ervin-Tripp & C. Mitchell-Kernan (Eds.), *Child discourse.* New York: Academic Press.

Brim, O.G. (1975). Macro-structural influences on child development and the need for childhood social indicators. *American Journal of Orthopsychiatry, 45,* 516–524.

Bronfenbrenner, U. (1979). *The ecology of human development.* Cambridge, MA: Harvard University Press.

Brown, P., & Levinson, S. (1978). Universals in language usage: Politeness phenomena. In E.N. Goody (Ed.), *Questions and politeness: Strategies in social interaction.* Cambridge, UK: Cambridge University Press.

Cazden, C.B. (1988). *Classroom discourse: The language of teaching and learning.* Portsmouth, NH: Heinemann.

Cronbach, L.J., Ambron, S.R., Dornbusch, S.M., Hess, R.D., Hornick, R.C., Phillips, D.C., Walker, D.F., & Weiner, S. (1980). *Toward reform of program evaluation.* London: Jossey-Bass.

Crystal, D. (1979). Prosodic development. In P. Fletcher & M. Garman (Eds.), *Language acquisition: Studies in first language development* (pp. 33–48). New York: Cambridge University Press.

Donaldson, M. (1978). *Children's minds.* Glasglow, UK: William Collins.

Dunn, L.M., & Dunn, I.M. (1981). Manual for Forms L and M: *PPVT-R.* Circle Pines, MN: American Guidance Service.

Edwards, A.D., & Westgate, D.P.G. (1987). *Investigating classroom talk.* London: The Falmer Press.

Fillmore, C.J. (1979). On fluency. In C.J. Fillmore, W. S-Y. Wang, & D. Kempler (Eds.), *Individual differences in language ability and language behavior.* New York: Academic Press.

Goetz, J.P., & LeCompte, J.P. (1984). *Ethnography and qualitative design in educational research.* New York: Academic Research.

Goodlad, J. (1984). A place called school. New York: McGraw-Hill.

Green, J.L., & Harker, J.O. (Eds.). (1988) *Multiple perspective analyses of classroom discourse.* Norwood, NJ: Ablex Publishing Corp.

Guba, E.G. (1987). Naturalistic evaluation. In H.S. Bloome, D.S. Cordray, & R.J. Light (Eds.), *New Directions for Program Evaluation, 34,* 23–43.

Guba, E., & Lincoln, E. (1981). *Effective evaluation: Improving the usefulness of evaluative results through responsive and naturalistic approaches.* Beverly Hills, CA: Sage.

Hammersley, M., & Atkinson, P. (1983). *Ethnography: Principles in practice.* New York: Tavistock Publications.

Hymes, D. (1974). *Foundations in sociolinguistics: An ethnographic approach.* Philadelphia: University of Pennsylvania Press.

Jones, R.L., & Spolsky, B. (1975). *Testing language proficiency.* Arlington, VA: Center for Applied Linguistics.

Karmiloff-Smith, A. (1979). Language development after five. In P. Fletcher & M. Garmon (Eds.), *Language acquisition: Studies in first language development* (pp. 307–324). Cambridge, UK: Cambridge University Press.

Mayer, M. (1973). *Frog on his own.* New York: Dial Press.

Mayer, M. (1974). *Frog goes to dinner.* New York: Dial Press.

Mayer, M., & Mayer, M. (1975). *One frog too many.* New York: Dial Press.

Powers, S., Johnson, D.M., Slaughter, H., Crowder, C., & Jones, P.B. (1985). Reliability and validity of the language proficiency measure. *Educational and psychological measurement.*

Purcell-Gates, V. (1988). Lexical and syntactic knowledge of written narrative held by well-read-to kindergartners and second graders. *Research in the Teaching of English, 22*(2), 128–160.

Robertson, G.J., & Eisenberg, J.L. (1981). *Peabody picture vocabulary test –revised: Technical supplement.* Circle Pines, MN: American Guidance Service.

Rosen, H. (1986). The importance of story. *Language Arts, 63(3).*

Slaughter, H.B. (1988). A sociolinguistic paradigm for bilingual language proficiency assessment. In J. Fine (Ed.), *Second language discourse: A textbook of current research* (pp. 89–123). Norwood, NJ: Ablex Publishing Corp.

Slaughter, H.B., Bennett, A.T., Arrieta, O., Santa Ana, A.O., Garcia, B., & Prather, M.B. (1982). *Methods of analyzing samples of elicited discourse in English and Spanish for determining student language proficiency* (Final report to InterAmerica Research Associates and the National Institute of Education, NIE Grant No. 400-79-0042). Washington, DC: National Institute of Education.

Watson-Gegeo, K. (1975). Transferrable communicative routines: Strategies and group identity in two speech events. *Language in Society, 4,* 53–70.

Wells, C.G. (Ed.). (1981). *Learning through interaction: The study of language development.* New York: Cambridge University Press.

Wilds, C.P. (1975). The oral interview test. In R.L. Jones & B. Spolsky (Eds.), *Testing language proficiency.* Arlington, VA: Center for Applied Linguistics.

chapter 7
Assessing the Written Language Abilities of Beginning Writers

Jo-Anne R. Wilson Keenan

ONE CHILD'S PERSPECTIVE

"That's all the words I know," Alejandro said as he put down his pencil. Alejandro is a first-grade Hispanic student from an integrated urban school. He speaks English in school and to his parents, but he speaks Spanish to his friends. He had just completed a writing task, adapted from Harste, Woodward, and Burke (1984), in which I asked him to write his name and anything else that he would like to write or pretend to write. Alejandro produced a list of eight words (see Figure 7.1). Alejandro did not talk while he was writing. When I asked him to read, he read his words for me: *after, hello, Holly, van, man, cat, dog,* and *can.* Alejandro said little beyond this, except, "That's all the words I know."

The idea that young children, and more importantly young minority children from urban schools, know how to write words and more complex units of written language is a relatively new concept for educators who have been accustomed to curriculum that focuses upon isolating discrete features of written language. For many years general assessments of children's knowledge of written language have centered upon the child's ability to match a picture to a spoken word, recognize letters, make letter–sound associations, and recognize lists of commonly used words. There was a time when Alejandro's ability to write the eight words would have been considered an impressive feat.

Figure 7.1.   Alejandro—First Sample. What he wanted to write or "pretend" to write.

Assumptions about children's knowledge of the workings of written language have changed over the past few years, however, and when Alejandro had completed his eight words, I invited him to "tell me more" of what he knew about written language. Later in this chapter, I present two more samples of Alejandro's work, and the work of two other writers. The purpose of this chapter is to help teachers and diagnosticians to see ways in which they can assist children in getting beyond the words they "know" and reveal more of their knowledge of the workings of written language.

BEGINNING LITERACY

My assumptions about children's knowledge of written language have changed because within the last two decades, researchers have been focusing upon the importance of the child's developmental history of written language as a basis for early language instruction. Researchers (Bissex, 1980; Clay, 1975; Ferreiro & Teberosky, 1982; Harste, Woodward, & Burke, 1984) have begun to uncover the knowledge that children have about written language before they begin formal instruction. Harste et al. (1984) have found that since ours is a print-filled society, children by the age of 3 demonstrate a personal as well as a social history of literacy. They further state that prior to coming to school, children are developing an understanding of the workings and purposes of the social process of written language.

Young children are discovering that symbols represent messages (Clay, 1975). They explore the ways in which messages are generated from a finite group of symbols, and how written messages are organized on the page. Children assume that symbols are intentional and use them as to produce texts that are appropriate within specific contexts.

Ferreiro and Teberosky (1982) have studied the literacy behaviors of 4-, 5-, and 6-year-olds in the urban areas of Buenos Aires. They found that children are learners who are actively making sense of the world and are not waiting for someone to transmit knowledge to them through an act of benevolence. They state that children are learning by constructing their own categories of thought while making sense of the world. Urban areas display print everywhere (toys, billboards, road signs, clothes, and TV), and the children who live in these areas, too, are making sense of print.

CLASSROOM CONTEXTS

There is a danger, however, that the sense that these children are making of the world will not be recognized once they enter school. Cook-Gumperz (1981) states that children upon entering school have had exposure to a range of literacy experiences, all of which have formed their preschool language capabilities. These skills may not be tapped by the more limited focus of the classroom curriculum with its emphasis on literacy training through simple expository prose. Gilmore (1984) adds that children should be seen, trusted, and evaluated as skilled language users and as individuals who have the right to instructional circumstances where pride and ownership are central features of learning. She says:

> Successful and respectful assessment and instruction must be responsive to what children are capable of doing with language across various contexts, not only in classroom or test performances. Too often teachers say the students can't, rather than students won't. The former implies skill deficiency, the latter an issue of social control. (p. 390)

Adults often fail to acknowledge children's texts because not all of the structures may appear in conventional form, but it is most important that teachers of young children are able to interpret these texts and help students build upon them. The challenge that teachers and diagnosticians now face is designing practical assessment strategies that disclose the range of written-language abilities of all young children.

LANGUAGE ASSESSMENT: CHILD AS INFORMANT

To help meet this challenge, I describe the writing samples of Alejandro and two other students who participated in a recently completed study of 50 first-grade students from integrated classrooms in a large city (pop. 160,000) in New England. This study is one of the first to attempt to tap the written language capabilities of a large number of African-American, White, and Hispanic first graders. The study analyzes the processes and responses of inner-city first-grade writers who were requested to write within three different contexts: writing anything of their choice that they could write or pretend to write; writing a known text, that is, a story, poem, song, rhyme, or jingle or part thereof that the writer has memorized or holds "in head"; and writing a story about themselves, a personal narrative. Based on a number of previous studies (Bonin, 1982; Cambourne et al., 1984; Dyson, 1984; Edelsky & Jilbert, 1985; Hall, 1985; Harste et al., 1984; Milz, 1985; Wilson, 1986), it was hypothesized that the participants would show variations in their responses when the writing task was framed in three different ways. As Edelsky and Jilbert (1985, p. 66) state, "When looking at one child's writing under different circumstances, it is possible to see that different contexts elicit different displays of what a child knows." I attempted to discover whether requesting inner-city writers to produce texts in different contexts revealed different understandings that the writer had of written language.

In contrast to assessments in which children respond to a number of evaluator-designed tasks, my goal for this study was to encourage children to create their own responses by engaging in the production of written language. The meaning of each piece of writing, and the way in which it was constructed, came from the children themselves—even though the writing was often unconventional. I placed value on content rather than form. Although adults frequently view children's early writing as erroneous, disorganized, or lacking meaning, researchers have found that children do indeed assign meaning and employ organizational strategies for nearly all of their writing—even markings that adults might regard as "scribbles." As Harste et al. state:

> Since access to the process can be gained through involvement in the process, strategies which allow language users to set aside perceived or real constraints and which permit engagement on the language user's terms are central to growth in literacy. (1984, p. 130)

REDUCING CONSTRAINTS

In order to encourage children to produce written language, it is important to set aside constraints and view the writing from the perspective of the child. I gave children plain paper on which to write, encouraged functional spelling, and gave them a choice of what to write about. My intent was to remove the constraint of correct spelling because many young children are fearful of misspelling even a single word. Harste et al. state: "The perception that when one writes one must spell correctly appears to be the single biggest constraint which 5- and 6-year-old children see as the reason why they can't engage in the process" (1984, p. 131).

Encouraging the participants to write in functional spelling adds a rich dimension to the production of a text and allows children to write more than just the words that they know how to spell. Through functional spelling, children bring into print words that previously existed only in their spoken vocabularies. Even children who can't spell any words yet can "pretend to spell." Functional spelling also gives the teacher information about the child's knowledge of alphabetic principles. Children's spellings can be categorized according to stages of functional spelling that the children used as Stages I through V as defined by Graves (1983), letter–name spelling, and transposed-recall spelling. Table 7.1 gives a brief explanation of these categories.

In addition to encouraging the children to write in functional spelling, I also suggested genres that the participants might select

Table 7.1.   Categories of Functional Spelling (adapted from Donald Graves)

Stage I	Words are represented by the initial consonant only—*m* represents the word *morning*.
Stage II	Words are represented by the initial and final consonants—*mg* represents the word *morning*.
Stage III	Words are represented by initial, final, and medical consonants—*mrng* represents the word *morning*.
Stage IV	Words are represented by initial, final, and medial consonants, and vowel placeholders.
Stage V	Conventional spelling.
Transposed-recall spelling	All of the letters in the word are included, but they do not appear in the correct sequence. A child who spells the word *said* as *siad* is using a transposed-recall spelling.
Letter–name	Using the sound of the letter name to choose appropriate symbol. The child who begins the word *what* with the letter *y* is spelling by letter name.

from in writing a known text: a story, poem, song, rhyme, or jingle, or part thereof. These suggestions made them rely on their stores of personal language. The participants were freed from the task of designing a text; they only had to transcribe one that they had already memorized. I did not know what these texts would be; only the writers themselves could bring them to the page.

As a result of reducing the constraints on the writers in the study and making them rely on personal texts, they were able to take risks and produce a different type of response than they had produced when asked to write anything they could. The participants moved from writing single word lists, copying, and drawing to writing connected texts that contained story language and some conventions of written language.

THREE WRITERS REVEAL UNDERSTANDINGS

The outcomes of Alejandro's writing a known text and a personal narrative illustrate that allowing children to set aside constraints and produce personal writing helps us see more of what they know. When I asked Alejandro what he knew by heart and suggested different genres, he nodded that he knew a joke. He was actually referring to the nursery rhyme "Hey Diddle Diddle." Alejandro recited the entire text before writing it and then recited it again as he wrote. Alejandro began writing without hesitation, but he labored over this piece, sound by sound, letter by letter. He looked to me for approval as he wrote. He would put down a letter and would then question me about whether or not it was right. Alejandro also tracked back to the beginning of the rhyme when he lost his place. He sounded out many of the words as he wrote. The following excerpt from the transcript of Alejandro's writing session shows how he went about composing the piece.

JWK: What joke do you know?
Tell me.
Alejandro: Hey diddle diddle [JW: Hey diddle diddle] and the cat and the fiddle a the cow the cow jumped to the moon. The dog was laughing because he wants the sports. The dish run away with the spoon.
JWK: Write that down for me as best you can. If you can't spell the words, pretend. OK? Go ahead.
Alejandro: Hey.
JWK: How would you put that or pretend to put it down?
Alejandro: I could put hey and then diddle diddle. [Out loud] Hey. [subvocalizing] Hey. How you write hey?
JWK: Show me what you've put.

Alejandro: H.
JWK: Um-hum.
Alejandro: H-e right?

He continued in a later part of the text.

Alejandro: Diddle and the [pausing, saying as he writes] cat and [JW: UM-hum] the fiddle/ĭ/e o right? [JW: Um-hum] fiddle and the cat cow How you write cow? Cow?
JWK: How do you think?
Alejandro: C-o-w.

When asked to write anything that he could, Alejandro produced the list of 8 words, but when asked to write a known text (Figure 7.2), he produced a personal version of the nursery rhyme, "Hey, Diddle, Diddle," which was 34 words long. Alejandro stood up and leaned over the paper as he wrote this piece. He tugged at the sheet with his left hand each time he completed a word. His words looped around the page as a result. When he finally came to the lower right-hand corner of the page, he rotated the page again and continued down the page in a column. In looking at this one piece of writing, it might appear that Alejandro did not understand how to organize words on the page, but this may not have been the case. The organization was not of primary importance to him at this point. The conventional organizational strategy of left to right and down the page may not have been present because Alejandro was concentrating on composing the rhyme and forming the letters.

When asked to write a personal narrative, Alejandro decided to write the story of how he had learned the nursery rhyme, which he said his mother had taught him when he was 4 years old. He said that she had written it down, that his father had written it, and that he had written it. The following is a brief section of the transcript of the conversation surrounding Alejandro's writing of the personal narrative (and see Figure 7.3).

Alejandro: When [subvocalizing] I I /w/ŭ/s/ 4 /y/-e-/r/z/ er, er-/z/ years /2/g/g/2g/-o/m/m/ my [subvocalizing] ago my mother tell told told me a d-/i/di/ĭi/ a/dĭ/t/t/1/ right two d's a diddle? [JW: Um-hum] Me when I was 4 years ago, my mother told me I me a diddle. And the-, the-, then my mother /m/ŭ/ d-/d/ĭd/ĭd did /ĭd/ĭd [JW: ĭd?] e-e/ĭd (JW: Um-hum) yeah, it and then my mother wrote, (pause) that's all.

Alejandro wrote four lines of print from left to right across the page and produced a 31-word repetitive text. He returned to the left-hand

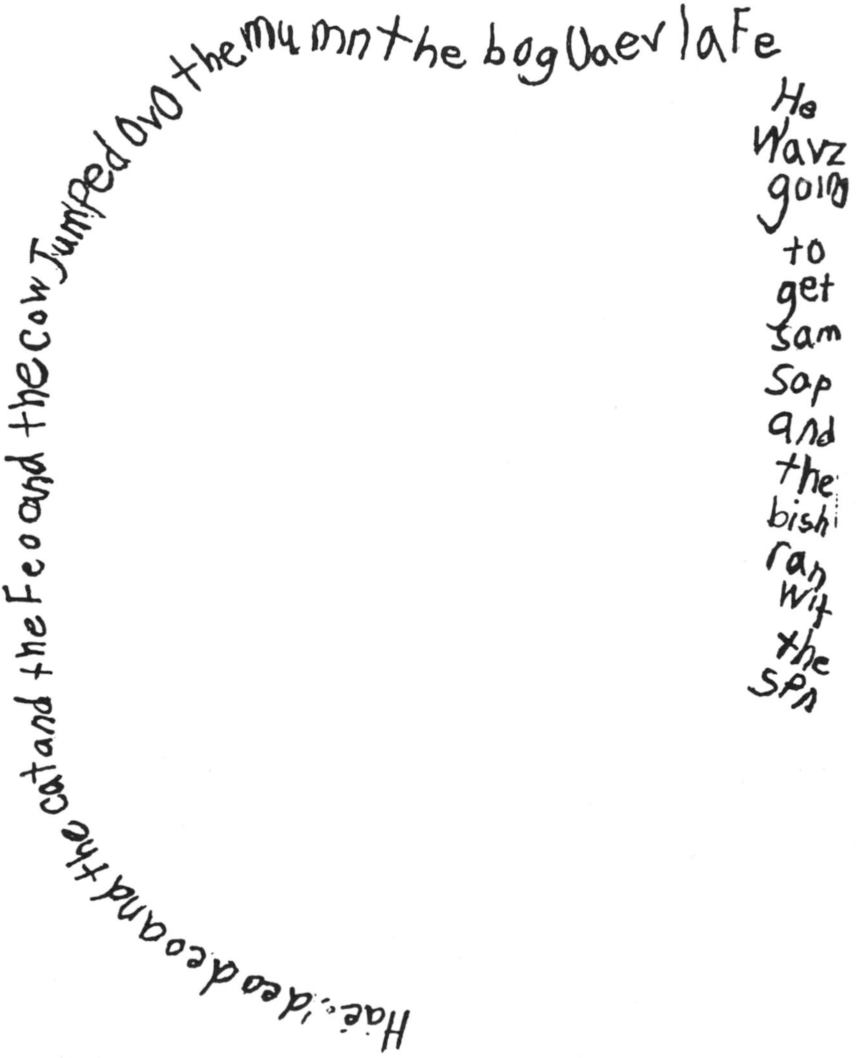

Figure 7.2. Alejandro—Second sample: known text. [Text: Hey diddle diddle and the cat and the fiddle and the cow jumped over the moon the dog was laughing He was going to get some sports and the dish ran with the spoon.]

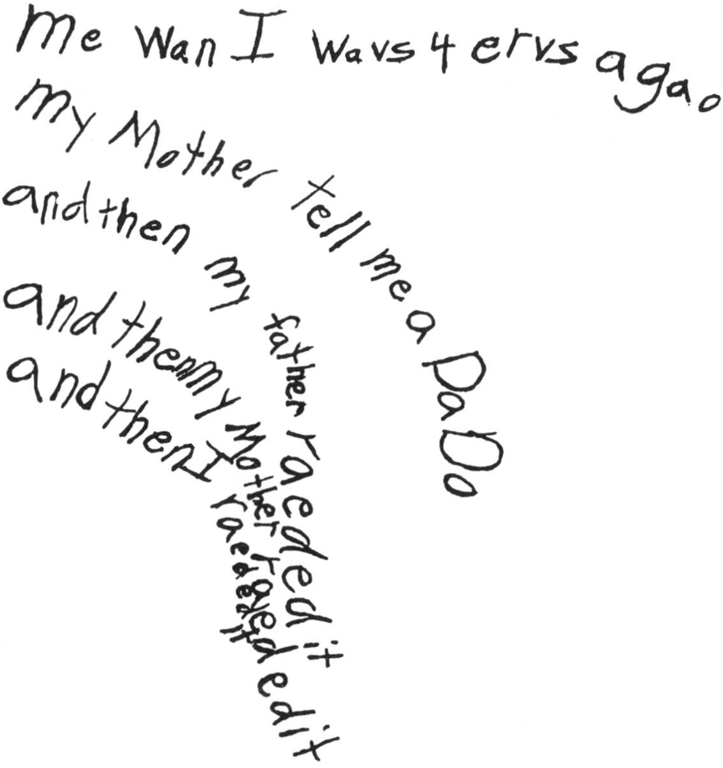

Me Wan I Wavs 4 ervs agao
My Mother tell me a PaDo
and then my father raeded it
and them my Mother raeded it
and then I raeaed it edit

Figure 7.3.   Alejandro—Third sample: Personal narrative text. [Text: Me
when I was 4 years ago/My mother tell me a diddle/and then my father
writed it/and then my father writed it/and then my mother writed it/ and
then I writed it.]

side of the page to begin each new line. Each of the sentences slanted
down the page. Alejandro sounded out many of the words while he
wrote this text also. Alejandro asked me for help with the spelling of
one word, and then he continued using the same process of sounding
each letter that he had used in the previous sample. He subvocalized
the piece as he wrote it. He then read the entire piece to me. When he
read the piece, he recalled the correct spelling of the word *it* and added
it on to the end of each line. He did not remove any other letters.

Alejandro's writing samples are some of the most important samples in the study, because they reflect the processes of several of the
African-American and Hispanic writers. At the end of the first piece,
it may have appeared that Alejandro's written language was limited to

the eight words that he said he knew. If I had not asked him to write anything else at this point, I might have thought that his knowledge of written language was extremely limited. His statement, "That's all the words I know," was apparently based upon the words that he could recall and spell nearly correctly.

Once Alejandro began to concentrate on recalling a connected text instead of individual words, he revealed much more than he had initially. This pattern was typical of many of the African-American and Hispanic writers in the study. Alejandro could both recall and write a text that he had stored "in my head." His recall strategies were to rehearse the text prior to writing it and to recite it again as he wrote. His memorized text helped him to read the written text and to discover the next word. Alejandro also had a firm understanding of letter/sound associations and used them to encode the words. He took words apart in the same manner that he took the entire text apart: he started with the whole, sounded down to the smallest part, and then said the whole word once again. Then Alejandro went back and read the third piece, and he made revisions by adding in the correct spelling of the word "it." Alejandro did his entire encoding process out aloud. At other points in his process, Alejandro spoke directly to me and questioned me as to the accuracy of the letters he was putting down. I did not make judgments about the accuracy of his word but rather nodded and assured him to keep going or rephrased his questions and directed them back to him.

Alejandro revealed that he understood the alphabetic context of written language. He was representing words in Stage IV (Graves, 1983) (near conventional) spelling, as did many other writers in the study. Other processes that Alejandro had in common with other writers were his use of recalling and reciting as "in head" text prior to writing and the use of letter/sound strategies to facilitate functional spelling. He also made revisions in his piece as a result of reading over the piece. He relied upon me for reassurance to keep writing. However, once again, the most important comparison with other writers is that at first Alejandro demonstrated a constrained ability and willingness to write, but then he revealed far richer language when the writing tasks were framed within different contexts.

Julian, like Alejandro, was hesitant to take risks initially (Figure 7.4). When asked to write anything he would like to write, he copied nine words and some pictures from the wall next to the table where we sat. These words were listed in a column down the page. When asked to write something he knew by heart, however, he recited a story that he knew and wrote it without hesitation (Figure 7.5). Julian was a quiet African-American boy with a soft voice, and I repeated each line

Figure 7.4. Julian—First sample: What he wanted to write or pretend to write. [Text: child copied from nearby wall—the A Lion Lamb like in wat to be.]

as he recited the text for the *Berenstein Bears' Trouble with Manners*. Once Julian had recited the text, he wrote it without hesitation. He wrote from left to right but altered the sequence of the lines somewhat. He continued down the page in a column when he ran short of space. The piece was 31 words in length. Julian said that he knew this story

Figure 7.5.   Julian—Second sample: Known text. [Text: there was trouble Big House deep in Bear country a sunny dirt road trouble with manners the Bear Family down a.]

because he had heard it on a tape that accompanied his book. The following is a brief excerpt from our conversation when he told me about how he knew the text.

JWK: Julian, how do you know this story? Have you read it yourself, or has someone read it to you?
Julian: I read it myself. I heard the tape.

JWK: When you first read it, did you have a tape?
Julian: Uh-huh, but now I can read it without the tape.

Now Julian can write it as well. When asked to write a personal narrative, Julian was able to continue writing a brief text in functional spelling (Figure 7.6). This was a two-line piece about taking out the trash for his mother. He was no longer copying, nor was he as hesitant as he had been initially.

Richard, another African-American student, was also a very hesitant writer. Richard had recently learned how to draw cartoon characters and interpreted writing as drawing cartoons. When asked to write his name and anything else he wanted to write, he would ask to draw cartoons. He then paused and drew silently. When Richard was not satisfied with the way his picture was turning out, he made changes. At one point he sighed and said, "I messed up on the shoe." He then erased it, making it slightly larger. Later, Richard added a skateboard and lines to show that a cat jumping in the air. Richard also added a dog, and said, "But I ain't that good at dogs." Richard said that he had practiced these drawings at home. He was incorporating demonstrations of drawings he had seen previously into the task. He made additional erasures when he wasn't satisfied with his product. He drew and revised his drawing constantly.

Richard then drew the cat and dog's owner. He looked at the man's eye, erased it, and changed it. Richard said, "Messed up in the eye." He had originally drawn slanted lines across the eyes, but changed these to single dots representing the pupils. Once Richard saw the eye, he recognized that it was not correct and changed it. This is similar to the process that other writers went through when they realized that a word that they had written down was not spelled correctly and then erased it and changed it. Later, he drew a house (see Figure 7.7).

When asked to write something that he knew by heart, Richard did not initially perceive himself as being able to write a story. I felt that he could, however, because he had already drawn characters and

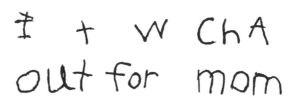

Figure 7.6.   Julian—Third sample: Personal Narrative. [Text: I put the trash out for mom.]

Figure 7.7.   Richard—First Sample

described the action that was taking place in his drawings. He resisted the writing by saying that he only knew how to draw, then he was hesitant to spell, and finally he said that he could not remember an entire text. He said, "I don't know nothin' except cartoons and all kinds of drawings." I coached him and offered him the options of writing only part of a story and "pretending" to spell. He interpreted this at first as writing in the air above the paper. He was gradually able to produce the story, *The Gingerbread Man*. The following is a brief excerpt from our conversation as I encouraged him to write.

JWK: What story do you know?
R: Gingerbreadman.
JWK: How does that start? Or what do you know of it? Any part at all.

R: Once upon a time there was an old man, a old man and a little boy.
JWK: Could you write that down for me? As best you can—pretend to spell it
        if you can't spell it? Once upon a time...
R: I don't know how to spell *once*.
JWK: Spell as best you can, pretend I'm not here.
R: I don't know how to write it. I don't know how ta...
JWK: Pretend.
R: [Writes in the air just above the paper.]
JWK: Let your pencil touch the page; it's ok. Once...
JWK: Um-hum, that's the idea.
R: I can't remember the whole story.
JWK: That's ok.
R: I don't even remember the first part.
JWK: Just put down what you just told me.
R: Once upon...(softly)
JWK: UM-hum
        [pause while he writes]

Once he acknowledged that he knew a story, he was then able to
begin to write it (Figure 7.8). Richard recited part of the text and then
wrote it. After that, he recalled the next section and wrote it. Richard
needed continued encouragement as he wrote. By remembering his
memorized text and accepting a great deal of coaching from me,

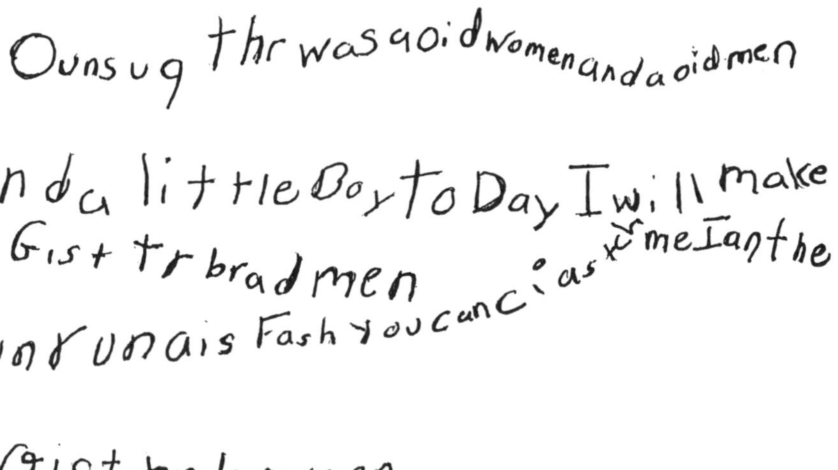

Figure 7.8.   Richard—Second sample: Known text. [Text: Once upon there
was a old women and a old man and a little boy today I will make a
gingerbreadman run run as fast you can catch me I am the
Gingerbreadmen.]

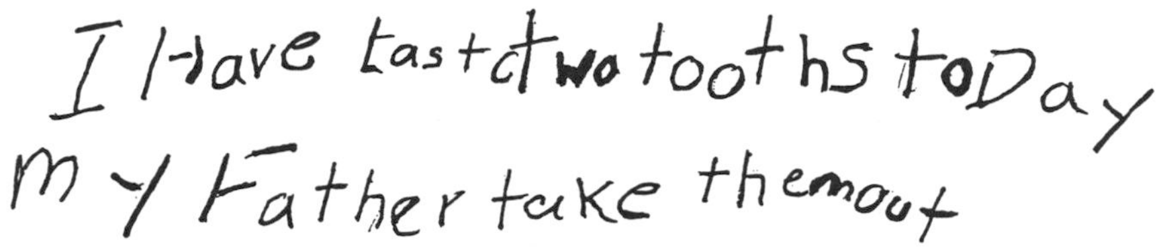

I Have Lastctwo tooths toDay my Father take themout

Figure 7.9.   Richard—Third sample: Personal narrative. [Text: I Have Lost to tooths today my father take them out.]

Richard broke through and was able to produce a 33-word text, using both conventional and functional spelling. This piece contained story language and capitalization. It was among the richest writing samples in the study. At one point, Richard was unsure of the exact text he was trying to remember page by page, but he was able to retell the part of the story when the gingerbread man popped from the oven. He sang the words of the escaping gingerbread man, convincing me that he was sure of that part of the text. I encouraged him to continue writing down that part of the story, which he was then able to do.

When asked to write a personal narrative, Richard continued to write in functional spelling. This time he wrote an 11-word piece about losing his teeth. By this point Richard was comfortable with his functional spelling and focused on the message rather than the spelling. He clearly enjoyed drawing, however, and seemed to prefer to draw rather than write, but he showed that he could indeed produce a written text (Figure 7.9).

AN ALTERNATIVE WAY OF ASSESSMENT

Alejandro, Julian, and Richard were initially hesitant writers who revealed richer knowledge of written language when they took risks because constraints had been reduced, and when they drew on their personal knowledge of memorized texts. The profiles of these writers show teachers and diagnosticians ways in which they can assist children in getting beyond the words they "know" and reveal more of their knowledge of the workings of written language. When I asked the children to write texts that they knew by heart, I suggested genres that the writers might select, but they had to rely on their stores of personal language. In writing the memorized texts they did not have to compose a new text; they needed only to transcribe one that they already knew. Once encoded, the texts became readily accessible reading material. I perceived, trusted, and evaluated these students as skilled language-users and as individuals who had the "behind the eye" (Smith, 1980) and the "behind the pen" information necessary to write texts. I also encouraged the participants to write in functional spelling. Once they felt comfortable, they made their own decisions about spelling and organization. They responded and revealed their knowledge of written language once they realized that they could produce the texts on their own terms.

Teachers and diagnosticians can use the procedures described in this study to maximize opportunities for children to reveal the broadest picture of their understandings of written language. The assessment strategies would probably be most beneficial to the diagnostician or teacher who is attempting to find out what reluctant writers know, but they could be used with any child. Assessments take approximately 20–30 minutes and should be done on an individual basis. The first step is to elicit writing samples from the child by providing unlined paper and a writing instrument and requesting him or her to write. The diagnostician should ask the child to write something that he or she knows by heart, because pieces that children already know and can recite "by heart" provide an immediate channel into text production, and link oral and written language. Diagnosticians can suggest a variety of types of texts that the child might write, including songs, poems, jokes, rhymes, oaths, and stories. Functional spelling and children's organizational structures should be encouraged. Children should also be given time to recite memorized texts out loud, as this type of rehearsal aids in the recall of the text to be written. These sessions should not be "testing" sessions that attempt to measure discrete skills, but should be viewed as an opportunity for interactive exchange between the child and the diagnostician. As shown in this study, sessions that allow time for conversation and clarification between the researcher and participant can result in extension of the knowledge that is revealed. This type of assessment session broadens diagnosis beyond the scope of questions or writing tasks that are framed solely in adult language.

EVALUATING FROM AN INFORMED PERSPECTIVE

The assessment procedures alone will not uncover extensive knowledge, however. In order for diagnosticians and teachers to be able to identify a child's knowledge of written language, they must first set aside the constraints of their own assumptions about children's knowledge of written language and gain an understanding of the milestones of written language development. The emphasis of the assessment must shift from children's knowledge of discrete sounds and skills to children's holistic understanding written language. This shift in emphasis requires that evaluators understand the variety of texts that children produce and the variety of ways in which they produce them, specifically risks taken, genre, organizational patterns, and spelling patterns. Once diagnosticians understand children's ways with written language, they will view children's writing from a fresh perspective. They can then encourage children to engage in the production of written language on their own terms, where the meaning of the pieces of writing and the way in which they are constructed come from the writers themselves. Those assessing children's knowledge of written language can then allow the child to present the text in functional spelling and with organizational structures that differ from adult forms. When these constraints are reduced, evaluators will seek understandings of written language that extend beyond lists of words and the surface features of texts and will ask children to "tell more" when they respond, "That's all the words I know."

REFERENCES

Bissex, G. (1980). *Gyns at wrk: A child learns to write and read.* Cambridge, MA: Harvard University Press.

Bonin, S. (1982). Beyond storyland: Young writers can tell it other ways. In T. Newkirk & N. Atwell (Eds.), *Understanding writing.* Chelmsford, MA: Northeast Regional Exchange.

Cambourne, B., Farrar, P., Hammond, J., Pretty, R., Stone, M., & Vine, E. (1984). *Process writing with English and non-English speaking children in kindergarten classes: A report on research in progress.* Wollongong, New South Wales: Centre for Studies in Literacy, University of Wollongong.

Clay, M. (1975). *What did I write?* London: Heinemann.

Cook-Gumperz, J. (1984). *Final report on school/home ethnography project,* Berkeley, CA: University of California Press.

Dyson, A. (1984). Emerging alphabetic literacy in school contexts: Toward defining the gap between school curriculum and child mind. *Written Communication, 1* (1), 5–55.

Edelky, C., & Jilbert, K. (1985). Bilingual children and writing: Lessons for all of us. *Volta Review, 87*(5), 57–72.

Ferreiro, E., & Teberosky, A. (1982). *Literacy before schooling.* Exeter, NH: Heinemann.

Gilmore, P. (1984). Assessing sub-rosa skills in children's language. *Language Arts, 61,* 384–391.

Graves, D. (1983). *Writing: Teachers and children at work.* Exeter, NH: Heinemann.

Hall, S. (1985). OAO MAHR GOS and writing with young children. *Language Arts, 62,* 262–265.

Harste, J., Woodward, V., & Burke, C. (1984). *Language stories and literacy lessons.* Exeter, NH: Heinemann.

Milz, V. (1985). First graders' uses for writing. In A. Jagger & M.T. Smith-Burke (Eds.), *Observing the language learner.* Urbana, IL: IRA and NCTE.

Smith, F. (1980). *Understanding reading.* New York: Holt, Rinehart & Winston.

Wilson, J. (1986). Unpublished comprehensive examination, University of Massachusetts.

chapter 8
Looking at Their Own Words: Students' Assessment of Their Own Writing

Susan Benedict

Story # 1

Luke wrote about things he liked: school, arcades, energizer battery advertisements, swimming at the local pool. In December of his second-grade year he evaluated *The Energizer* as one of his best pieces of writing. He explained, "Well, I like how they advertise it."

Benedict: You mean the batteries they advertise on TV?
Luke: Yeah, well this [character] is a battery too, but it's a live battery. I wanted to write a piece about it, and I really like it. I like [the part] (reads) 'One day the Energizer had a problem. He had nothing to do. He was bored. Then he had an idea. He would go swimming at War Memorial Pool. He swam into the afternoon.'...I like when he was swimming. I also like swimming in the afternoon and doing a lot of swimming.

Story # 2

Eight-year-old Jane and Beverly explain why a newspaper they have written for their classmates about school events is a good piece of writing:

Jane: We saw the *Scholastic News* and saw what they had and then we decided to do something like they did, but we made up new stories. We looked in a variety of newspapers before we found the *Scholastic News*. The others weren't very helpful.

Beverly: [This article] is good because of the names. I saw "The Brady Bunch" once, and he was a newspaper reporter, and he mentioned a lot of names and people liked that. So I mentioned a lot of names. That's important to do if you're a reporter.

Story # 3

As an 8-year-old, Luke understood that his teacher was concerned about the surface features of texts. He said he didn't take the time to attend to the surface features of text as he drafted. He explained his process as follows:

Luke: If I want to publish it, then you put in quotation marks. You don't have to bother if you don't want to read it again. I think that you shouldn't [bother] 'cause it's going through a lot of trouble while you could be writing a very good story and publish that. It's easier to figure out where the punctuation goes after you finish writing it.

The previous stories show examples of children evaluating their own writing; all have evaluated their writing using criteria they feel strengthen their writing. Luke, as an 8-year-old, speaks to the importance of producing a large quantity of writing in order to get to the good stuff. Jane and Beverly are particularly concerned with the appropriateness of their content in relationship to what they see as the constraints of a specific genre.

Flower and Hayes (1981) note that "sub-processes of revising and evaluating, along with generating share the special distinction of being able to interrupt any other process and occur at any time in the act of writing" (p. 374). Hilgers (1984) adds that "neither revising nor generating is likely to occur except in response to evaluation" (p. 366). Evaluation is not, then, only within the domain of what teachers do even in "assign-assess" environments. It therefore seems fruitful to examine the evaluation criteria students employ.

Graves (1983) states, "If teachers are to help children control their writing, they need to know what children see and the process and order of their seeing" (p. 151). There are no better informants about what students see in their writing or their perceptions of themselves as writers than students themselves. Teachers' careful listening and questioning can provide a much fuller and more accurate picture of what children know, are grappling with, or are yet to discover about their writing than can all the more formal methods of assessment.

Close observation, listening, and questioning instructs teachers about the writing decisions, assessments, and evaluations individual students make. Finally, and most importantly, students' assessments of their own writing have the potential to provide insights for the student writer, by bringing her evaluative criteria and decision making to a conscious level.

The information that follows is drawn from a qualitative, 3-year longitudinal study of seven children's and four teachers' evaluative statements about student writing (Benedict, 1987). Data were collected in the children's second-, third-, and fourth-grade years from the children themselves and from their third- and fourth-grade teachers. (Data were not collected from their second-grade teacher, since I was their teacher.) The data collected included: interviews, children's evaluations of their year's work, children's evaluation of classmates' texts, audio tape recordings of large group shares, participant observation notes of small group shares, reader-based feedback sessions (Elbow, 1981), evaluations of two unknown texts by students and teachers (Newkirk, 1984), and teacher evaluations of student-authored texts.

The purpose of this chapter is to underscore the assessment lessons to be learned from these children and to suggest alternative ways of assessing students' strengths and growth as written-language users. Hilgers (1984) suggests that there may well be evaluative stages through which many students pass as they write. My findings would support Hilgers' (1986) later questioning of the existence of stages. Data from this present study suggest that evaluation is highly individual. Equally, if not more important, is the finding that students' assessments were in many cases dependent on the social and situational context in which the students worked.

FINDINGS

The classrooms in which these seven children worked over the 3 years of the study varied, and yet similar findings seemed to emerge from each of the years. Among those findings are the following:

1. children use a wide range of criteria to evaluate their written texts;
2. the criteria children use can vary from child to child;
3. a child may use the same criteria in different ways across time;
4. children's evaluative criteria are affected in part by the social environment in which they work;

5. there are differences among the criteria employed by children and their teachers.

In the pages that follow, I examine each of these findings by giving examples from the data to amplify their meaning.

Children Use a Wide Range of Criteria to Evaluate Their Written Texts

Even as a second grader, George had strong opinions about his writing. He and I were reviewing the work in his folder; he was looking for those pieces he considered his very best. He discarded one, saying, "This doesn't make sense, the pictures aren't too good, it's very short, and I think it's too pretend. No one would believe it." At 7, George was more than capable of evaluating his own writing and, in addition, giving me insight into criteria he felt helped to make writing good. In this case: the importance of making sense, the quality of the illustrations, the length, and conventions of genre—even in fantasy the action in the story must be believable, given the context of the story.

During the next 3 years George and his classmates used a variety of criteria to support their evaluations of student texts. Among the criteria the students used were: the inclusion of excitement or action, the appropriateness of details to the text, the adherence to the standard form concerning surface features of text, the liveliness of leads and the satisfaction derived from endings, the degree to which the author adhered to the student's understanding of the conventions of genre, the content, and the inclusion of humor to name a few.

Beverly's explanation in her fourth-grade year about how she felt a writer ought to determine what details were important to a piece of writing and which were extraneous and perhaps interfered with the story is typical of the data collected across the children concerning the criteria listed above as well as many additional criteria.

Beverly: Like if you wanted to tell about an old lady who lived in a house. If the lady wasn't in the house a lot, if she was mostly out in her garden, you wouldn't describe the house, but you wouldn't also describe the whole garden. You'd think about the garden—what parts she was working in most or were most important to the story, and you might put in a lot of detail about that.

Benedict: Why is it important to do that?

Beverly: You might want to put the house was a medium-sized house—just enough for the old lady, 'cause it won't have a lot to do with the story. It's not the setting that the old lady's in the most or anything.

The depth of some of the children's explanations of their application of criteria for good writing, and the breadth of those criteria, point to the lessons we can learn from children if we will make time and insure that there are opportunities for conversations of this nature within our classrooms.

The Criteria Children Use can Vary from Child to Child

Figure 8.1 demonstrates the wide range of text-related criteria the students used over the course of the study. Examination of the chart will show, for example, that Beatrix, Beverly, George, Jane, and Luke spoke of the use of language when they evaluated texts. Neither Jack nor Sarah used this criterion. In the same way, only Beatrix and Beverly considered plot when evaluating fictional writing.

Figure 8.2 is the lead to Beverly's story *The Swinging Door.* This is a story Beverly wrote as a third grader. She discussed it in process. In addition several of her peers also discussed this story. First, let's look at Beverly's evaluation of this piece.

Beverly: I like doing dialogue when I start because it doesn't start at the very beginning...and I just put in what a real kid might say. Like the "Aw." It makes it plainer. If he said, "Mother, Father, I'm all together old enough," you might put a different voice than if you wrote, "Aw, Mom, Dad, I'm plenty old enough."

Benedict: Is there anything else you did that makes this good?

Beverly: I liked how the mother was so positive about making her decision, and it didn't go on and on about something that has about this much (motions with thumb and index finger) to do with the whole piece...if I know something is a real important part of the story, I should put a lot of detail in.

Beverly has evaluated the success of this piece by using a number of criteria, namely, the lead, dialogue, details, and suspense. Now let's turn to a discussion of this story that involved several of her peers:

Jane: I just liked the excitment of that—at the beginning especially.

Beatrix: It's like a mystery. I like mysteries.

Jane: I like how at the beginning when the eyes came out on the door, and he was so scared and he picked up the phone and he said, "Now I won't call, I won't." Then the second time when he hid under the table.

Benedict: Are you saying that you like the way she built the suspense?

Jane: Yeah.

Luke: It could happen, and also I liked the eyes and how she make the story.

Figure 8.1. The Use of Text-Related Criteria in Grades Two, Three, and Four

	Beatrix			Beverly			Geroge			Jack			Jane			Luke			Sarah		
	2	3	4	2	3	4	2	3	4	2	3	4	2	3	4	2	3	4	2	3	4
Language	□	□	■	□	■	■	□	■	■	□	□	□	■	■	■	□	□	■	□	□	□
Experience	■	■	■	□	■	■	■	■	■	■	□	□	□	□	□	■	□	□	□	□	□
Surface Features	■	■	■	□	■	□	□	■	■	□	■	■	□	■	□	□	■	■	□	■	□
Realism	□	□	□	□	□	■	□	■	□	□	□	□	□	■	■	□	□	□	□	□	□
Plot	□	□	■	□	■	■	□	□	□	□	□	□	□	□	□	□	□	□	□	□	□
Illustrations	□	□	□	□	□	□	■	■	□	□	□	□	□	□	□	■	■	■	□	□	□
Action	□	■	□	□	■	□	□	■	□	□	■	■	□	■	□	□	■	□	□	■	□
Content	□	□	□	□	■	□	□	■	□	□	□	■	□	■	□	□	■	□	□	□	□
Dialogue	□	■	□	□	□	□	□	□	□	□	□	□	□	■	□	□	□	□	■	■	□
Effort	□	□	□	□	■	□	□	□	□	□	□	□	■	■	□	□	□	■	□	□	□
Genre	■	■	□	□	■	■	■	■	■	□	□	□	□	■	□	□	■	□	■	□	□
Humor	■	■	□	□	□	□	■	■	■	□	□	□	□	■	□	□	■	□	□	■	□
Leads/Endings	□	■	□	□	■	□	□	■	□	□	■	■	□	■	□	■	■	■	■	□	□
Point of View	□	□	□	□	□	■	□	□	■	□	□	□	□	□	□	□	□	□	□	□	□
Purpose	□	■	□	□	■	□	■	■	■	□	□	□	■	■	□	□	□	□	□	□	□
Sense	□	□	□	□	□	□	■	□	□	□	□	□	□	■	□	■	□	□	□	□	□
Show not Tell	□	□	□	□	□	□	□	□	□	□	□	□	□	□	■	□	□	□	□	□	□
Surprise	□	■	□	□	□	□	□	■	□	□	□	□	□	■	□	□	□	□	□	□	□
Suspense	□	□	□	□	□	□	□	□	□	□	□	□	□	□	□	□	□	■	□	□	□
Titles	□	□	□	□	■	□	□	□	□	□	■	□	□	□	□	□	■	□	□	□	□

Note: Sarah had no criteria listed for the fourth-grade year. This is due to the fact that no text-related criteria were apparent or inferrable from the fourth-grade date.
■ criterion used repeatedly by student at this grade level
□ criterion not used by student at this grade level.

Beatrix: I liked how the guy said "PLEASE."
Benedict: Oh, about being left alone?
Beatrix: Yeah. He sounds like a real kid. I always do that to stay up late.

What strikes one reader about a piece of writing may or may not strike another. In the same way, readers often look for different

Figure 8.2.   The Swinging Door

Aw, Mom, Dad, I'm plenty old enough!" protested Adam MacClaine, who everyone called Ace (goodness knows why).

"But, Adam, you know perfectly well last time we left you alone you called up, and we had to come home," remembered his mother.

"At my boss' house you called us to come home," added Mr. MacLaine.

"What if I promise not to call?" asked Ace.

"Adam," Mrs. MacLaine started to say hesitantly, breaking the silence. "I think George, and I should let you stay home along tonight."

"You won't regret it, Ma!" Ace cried.

"Shirley, are you sure you're makeing the decision that's right?" questioned George MacLaine.

"Positive."

"Hmm, well, OK."

About a half hour after his parents left, Ace started getting a little bit scared. He had finished his homework and was walking into the kitchen to get some milk and cookies. He walked through the seinging kitchen door and retrieved the cookies and milk which had somehow gotten to the back of the refrigerator. As he sat down he suddenly was aware that someone or something was watching him. He whirled around just in time to see ONE smooth swing of the kitchen door.

He jumped up, picked up the phone, then calmed down and put the phone back on the hook. He wouldn't call. He wouldn't call. "Ace MacLaine is not a scardy-cat, Ace MacLaine is not a scardy-cat," Ace kept saying to himself.

He looked for a game in his head. Finally, he decided to describe his surroundings. "A dark house with shadows dancing everywhere, three chairs and a table that his mother had refinished, a couple of yellow glowing eyes...A Couple of yellow glowing eyes wigh black line in the middle! Oh, my gosh!"

Ace ran to his favorite hiding place under the coffee table.

---

qualities in writing. While Beverly evaluated her text on her success with getting the desired voice into her dialogue and the appropriateness of her use of details, Jane was most immediately struck by the excitement and suspense, Luke was drawn to the realism in the writing, and Beatrix was predisposed to like the piece because it read like a mystery.

This finding points to the wealth of information a teacher can be afforded if groups of students discuss students' writing. The wide range of criteria these students held would not have been as readily apparent if students only assessed their own writing. Some students may well experiment with writing that their classmates do not. By examining samples together, students may well make assessments about writing that they otherwise would not make due to the fact that their own writing might not contain the qualities a fellow student's writing does. These students were often able to make assessments about their peers' writing that they did not make about their own writing. Assessing student writing sometimes has the added benefit of encouraging students to try something in their own writing they might never have considered.

A Child May Use the Same Criteria in Different Way Across Time

The changes in the way Luke used the criterion of illustrations to evaluate student-authored texts is an example of the long and subtle changes that were taking place with many of the students' criteria. In the late fall of his second-grade year Luke frequently identified the best parts of his stories as those where he liked his illustrations. In the case of the following illustration, he felt no need to add text because he'd already told his story in his drawing (see Figure 8.3). In May we talked about this piece again; his evaluation changed.

Luke: It barely has anything.
Benedict: You have lots of detailed pictures.
Luke: There's not that much words in it.
Benedict: Do you have to have words to make it good?
Luke: Yeah. 'Cause it tells it better that way. 'Cause if you have no words and say somebody's in the building taking a drink—you'll probably think someone's brushing their teeth in the building.
Benedict: Someone might misinterpret your picture if you don't tell what's happening in the words?
Luke: Yeah.

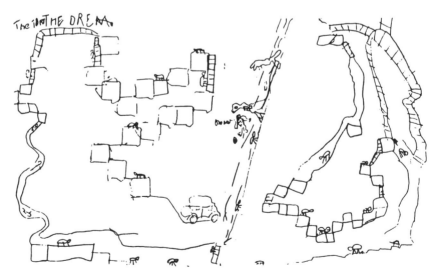

Figure 8.3.   The Turtle: The Dream

In his third-grade year Luke was still grappling with the need for the author to use words to accurately tell his story, but on the other hand he still relied heavily on illustrations and felt that writers should use illustrations to support the written text. Luke was a visually oriented child. Stories developed out of graphic images in his mind's eye, and yet he increasingly felt the need to communicate his ideas in written text. For example, he evaluated one of his pieces as poor because it was a comic book.

Luke: People will understand if you write. If you just draw, people will say, 'What's happening?' Like I think books are better [than comics] 'cause they can tell more about things. With comics you don't have that much room to put anything in.

Although Luke stated that the words were more important in a story than the pictures, he did not eliminate illustrations altogether. For him they played a crucial role.

The balance between writing and drawing continued to be a source of concern for Luke even in his fourth-grade year. Although he expressed the desire to tell his stories with text, the freewheeling adventure stories he liked to write still developed from the illustrations he drew. Drawing was one of his major sources for topic selection and development of story. In second grade Luke seemed to feel he had already told the story through his illustrations and saw little need to repeat in writing what he'd already done with his drawing.

By fourth grade, although Luke seemed to continue to use drawing for planning purposes, he wanted to tell his stories in the text. He began to see the value of multiple drafts. He shared his drawings and limited texts with his peers; the talking and the listening seemed to help him to reexamine his initial story plan and make telling his story in prose approachable. Figure 8.4 is Luke's original draft of a science fiction piece called *The Transformers*. Figure 8.5 shows his revision of the same part of the text.

Luke's continued examination of the role of illustrations in his fictional writing changed from "I've told the story with pictures—I'm done," to an awareness that the text did not match the extravagance of the illustration, to an effort to tell his stories in text. It is important to note that these changes did not happen quickly.

The discussion above was typical of the kinds of changes which were taking place in the children's criteria as they continued to write and evaluate their texts. The students seemed to need the time to work through their writing concerns and arrive at comfortable decisions. For Luke that work concerning the role of illustrations in his writing was still in process late in his fourth-grade year.

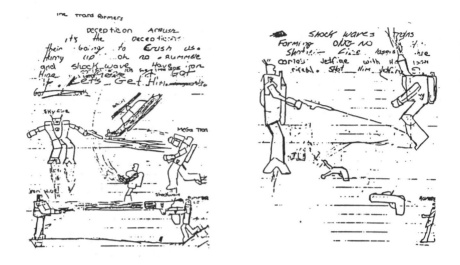

Figure 8.4.   Original Text: The Transformers

Because students' growth in writing does not always fit neatly into academic calendar years, it is important for students' assessments of their writing to be ongoing. The slow, subtle changes Luke made in his evaluation of the role and significance of illustrations would not have been apparent had a portfolio of his evaluative criteria not been established. Often it is only over time that we can observe growth and change.

Its the Decpticons thier going to crush us says twirl: lokli ... rummble and shock wave have iron hide in a corner lets . get: iron hide ohno shock wave. is trans forming to his robot form ya to Jetfires here shoot him down Jetfire now it an even battle says twin twist to bad megatron says to twin twist your Jetfire is losing why dont you send out for wheel Jacks new invention say Jet fire to twin twist ok dino bots form supirion

Figure 8.5.   Revised Text: The Transformers

Children's Evaluative Criteria are Affected in Part by the Social Environment in Which They Work

The following story illustrates how interaction with peers can favorably influence the decisions a young writer makes.

Seven year old Beatrix came to share her writing at the authors' circle one day. She was stuck and needed ideas from her classmates. She began to read (see Figure 8.6). She finished reading. She sat on the edge of the chair, her feet entwined in the rungs. Although at other times she kept a low profile, in the author's chair she orchestrated a dialogue with her classmates. First she answered questions:

Beverly: Is it like a regular typewriter or does it have titles on the keys?
Beatrix: It's like a regular typewriter.
Soda: Is this a true story?
Beatrix: [immediately and a little surprised] *No!*

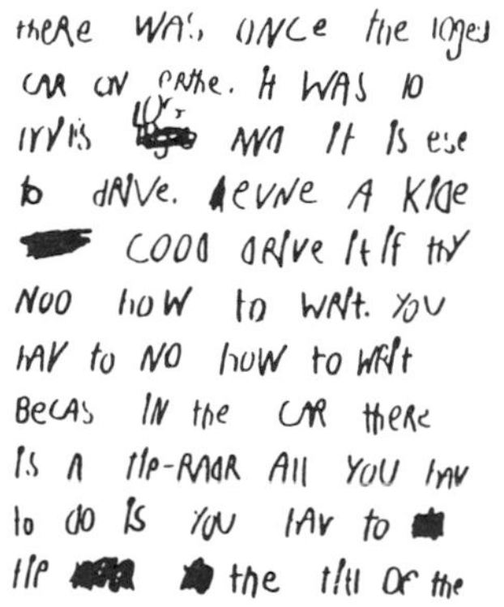

There was once the longest car on earth. It was ten miles long, and it is easy to drive. Even a kid could drive it if they knew how to write. You have to know how to write because in the car there is a typewriter. All you have to do is you have to type the title of the

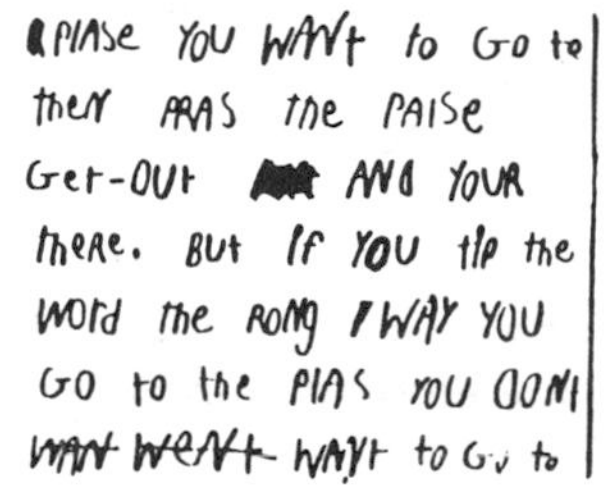

place you want to go to. Then press the pedals, get out, and you're there, but if you type the word the wrong way, you go to the place you don't want to go to.

Figure 8.6. Lead of The Longest Car

Then the suggestions came:

Keith: You could add that you were in it and that you by accident typed the wrong place and went up-side-down and you fell out of the car.
Beatrix: [now seeks to clarify] At the wrong place.
Benedict: I wondered if you had any plans to put characters in your story.
Beatrix: Well, I have an idea of a little kid came along and he got in and started to play and he got into the little car and started to fool around with the buttons and by accident it typed *The Fair* and the car went to the fair.
Jack: Did he have a good time?

A few seconds later Keith sees her theme and is building an adventure. The boy's father enters the story:

Keith: ...and the father starts to type, and he types a story and he goes into that land and all those things happen.

During this author's circle discussion there were other suggestions:

* the car couldn't get around corners
* the car could end up in a swimming pool
* the driver of the car wanted to go to a restaurant named the Roon but by mistake ends up on the moon.

The following day Beatrix listened to a tape recording of her authors' circle discussion and then resumed work on her draft. It was her decision to accept or reject the suggestions she received. "I read my piece with the suggestions, and if it works sometimes I put them in and sometimes I don't," she stated of her strategy. She rejected most. On this day she went with her own idea about the fair. The father's voice, an "I'm the expert" adult voice, was a result of a suggestion from Keith. She included it. Her additions include instructions on how to drive a car from Beatrix's perspective (see Figure 8.7).

Beatrix had many questions and suggestions to consider after she shared her writing. She then evaluated the feedback and made decisions about which ideas she would incorporate in her writing and which she would disregard.

Sarah's interpretation of the social environment paints a very different picture. Although the social interaction seemed to enhance Beatrix's evaluations and decisions, the same environment seemed to inhibit Sarah.

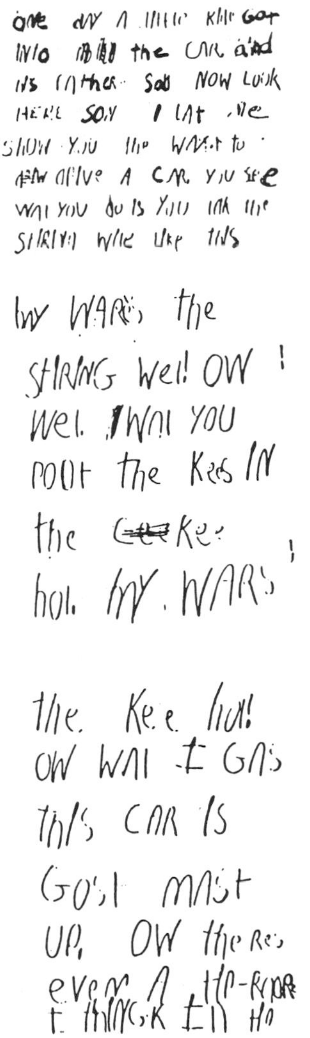

One day a little kid got
into the car and
his father said, "Now look
here, Son, let me
show you the way to
drive a car. You see,
what you do is you take the
steering wheel like this

Hey, where's the
steering wheel!   Well, oh
well.   When you
put the keys in
the key
hole.   Hey, Where's

the key hole?
Oh, well, I guess
this car is
just messed
up.   Oh, there's
even a typewriter.
I think I'll type...

Figure 8.7.   Additions to the Longest Car

In the first year of the study Sarah read her work to others to receive praise. In her third-grade year she continued to use the opportunities to share for the same purpose. When praise was not forthcoming, she sometimes changed her evaluation, but did not use the feedback as a basis for revision. Evidently one criterion she used to evaluate her texts was peer approval.

Sarah: They like it. A lot of people said, 'What do you mean when it goes meanwhile Martha had found the rubies then she had to find Tom.' And they didn't get the part where it said they're outside the black limo. People asked, 'Who was in the black limo. What was the black limo doing there?' I didn't want to answer: I just wanted to put that there.

Benedict: When people ask you questions like that, how does it make you feel about your writing?

Sarah: I don't like it when they ask me those kinds of questions, because they make me feel like I did something wrong in my writing.

She said she liked to read her writing to people but didn't like it when they asked questions. This put her in a bind. She didn't want her peers to ask questions; she wanted them to listen to her writing and give her positive feedback.

Benedict: When you shared this story, had you already written the ending?

Sarah: [Nods]

Benedict: How did you feel about the ending before you read it?

Sarah: Good.

Benedict: When people questioned you about the ending, it made you change your mind about the piece?

Sarah: It does—it [heavy breathing] I mean—I don't like changing things in my pieces.

Benedict: Oh, why's that?

Sarah: 'Cause I just—if it's bad, it's bad. If it's good, it's good.

Before Sarah read her piece to the class she felt successful. Because her classmates questioned her about her story, she changed her evaluation of the piece. The ending that had been fine, now, in her mind, had serious problems. Her classmates' questions only served to point out her lack of success; they did not point the way for her to make changes that would remove doubt and questions from her readers' minds. Sarah shared her writing to win academic and social approval. If in her mind that was not forthcoming, she changed her evaluation.

The text-related criteria the children applied were the criteria that, at the time, they held within themselves and used to measure the success of their own and their peers' writing. They then used the classroom social environment as a barometer to measure the effectiveness and appropriateness of their application of these criteria. When the people in the social environment were saying, "Yes, we think that's good too," the individual continued to apply his or her own criteria. If the group or individuals within the group indicated that the writing did not meet their criteria, the writer then seemed to examine his or her own criteria and make decisions based on his or her own evaluation criteria and the information coming from the social environment. These decisions appeared to take two forms. In some cases, like Sarah's, the individuals questioned and abandoned their own criteria in exchange for what they perceived were either the group's or respected individuals'. Sarah did this to such an extreme that, by the third and final year of the study, it was impossible to glean what her own text-related criteria even were.

In other cases the students apparently used the feedback from the social environment to reassess and reshape their own criteria. This was most apparent with George, who did not often revise individual pieces of writing, but rather used feedback from teachers and peers to revise his writing in general.

For example, when he was 10 he brought his story *The Planet of Eternal Day* to his response group for feedback. He had told me one of his major concerns was the words he had used, and yet he did nothing to seek help to change the language, nor did he make any effort to change the language when he reworked his draft. I asked him about that:

Benedict: I'm curious. You don't want to go back and change the language in this piece, even though that was what you wanted to do originally.
George: I think I'm taking care of it in another story I'm writing.
Benedict: Let me check this out. I've noticed that, when you get feedback, you don't tend to do a lot of changing of the piece you got the information about, but you tend to use that information the next time you write and change, not a piece of writing, but the way you write.
George: Yeah, yeah. You're right. I think you're right. I think that's what I do.
Benedict: Do you consciously do that, or is that a new idea to you?
George: Well, actually I sort of knew I did it, but I never really thought about it.

Although all of the participants seemed to make writing decisions by interpreting the relationship between their own criteria and what they perceived were the criteria employed within the social environment, the decisions they made appeared to reflect, not only their own criteria, but their senses of themselves as writers as well. Those who recognized the potential of receiving text-related feedback from their readers, and interpreted that feedback as information that might be useful while working on a current or on a subsequent draft, seemed better equipped to weigh the value of information and feedback from the social environment. They more often evaluated their writing and the feedback they received through the lens of their own evaluative criteria, making decisions to satisfy first themselves and secondly their readers. For example, Beatrix received feedback from her peers relative to her story *The Longest Car.* Following the author's circle, she listened to an audio recording of the discussion and made decisions about how the story would proceed. This strategy worked for Beatrix.

Those who generally used opportunities for feedback for purely social purposes more often abandoned their own criteria and tried first to satisfy their readers' needs. Because they seemed relatively out of touch with their own criteria, the result, more often than not, was that their writing satisfied neither themselves nor their readers.

It is interesting to consider what enabled some students to respond to feedback and decide what they might do as a result of the feedback, while others tried only to meet the needs of their readers or to abandon the writing altogether. Clearly, the students' interpretations of the decisions concerning the events and structures of their classroom environments did not always coincide.

Students' assessments of their perceptions of themselves as writers, and of the relationship of the individual writer to the social environment, are a bit more elusive than their assessments of text-related criteria. However, the pervasive effect of the social environment which may result in positive or negative influences on a student's writing make it imperative that teachers not ignore this aspect of assessment.

There are Differences in the Criteria Employed by Children and Their Teachers

The criteria which the students and the teachers used to make their evaluative decisions were often different. On the whole, each teacher used more criteria when evaluating a text than individual children did when they evaluated the same text. Additionally, the actual criteria themselves were different. For example, when both the teachers and the children evaluated two of the same texts written by student writers unknown to them, their evaluations had different flavors. The teachers' evaluations were characterized by comments like the following:

• It was an interesting way to use research material.
• I felt the whole piece was clever.
• No central thread to tie piece together.
• This piece is intriguing.

The following comments characterized the students' evaluations:

• A major strength is the lead and ending.
• Some of the frog story I didn't understand.

- It had no action in it.
- I like the way the beginning sounded like a story.

The most striking difference between the students' and the teachers' evaluative criteria was that the students more often cited criteria related to specific aspects of the texts to support their evaluations, and the teachers first offered criteria reflecting a more global reading of the texts. The teachers were concerned with the way the writers organized a paper, approached a topic, and included a central theme. Hilgers (1984) suggests that professionals most frequently evaluate texts using criteria that "require complex cognitive ability" (p. 381). He states that their evaluative statements include such descriptors as: "coherent, consistent, complete, creative, nicely paced, clever, moving, and it really worked" (p. 379). If this is true, and there are similarities between Hilgers's descriptors and those applied by the four teachers in this study, the students may not yet have been able to apply criteria their teachers applied.

The criteria most frequently applied by the students in the first year of the study, experience and length, were not within the most frequently applied criteria in the second year. This finding indicates that the students' criteria were changing. The data suggest that the impetus for the changes came from several sources. First, several of the criteria from the students' list also appear on the teachers' list. This result, coupled with supporting data from the students concerning their perceptions of their teacher's expectations, points to the possibility of the teachers having influence on the students' evaluative criteria. The criteria of leads and endings and supporting details or description are most apparent. This finding would support Newkirk's (1984) finding that students' evaluations may, in part, be a result of previous schooling.

Newkirk goes on to point out that previous schooling cannot be the only factor contributing to students' evaluative criteria. "Such an explanation," he says "does not answer the question of why [a] particular injunction 'took' while others, did not" (p. 294). It is interesting to look at Newkirk's statement in conjunction with the two criteria the teachers used most frequently: development of a piece of writing, and organization. If these were criteria the teachers most valued, it is interesting to wonder why organization does not appear among the criteria the students employed, and development occurs in the second and third year of the study among Beverly's criteria alone and in the third year of the study is mentioned only by Beatrix. It seems possible that one explanation for why some injunctions "take" and others do not may be a child's maturity and development.

These children and their teachers did not always use the same criteria to evaluate texts, nor did each group always place the same value on the criteria they employed. There does, however, seem to be a relationship between those criteria both groups applied. It appears that, if the student is capable of employing a specific criterion, his or her teacher may have some influence in the application of that criterion. On the other hand, there seem to be criteria teachers hold that their students are not ready or able to apply. In other cases the teachers may have failed to communicate to their students sufficient information concerning the criteria they apply. Once given the suggestion, students may well be able to apply these criteria effectively themselves. In addition, there seem to be criteria children apply and value that are not employed by the adults who teach them.

This finding points to the need for teachers to assess their own evaluative criteria as well as those held by their students. This examination might help a teacher to judge the significance and appropriateness of the criteria he holds in relationship to the students he teaches. Comparison of evaluative criteria held by a teacher and her students might suggest to that teacher times when challenges might be made or patience might be employed.

CONCLUSION

The findings of this study suggest that the writing decisions that students make that result in growth and change in their written products do not happen automatically. Writers are constantly moving between writing and assessing (Flower & Hayes, 1981; Hilgers, 1984). Evaluation drives the writing decisions writers make. Teachers might, therefore, find it fruitful to determine the evaluative criteria their students are employing and to provide opportunities for their students to become more aware of their evaluative processes in order to improve the quality of their students' writing. There are many ways teachers can do this within the contexts of their classrooms.

Students, regardless of our awareness of unawareness, assess their own writing, their peers' writing, their teachers' criteria for good writing, and the social environment in which they work. Since this is the case, it is important for teachers to train their ears and eyes to observe the assessment that is already occurring in their classrooms. One of the easiest ways to begin to do this is to take a half-hour or so a week to watch, listen to, and record observations about what students are doing as they write and talk about their writing. This task is simplified if a teacher lets her students know she will be observing to learn what the students do as they write, and that the teachers cannot be interrupted during this time.

The writing conference is a good place to listen to students' assessments of their own writing to ask questions about assessment issues that may not have occurred to the students, and to suggest goal setting for future writing based on the students' current assessment. At these times the teacher can elicit the students' responses to criteria related to the text itself as well as take a reading on the social barometer as it relates to the students' writing.

Small, consistent response groups serve to build a safe forum for students to read and react to the writing that the individuals within the group produce. Response groups provide writers with texts in which their fellow writers are wrestling with similar and dissimilar writing celebrations, decisions, and problems to those they are confronting in their own texts. These groups help writers to confirm and question their own assessment criteria and to try writing challenges they might not otherwise have considered. A teacher can often benefit students by determining the membership of groups and including students who might not otherwise have had occasion to hear the writing of specific members of the group. As a participant in the group, a teacher is afforded an opportunity to maintain a weekly assessment of his or her students' writing growth, as well as encourage the group, and individuals within the group, to address questions and view writing in ways they might well not have considered on their own.

Whole-class shares have similar benefits to response groups. They provide students with a wider range of writing to assess. Some students, like Beatrix, prefer the whole-class share because, in addition to the feedback they receive, they are provided an opportunity to assess the pieces read and collect the much needed grist for their own writing mills.

Folder reviews provide students and teachers with an additional window on assessment. Distance and comparison often provide writers an opportunity to assess their strengths and successes more objectively. Sorting writing into piles that are categorized by varying levels of success is often effective for young writers. Oral assessment of pieces of writing encourages students to articulate their criteria and thus raise those criteria to a conscious level, and also reminds writers about the aspects of their texts that strengthened their writing. As writers mature and the very act of encoding is not burdensome, written evaluations of the most successful pieces of writing can provide a record for the student and the teacher of the student's growth as a writer and as an evaluator. The establishment and maintenance of writing portfolios over individual school years and across school years makes it possible for students and teachers to readily assess students' growth in writing.

Assessment is happening in writing classrooms already. It is not necessary for us to impose additional assessment measures that are generated and evaluated outside the context of the classroom where the writing is taking place. Our energies would be better spent by honing our abilities to observe our students as they naturally assess their writing, their writing processes, and the effects of the social environment on their writing and evaluations, and to use the structures already in place in writing classrooms to collect assessment data. It is by examining the evaluations our students are making about their writing that we are most likely to gain entry into the very thinking processes that will result in improvement in writing in our classrooms.

REFERENCES

Benedict, S. (1987). *The evaluation of student texts by second, third, and fourth grade students and their teachers.* Unpublished doctoral dissertation, University of Massachusetts, Amherst.

Elbow, P. (1981). *Writing with power: Techniques for mastering the writing process.* New York: Oxford University Press.

Flower, L., & Hayes, J.R. (1981). A cognitive process theory of writing. *College Composition and Communication, 32,* 365–387.

Graves, D.H. (1983). *Writing: Teachers and children at work.* Exeter, NH: Heinemann.

Hilgers, T.L. (1984). Toward a taxonomy of beginning writers' evaluative statements on written compositions. *Written Communication, 1,* 365–384.

Hilgers, T.L. (1986). How children change as critical evaluators of writing: Four three-year case studies. *Research in the Teaching of English, 20,* 36–55.

Newkirk, T. (1984). How students read student papers. *Written Communication, 1,* 283–305.

Discussion: Making Assessment a Process

Nina Tepper and Rocio Costa

It is not uncommon for most teachers to question the results of standardized testing. However, even with this subtle skepticism, we continue to seek out and rely on assessments as a means to determine students' strengths and weaknesses. We know that some students "do not test well" or are culturally alienated by the content and context of a particular test, but assessment is still a valuable tool for determining instructional needs. The issue is not whether we should assess; rather, it is how to obtain samples that most closely reveal a student's natural developmental abilities within social contexts of authentic communication.

After reading Slaughter's, Wilson's, and Benedict's chapters on the importance of naturally assessing oral and written language, we discussed ways to apply these ideas to our inner-city, multicultural school system with a largely traditional workforce not fully conversant in holistic language assessment. With this in mind, we arrived at the following thoughts and suggestions.

First, like Slaughter, we recognize that the test setting may have an impact on assessment results. It would be contrary to the concept of natural assessment to set up an artificial environment in which we attempt to gain a sample of oral or written language. But even the most holistic test prompt can elicit a stifled response if the students are attuned to the fact that they are being assessed. Therefore, it is important to take many samples to evaluate over time.

Language acquisition, being a natural process from infancy throughout life, can accommodate assessment as part of this ongoing process. It would be limiting for educators to take one sample and say, "This is where the child is." Rather, it would be more valid to participate in a constant process of assessment. For example, a child who may not be fully comfortable with certain oral or written aspects of language might develop confidence and show higher skills just a short time later or in a different social setting. One of us had a special needs student who showed severely limited reading skills in a group setting. After establishing a relationship with the teacher, however, he was asked to read one of his favorite stories to her individually. His reading was very slow but showed that he had successful strategies for using syntactic and semantic information to decipher print.

Oral language is difficult to assess in one sitting or by using one standardized assessment test. In our school district, for example, bilingual students are rated by using the *Bilingual Syntax Measure*. As the title indicates, the test focuses on measuring the syntax of the child; it does not measure the multitude of qualities that make up oral communication, such as intonation, semantics, or even nonverbal communication. Many students, therefore, appear incapable of participating in language experience activities and integrated learning environments that might facilitate more natural second language acquisition. In more naturalistic, ongoing assessment, teachers can rely on their observational skills to assess students in natural conversations with peers, in classroom activities, or in teacher/child conferences. Teachers can also rely on input from parents during parent/teacher conferences and/or home visits.

Second, the prompt used in any assessment process must be carefully selected to elicit the most natural and least inhibited response. In particular, we were struck by Wilson's finding that "Alejandro's writing samples...reflect the processes of several minority writers." We wondered if the reluctance of minorities to write was a cultural characteristic, or if it was a response to the social setting of school, or both. If children culturally interpret the social setting of school as a place where they should try to do their best, show what they know, and try not to make mistakes, it is likely that teachers will get only short, but perfect, lists of the words children "know" how to spell, not what they really know about written language.

In order for children to take more risks and reveal their fullest potential, the test prompt can be as open as: "Write anything you want in any way that you want to write it without worrying about spelling." We agree that freeing the child of all obstacles is crucial; therefore, memorized texts, drawings, and creative writings are all valuable suggestions. However, even in the best of all testing environments, it is possible that some children will be stifled by insecurity about spelling. One of us has a daughter who, at age 7, is an excellent reader with a broad vocabulary and imagination, yet is reluctant to use invented spelling in her writing. She may need time in a classroom where editing is taught as part of the writing process before she comes to expect that her first drafts will always need editing and reveals her capabilities with written language more freely.

A great deal of what children expose of themselves, both academic and personal, evolves from trust and a positive self-concept. During our years of teaching, for example, we have observed that many poor readers show low self-esteem around reading. Rarely do they volunteer to read anything aloud, and they expect to be wrong when they confront a new word. They are the first to close a book during silent reading time and are reluctant to choose reading during free-choice periods. One student who fit this profile, for example, was reading aloud. He stumbled and mumbled over words, even though he knew them. When he came to the word *necessity,* he quickly said, *necessary.* Then he stuttered another version of the word and stopped, saying, "Oh, whatever, I don't know." He was on the right track, but he felt insecure with reading and therefore would not trust a guess. Years of struggle and "failure" with reading had taken their toll. The challenge for teachers is to develop approaches to instruction and assessment which acknowledge the wealth of language and literacy experiences children possess. For these experiences, if acknowledged, support the development of positive self-concepts so necessary for success as readers and writers.

Before teachers can be expected to openly adapt to any new program of language development and assessment, teacher training and support mechanisms must be in place to allow an easy transition. We suggest portfolios with a formal checklist of criteria to be assessed and ways to analyze oral and written language be devised using some of those mentioned in Slaughter's article. A student profile that cites information collected over time, including classroom measures, checklists, writing samples, and narrative observations, may provide a way to analyze student growth while deemphasizing the results of standardized testing that may still occur in some school systems. For teachers who are less familiar with the terminology, theory, and practice of process approaches to teaching and assessing, a formalized checklist and portfolio system that follows the student through the years might help place natural, holistic programs and assessment on a more concrete foundation. Similarly, having student writing folders follow the students through the grades would facilitate our understanding of each student's skill progress and personal literacy process.

In keeping with Benedict's emphasis on student self-assessment, we believe that both teachers and students should have input into the formulation of an assessment criteria checklist. Staying in tune to our "adult" criteria while listening to the children will help guide the assessment to more objective levels. Although we want to see each child's strengths, we also want to understand the weaknesses. Making the criteria clear will help students be aware of their own and their teacher's expectations. If, for example, children are taught to be aware of their teacher's, peers', and personal criteria, they may be able to articulate what they cannot do now but will strive for in the future. As teachers, we can guide children toward their goals. In this way, children are seen as having more skill awareness than the actual oral or written language samples show.

As an example of involving children in assessment criteria, one of us sought student input about making their daily journals more meaningful. The project was initiated in the belief that students could be more descriptive and productive in their journals. After weeks of conferences with students about their journals, we were pleasantly surprised to discover that most students liked their journals and that they had meaning for them, however brief the entries might be. Since the majority stated that they wrote in their journal special events to remember, we discussed whether the entries would spark their memories ten years from now. Using the student's goal of remembering enjoyable events and our teacher's frame of mind, we discussed ways to expand on our thoughts in writing. Many children suggested that they could to back to certain pieces and add more details. The new criterion came from the students' personal goals, which helped make the new expectation both clear and meaningful.

Our final suggestion involves the point in the development of a holistic language program at which an assessment model should be introduced. Based on our experience with one such program in our district, we believe assessment criteria must accompany the program in the initial stages. In this program there were no means of assessment compatible with the theory behind the whole language model that was being implemented in some classrooms. As a result, it was decided to evaluate students at the end of the year using a standardized basal reading test.

This standardized test only assessed the knowledge the children acquired in terms of letters and their sound associations. It did not reflect the children's knowledge of literature, writing, and other communication aspects of language. Nor did the test show the greater risks taken and the positive attitudes developed towards reading and writing.

Developing assessment and evaluation criteria before the program was implemented might have made the holistic language approach more conscious and less improvisational. Clear criteria early on are important so that both teachers and students are aware of where they are heading. Because we are proposing a process approach, we stress being both flexible and individual in the program development and the assessment of each child, leaving room for change.

Dramatic change is rarely accomplished in isolation. We hope teachers will feel confident knowing that great progress may not happen in the first year, but that they play an important role in defining and developing holistic language and literacy programs. Such programs will be actualized only when a systemwide effort is introduced to train and support teachers in process approaches to instruction and naturalistic assessment methods.

We are encouraged by these chapters to continue and expand our efforts to make assessment of language and literacy an ongoing process in our classrooms. We have learned that this process must take into account the social context of language and the ways we use language with students, as well as the ways they use language with each other. In addition, we believe that it is important to consider the development of appropriate assessment strategies within a school system as a social process that supports teachers in moving toward holistic language and literacy programs.

Part IV
Reader Response Perspectives on Assessing Children's Language and Literacy

Do we dare reconsider traditional contexts for assessment of literary language? By making use of perspectives from reader response theory in natural social contexts for assessment, can teachers help children relive, recreate, and savor their own unique responses to literary language?

Reader response theory traces its roots to the work of Richards (1929), who emphasized the influence of the reader's past experience and personality on the interpretation of literature. He saw that influence as problematic, in that reader inadequacies gave rise to critical concern with the importance of text and the shaping of taste. In contrast, Iser (1974) promoted the idea that reading is a dynamic process in which readers set texts in motion. He suggested that texts themselves are sets of component parts to which readers make connections on the basis of their own perspectives, preintentions, and recollections. Readers complete that which texts suggest but do not make completely explicit.

In this section of the book, we have chosen to explore evaluation of literary language from the perspective of Louise Rosenblatt, a reader response theorist who has focused our attention on students' literary experiences within educational contexts. Over 50 years ago, Louise Rosenblatt (1938–1976) first published her classic response work, *Literature As Exploration,* which challenged educators to consider that each student has his or her own unique response to any literary work. Thus she placed emphasis on the possibilities inherent in releasing multiple meanings among students from the same text. Rosenblatt saw reading as a transaction, a two-way process, involving a reader and a text, at a particular time under particular circumstances. Early in each reading event the reader must choose a stance, or mental set. If the efferent stance is chosen, readers will focus their attention on building up meanings, ideas, and directions to be retained. In this stance, readers focus on accumulating what is to be carried away at the end of the reading. Conversely, if the aesthetic stance is chosen, readers seek whole texts and shift to an inward focus in an effort to center on what is being created during the actual reading. Personal feelings, ideas, and attitudes will be allowed to rise into consciousness as the text is shaped and lived through by readers.

Traditional literary evaluative measures—multiple choice tests, essay questions, literal book discussions, and book reports—all stress the efferent response stance at the expense of the aesthetic response stance. Therefore, it is not surprising to recognize that the efferent stance, with its emphasis on parts-to-whole response, fits more easily into traditional assessment strategies that quantify, test, and measure literary language. So, in scores of classrooms, students are learning to adopt the efferent stance without ever acknowledging their own unique aesthetic responses to literature.

The more elusive aesthetic stance has long been neglected within traditional evaluative contexts. The challenge which lies before us now is not only to recognize and validate aesthetic responses, but also to reassess the ways we have traditionally evaluated the efferent stance. Although we are presently out of balance between the two stances in the assessment of children's literary language, there is tremendous potential within teachers, students, and natural classroom social contexts for unleashing alternative assessment directions.

The possibilities of positive assessment strategies for literary language seem to lie within our need to emphasize balance between aesthetic and efferent stances as well as our attempts to vary natural classroom social contexts. In the first instance, a balance of aesthetic and efferent stances would occur if students were allowed to choose among many response mode choices: oral language usages, art/media projects, drama/dramatic play, and writing. By allowing students choice among response modes, multiple meanings of the same texts can be shared and validated. Many times students may work through more than one response mode to deepen their responses. Hickman (1979) found that elementary students often worked through oral language along with art/media projects and/or drama/dramatic play before tackling the written response mode. Students seemed to use this time to sort out their feelings and ideas about the literary work and connect it to their own life experiences before actually putting their unique responses into written language. Further, students would be observed and assessed in many social contexts within the classroom, such as whole-class discussions, individual conferences, collaborative groupwork, oral and written language processes, art/media projects, and drama/dramatic play. Thus, within a variety of contexts for literary responses, the balance of power shifts into student chosen response modes and varied social contexts which recognize and validate student constructed meanings.

All three of the chapters in this section challenge us in different ways to develop evaluative contexts which balance both aesthetic and efferent response stances. A second theme concerns the establishment of a diversity of social contexts in which we might assess literary language.

In the first chapter, Susan Lehr and I establish a theoretical basis for assessment of literary language. Through analysis of the responses of both primary- and intermediate-aged children, we attempt to shift the focus of evaluation away from "products" to an emphasis on the "process of response within natural social classroom contexts." From this perspective, we show that the teacher is often an observer, supporter, and active listener. Children are active, collaborative, confident, connected to their own backgrounds of experiences, and able to make their own response choices. We argue that children need to feel "ownership of their responses" to experience meaningful and unique responses to literature.

In the second chapter of this section, Carlisle presents practical assessment strategies for classroom discussions of literary texts. She argues that everyday oral responses within classroom book discussion contexts can become the best natural assessment context. When students are actively and purposefully responding to literature through oral discussions, they often talk to each other as well as the teacher. By observing and listening to oral discussions of literary texts, teachers can gain insights about students' strengths and weaknesses within the social context of classroom talk and collaborative construction of meaning.

Golden's chapter extends and supports the need to expand the range of social contexts for response choices within assessment of children's knowledge of literary language. Using an interpretive response context, students are able to construct meaning of a literary text through "cooperation and collaboration." As students explore their individual and collective interpretations of a novel and prepare an actual dramatic presentation, we see that the students' processes of discussing their responses to the novel's characters and scenes are far more crucial than the final performance itself. Based on her work with upper elementary grade students, Golden recommends that teachers become active listeners, observers, and collaborators in creating frameworks for children's oral responses to literary language.

The discussion entry in this literary section is a collaborative venture among three public elementary and high school teachers: Leslie Shaw, Deborah Jacque, and Cheryl Taylor. These classroom teachers reflect upon ways to enhance children's diverse responses to literature and social constructions of meaning. They emphasize the need of all of us to acknowledge and value diversity among the responses of our students. In her case study of an African-American girl's responses to strong African-American characters, Sims (1983) has explored social and literary contexts which recognize and validate culturally constructed meanings and responses. Therefore, the teachers actively support the need for more teachers-as-researchers like Egan-Robertson (1993) to further explore children's cultural responses to literature. The three chapters within this section challenge us to reconsider traditional contexts for assessment of literary language. By incorporating reader response theory into natural social contexts for assessment, teachers can help children relive, recreate, and savor their own unique responses to literary language.

REFERENCES

Egan-Robertson, A. (1993). Puerto Rican students respond to children's books with Puerto Rican themes. In K. Holland, R. Hungerford, & S. Ernst (Eds.), *Journeying: Children responding to literature* (pp. 204–218). Portsmouth, NH: Heinemann.

Hickman, J. (1979). *Response to literature in a school environment, grade K–5*. Unpublished doctoral dissertation, Ohio State University, Columbus.

Iser, W. (1974). *The implied reader: Patterns of communication in prose fiction from Bunyan to Beckett*. Baltimore: Johns Hopkins University Press.

Richards, I.A. (1929). *Practical criticism*. New York: Harcourt Brace.

Rosenblatt, L. (1976). *Literature as exploration*. New York: Noble and Noble. (Original work published 1938.)

Sims, R. (1983). Strong black girls: A ten year old responds to fiction about Afro-Americans. *Journal of Research and Development in Education, 16,* 21–28.

chapter 9

Children's Response to Literature: Isn't It About Time We Said Good-bye to Book Reports and Literal Oral Book Discussions?

Kathleen E. Holland

Amherst-Pelham Public Schools

Susan Lehr

Skidmore College
Amherst, MA

How do teachers evaluate children's responses to literature in elementary classrooms? Two evaluation devices frequently used are book reports and literal oral book discussions. These two means of evaluating comprehension are premised on the notion that the only way to "be sure" that children have understood a book is to have them review the book orally or in writing. Typically, children are told to list the book's title, author, publisher, and date of publication, and to summarize the plot. Then children are told to state whether they liked the book and to give reasons for their choice. In a similar manner book discussions often consist of plot summaries, evaluations of characters, and the provision of factual detail.

Are these meaningful ways of evaluating a child's comprehension of literature? We will suggest that they are not, and that they may miss the potential of literature's place in a classroom literacy program. Literature has the power to touch the reader's feelings and to elicit responses that indicate what meanings children have constructed from the book in relation to their own experiences. In contrast, asking children simply to repeat the plot of a story or to fill in the missing details is neither challenging nor will it stretch the child into new avenues of critical thinking.

In contrast to the narrow assessment focus of book reports and oral book discussions, we will suggest that evaluation of children's literature experiences should begin with a clear understanding of reader response theory and literature's functional place in children's language use across the curriculum. Following this theoretical perspective, a closer developmental investigation will explore evaluative approaches within reader-response-based book discussions with elementary children. The third section of this chapter will present intermediate grade children's responses to a shared chapter book. Assessment aspects will be emphasized both during and after the students have read the chapter book. In our concluding section, we will suggest implications for assessment of children's literature by classroom teachers based on reader response theory, research, and practices.

Language Across the Curriculum

Literature first of all must be accepted as a language, specifically a narrative and textual language. Thus, when we assess children's understandings and uses of literature, we are assessing their understanding and uses of narrative and textual language. To understand literature's potential and place in classroom literacy programs, Britton (1971) suggests that school curriculums have three language functions: transactional, expressive, and poetic (see Figure 9.1).

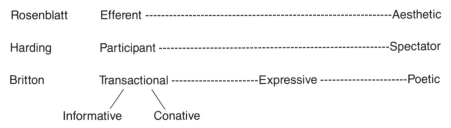

Figure 9.1. Britton's Theory of Language Across the School Curriculum in Conjunction with Theories of D.W. Harding and Rosenblatt

In transactional speech one gives and seeks information and tries to persuade through the use of language. This language is that of the participant role (Harding, 1977) where the user operates directly on the real world. It is used in piecemeal contextualization, as form is relatively unimportant to function. Transactional speech subdivides into two subcategories: conative and informative. The *conative* involves language used to regulate and to persuade; whereas the *informative* is language used to record, report, analyze, speculate, and theorize. Transactional language is an immediate means to an end outside the speaker/writer. Britton (1971) suggests that speakers (writers) are concerned that utterances enmesh with their listener's relevant knowledge, experiences, and interests; and listeners are at liberty to contextualize selectively what they find relevant.

The expressive function is the language of everyday conversation and writing, that which is closest to self. It is relatively unstructured, so that it relies on the listener/reader to construct meaning from common understandings between speaker–listener or reader–writer. Common written forms within this category are diaries, letters, journals, free writing, and some autobiography. Expressive speech helps us to get to know one another through our unique identities. When young children enter school, expressive speech is the language closest, most familiar, and most frequently used, because it springs from the very core of the child's badge of identity. Therefore, the potential for extending the child in the classroom through the use of the expressive mode is great, both on oral and written levels of response, for this is the language which the child uses spontaneously to share thoughts and reactions.

Poetic language is the language of *whole texts:* narrative, drama, poetry, prose, and literary fictional genres. Poetic language is language for its own sake that occurs in global textualization where form and function are crucial to its meaning. Britton (1971) suggests that the speaker or writer is concerned in the creation of relations internal to the speech or written text. They attempt to achieve a unity or a construct that is discrete from actuality. Thus, when students listen to a picture book in the early grades or independently read a chapter book in later grades, they are often engaging in poetic speech. They also enter the spectator role (Harding, 1977), because they are inside the whole story yet standing back reflecting on and feeling the events without actually being involved in the events occuring within the story.

What do these models of language have to do with book reports and oral book discussions? Book reports and oral book discussions, as described earlier, stress transactional evaluative functions of language at the expense of the poetic evaluative functions, thus limiting the spectator role and the opportunity for in-depth reflections in relation to what is read. Furthermore, this type of literal stance toward literature does not encourage the child to engage in meaningful transactional language; in that the teacher selects which information will be given, her purposes rather than the child's are central, and there is a limited amount of persuasive language in use.

In order to be fairly and reasonably assessed, children need to experience both ends of the continuum in meaningful contexts as they formulate their responses to literature in order to become competent language users. While being assessed, children should have experiences with written and oral language both as participants and observers. In the participant role, the writer or speaker may describe what is seen using the language of reports, such as that used by newspapers, whereas writing in the spectator role may produce a story based on what was seen. The use of expressive language may encourage the child to link both the participant and spectator modes through a personal reflection of what is read, for example, a reflective diary that contains thought ramblings about characters and events in books read.

Children's Responses to Literature

Rosenblatt (1976, 1978, 1982) suggests that children respond to literature efferently or aesthetically. In the *efferent* stance, the reader may be seeking information and may focus attention on an accumulation of what is to be carried away at the end to the reading. In the *aesthetic* stance, the reader focuses attention inwardly and centers on what is being created during the actual reading. When reader and text unite, a transaction occurs which allows the reader to take a stance toward the text, and that stance will vary depending on the background knowledge and intentions of the reader. Rosenblatt (1982) believes that understanding the transactional nature of reading would correct the tendency of adults to look only at the text and the author's presumed intention, and to ignore as irrelevant what the child actually does make of it.

Concerning children's experiences with literature, Rosenblatt argues that the entire educational process signals one major message to children—adopt the efferent stance. "What can be quantified—the most public of efferent modes—becomes often the guide to what is taught, tested, or researched. In the teaching of reading, and even of literature, failure to recognize the importance of the two stances seems to me to be at the root of much of the plight of literature today"

(1982, p. 274). When one considers Bloom's (1956) taxonomy, the regurgitation of information is found at the lowest levels of abstract thought.

One focus of theorists and researchers (Applebee, 1978; Hickman, 1981; Hickman & Hepler, 1982; Holland, Hungerford, & Ernst, 1993; Rosenblatt, 1982) is the use of story in the literacy program. Which stance do we help children accomplish? Can we assist them to become familiar with both the aesthetic and efferent stance? Thus, can we encourage children within classroom settings to explore the various entries into text, and thus the reasons for assuming them to accomplish literacy tasks at hand. Or conversely, do we gain the children's interest through the use of story and then make sure that it has to be literally understood? In this scenario, students become confused because their natural aesthetic stances are diminished through current questioning techniques that elicit highly specific factual details and encourage labeling and summarizing as a means of evaluating comprehension. As a result, in schools, the efferent stance is often misused in approaching and evaluating responses to literature, while the aesthetic stance is frequently neglected when asking children to respond to literature and when teachers assess children's responses to literature.

We are suggesting that teachers need to help children develop both stances, and their awarenesses of the distinctions between them from the very earliest grades forward through to the end of formal schooling. We contend that, if the texts are presented in meaningful classroom contexts, the efferent and aesthetic stances should naturally emerge and become more easily evaluated by both teachers and children. Literature should be used with children as means of encouraging the aesthetic stance. Yet the aesthetic stance is often the most elusive stance to assess. Where trust, acceptance, and spontaneity during storyreading are allowed, children will be able to deepen their experiences with literature, and teachers will begin to see aesthetic responses that may or may not be evaluated. Whether or not teachers are evaluating children's responses to literature, we want children to go back, recapture, reflect, and enjoy their reading experiences.

ORAL LANGUAGE IN BOOK DISCUSSIONS

How might teachers present texts in "meaningful situations" so that their students can allow the merging of both stances naturally? Discussions are central to the construction of meaning that children build in relation to books and are crucial to the development of critical thinking skills in relation to reading and understanding literature. If the ability to integrate new and existing knowledge is central to comprehension (Pearson & Johnson, 1978), children need opportunities to talk about what they read. How are children to respond in an interested and critical manner to what is read if their perspective of meaning is not central to the discussion?

Framing the Question

It is important to note that the questions are as important as the answers in evaluating children's responses to literature. Without thoughtful, as well as open-ended questions that encourage diversity in response, children will not necessarily stretch themselves as they reflect on what they read. In many approaches to the teaching of reading, children's perspectives of meaning are not encouraged. Because children's individual responses to what is read are not easily evaluated, measurable responses in instructional materials can nurture a right/wrong attitude, because they are efficient; this can severely limit children's responses to literature and can inhibit children's constructions of meaning.

For example, answering literal comprehension questions after a story is one way that classroom teachers determine whether children have understood a story. Typically, the answers either match and are correct or they contain misinformation and are incorrect. In this instance, children have taken on the purposes of the teacher (Rasinski, 1988) and are not actively engaged in the construction of personal responses to the story. Questions that begin with "What do you think?" can free children from our purposes and encourage an answer which is aesthetically based. Furthermore, children can be encouraged to support their views with the text. Within this framework evaluation is based on the child's own construction of meaning and the text is viewed as scaffolding the child's response. The resulting transaction is the "poem" to which Rosenblatt refers.

The Child's Perspective of Meaning

Piaget's (1926/1968) studies of children have long influenced our attitudes toward the child's ability to build meaning. Children do have difficulty retelling logically sequenced information and have certain limitations in abstracting relevant thematic information. However, this is not to say that children are unable to talk about stories, themes, and actions of characters. They are not latent thinkers until they reach the golden age of reason. If schemata are the "building blocks" upon which all information processing depends (Rumelhart, 1980), the young reader, who has not taken on the complete values of society and is said to be in a formative stage of growth, will most certainly offer perspectives of meaning that differ from that of the adult. Children talk about concepts that are relevant to their own lives and that are within the range of personal experience, therefore, we can not assume that children are incapable of abstract thought, nor can we assume that young readers cannot talk about themes or overarching concepts of stories, or evaluate the internal motivation of characters. When assessing children's responses to literature, it is critical to consider and value the perspective of children, and it is helpful to know that perspectives will frequently challenge adult perspectives (Paley, 1981).

Children Respond to Picture Books

In a study with 60 kindergarten, second-, and fourth-grade children, picture books were read aloud in small groups and children were asked open-ended questions about the books from a variety of perspectives (Lehr, 1988a, 1991b, 1993). To focus the children, time was given for a drawing activity in which children drew a picture that told what the stories were about. The children were then interviewed individually based on a retelling guide written by Goodman and Burke (1972) (see Tables 9.1 and 9.2). All answers were acceptable; children's responses were not matched to a preconceived set of answers (Paley, 1981). In reaction to assessment, what emerged was a picture of children with the ability to construct meanings for books that differed from adult perspectives but were consistent with information in the book. The children were persuasive, informative, and talked about the books from an aesthetic stance. Their verbalizations included statements of theme, character development, awareness of character motivation, summarizations of the stories, an ability to alter events in the story and to talk about the way they would like to see characters behave, and an awareness that their experiences were similar to those of characters in the stories. Likewise, children talked about events in their lives and related them to characters in stories. At the same time they offered moral statements of theme that cautioned others about mistakes made by characters in the stories.

This awareness of story suggests a developing sense of theme which begins with the child's earliest encounters with books. This sense of theme develops over time and is augmented in nurturing classrooms

Table 9.1.   Books, Grade Levels and Genres Used for Reading Aloud

BOOKS READ ALOUD

Realistic fiction

KINDERGARTEN:	TITCH by Pat Hutchins THE CARROT SEED by Ruth Krauss NEW BLUE SHOES by Eve Rice
SECOND GRADE:	THE HATING BOOK by Charlotte Zolotow LET'S BE ENEMIES by Janice Udry SAY IT by Charlotte Zolotow
FOURTH GRADE:	STEVIE by John Steptoe THY FRIEND, OSADIAH by Brinton Turkle WHEN I WAS YOUNG IN THE MOUNTAINS by Cynthia Rylant

Folktales

KINDERGARTEN:	THE THREE LITTLE PIGS by Paul Galdone THE THREE BILLY GOATS GRUFF by Marcia Brown THE GINGERBREAD BOY by Paul Galdone
SECOND GRADE:	TATTERCOATS by Flora Steel SNOWWHITE by Trina Hyman THE SWINEHERD by Lisbeth Zwerger
FOURTH GRADE:	DAWN by Molly Bang A JAPANESE FAIRY TALE by Jane Ike THE STONECUTTER by Gerald McDermott

where children are encouraged to explore meaning. This suggests that teachers must alter their assessment strategies when working with children's responses to literature. Preconceived answers will narrowly evaluate what children know and how they comprehend. Conversely, an open-ended attitude toward responses will encourage diversity in thinking and will focus assessment on what children know and how they interact with books as well as with each other. What follows is an

Table 9.2.   Individual Interview Questions

1. Match two titles. Why did you choose these two books? What are they both about?
2. Can you tell me what the whole story was about, in a few words or in short form?
3. Are these stories similar to any other stories you have read? How?
4. What were the authors trying to teach you when they wrote these stories?
5 What are the most important ideas in these stories?
6. Pick a story. Why did it end like that?
7. Is there anything you would have changed?
8. Did you like the story? Why or why not?
9. Would you have changed the ending?

attempt to characterize the child's verbalization of themes in book discussions with picture books, based on a model of evaluation that encourages children to explore meaning in books and to use the books as referents.

TALKING ABOUT THEMES OF BOOKS

Ability to summarize. Children in all three age groups were able to summarize stories. Embedded in some of these summaries were thematic statements. Kindergarten children who were able to summarize stories included concrete themes which were main idea statements. Some of the statements were given when the children were asked the following question: "Can you tell me what the whole story was about, in a few words or in short form?" Asking children to respond to specific questions related to the story gave them a focus for constructing meaning.

In talking about the book *Titch*, by Pat Hutchins, Mary (age 5:6) explored the theme after talking about the plot of the story.

> They both [child refers to two books in front of her] have a plant that grows....They [points to older brother and sister in *Titch*] get all the biggest things. He [points to Titch] ends up with the biggest.

When asked why the story ended as it did, she responded: "He needed to have something that was bigger. He wanted it to grow." Mary summarized the story, was aware of character motivation and made a concrete statement of theme. She was dependent on the physical text to help order her statements and identify her use of referents. Without the text physically present, Mary's explanation may have been quite different.

Beth (age 5:11) also summarized *Titch* and said this in response to the question: "Why do you think the story ended like it did?"

> Like older brothers and sisters had bigger things. All their stuff is bigger. She only got the littlest things. [But in the end] she got one of the biggest things...cause they all got the big stuff and she wanted something big.

Beth's words show that she not only comprehended the plot of the story, but she also responded critically to the actions of the characters. Beth empathized with Titch and moved from the spectator role to that of an emotional participant, which reflected her perspective of the world. Good literature has the capacity to take the listener on more than a ride. It has the capacity to pull us in and make us reflect on the lives of characters in relation to our own. Likewise, evaluative questions that ask the reader to respond to a book situation have the capacity to focus on what children know and encourage them to explore new avenues of thought. Asking children to summarize stories briefly, or to react to endings of stories, are determining what has been gained by the book experience. Children will ostensibly focus on different aspects of any story; however, whether a child can relate a story with threads that hold it together to create a cohesive narrative will be revealing about the child's transaction with the story. And asking for a critical response to the conclusion of a story focuses the child on relevant episodes and also forces him or her to consider why characters responded as they did.

Awareness of character motivations. Children in all three grade levels talked at length about characters and their internal motivations. Responding to how characters behaved or exploring what they needed was frequently included in summary statements that often involved following a character's actions through the plot of a story. One kindergartener enlarged upon the theme of sharing in *Titch*:

> They're going real fast up the hill. And here they won't let him try to fly the kites. Here they couldn't let him try their instruments. Here Titch he had to hold the nails and they had the hard jobs. That's not fair...right there they won't let him put any dirt in or hold it. They only let him handed the seed...it grew bigger until it was bigger than them...at the ending the plant grew out and it got those two.

This answer indicated an awareness of internal reactions and a sensitivity for Titch's plight as the youngest child. This child's view of being the smallest included a level of frustration with an added form of retribution. His world view included a system of concrete rewards and punishments and provided a satisfying ending. This sensitivity to the character in the story indicated a clear understanding of what the story was about. The entire response to the character of Titch showed how the child was reconstructing the plot in a way that was meaningful for him. One could almost imagine that this child had experienced life in a manner similar to that of Titch. This merging of the spectator and participant role is powerful and literature can broaden the child beyond his or her narrow life experience.

In response to *The Swineherd* Cary (age 8:0) stated:

> The princess learns a lesson...she was someone that wanted just about everything and that's how she learned her lesson...you don't get everything and that's how life goes.

The preceding sentences illustrated a concise understanding of the folktale, through analysis of the character's internal motivation. This response was also a summary statement of the story. The question asking to tell what the story was about provided a forum for this child. She clearly understood that there were pitfalls involved in getting everything you wanted in life. She related this to the story, and the result was a critical statement in reference to the story and life in general. This child was able to grapple with the theme of this folktale at an analytical level. Whether this girl remembered the color of the princess' dress, or the 5-year-old child above recalled all of the things that Titch's brother and sister owned, is less important in assessment than the insights that both children were able to offer in relation to these characters. Both children had a clear focus regarding character-ization and its relation to the theme of their respective books, and were able to relate that information to events in real life.

Talking about characters in relation to personal experience. In talking about characters and their actions, children were able to link the book experiences to their own lives. Titch was viewed sympathet-ically by many kindergarten children because he was little and "big kids have big things and little kids have little things," but "it doesn't matter if you're little or not... cause if you're little you might get better things." These children were aware that they were close chronologi-cally in age to Titch, and they championed him with their answers. They identified strongly with Titch and were able to offer fresh perspectives regarding his plight as the youngest child. Assessment must have room for the child's own personal accounts, because children experience books directly and become a part of the proceedings.

Older children talked about books and the experiences of characters in a similar fashion. Benny (age 8:0) stated that "you can't always have things your own way... cause you have to let your friends have things their way sometimes." His analysis referred directly to *Let's Be Enemies*; however, his words also came out of his own experiences with friends, which he talked about at length. In responding to *The Hating Book* and *Let's Be Enemies*, another second-grade boy gave a lengthy discussion of his neighborhood peer structure and how he and his little sister related to other children and handled disagreements. Both children understood the book they had heard and made connections between what was heard and their own personal experiences. Tradi-tional assessment has had a tendency to ignore the child's experiential base; that is not to say that it should be ignored. Rather it should be valued, for it is an indication of the child's ability to make connections between what is read and what is experienced, the application level on Bloom's taxonomy (1956).

Moralistic language. At times children offered responses that were stated in absolute terms. The answers offered no alternatives or choices for characters and were often stated in negative terms.

Children offered statements that reflected personal value systems such as "Don't run away from home" (kindergarten response to *The Gingerbread Boy*) or "Share whatever you're doing" (kindergarten response to *Titch*). What was noteworthy was the child's attitude toward life, the definitive black/white value system that emerged when talking about stories and how characters behaved. At this level of response children viewed events rather undimensionally. Rather than seeing life choices as a complex weave, they tended to react moralistically, almost parallel to morals given for fables. For example, Tana's (age 9:7) response in reference to *The Stonecutter* was: "Be what you are and don't change it." This type of decisive statement was meant to be an endorsement of how things should be. It became an overstatement of the stonecutter's dilemma, a static state in order to avoid problems. It is an indication of the child's view of the world and provides the teacher with a rich backdrop of information. Through open-ended questioning techniques this child could be led to confront her own lack of logic and conclude she didn't exactly mean that people could never change, but that the stonecutter's greed led him to change something that was better left unchanged. Encouraging contexts allow children to explore their own feelings with regard to a character's actions and provide an acceptable forum for changing one's opinion.

By contrast, other answers showed a delicate sensitivity to the themes of the books. "Well, don't underestimate your friends; they can be nice people." (Dave 10:1; in reference to *Thy Friend, Obadiah* and *Stevie*). Statements like these tended to include qualifiers, which revealed that the students were aware of other options or other choices available.

Children also offered warnings, which could be characterized as being similar to adult admonitions that are typically given to children of this age. This was most apparent with folktales. Pete (age 5:0) stated that you should "be careful walking on bridges" (in response to *The Three Billy Goats Gruff*), and that you should "stay away from wolfs" (in response to *The Three Little Pigs* and *The Gingerbread Boy*). The statements had several layers of meaning and at a very literal level were a caution to the billy goats, gingerbread boys, and others in a similar position to remain alert in dangerous situations, as well as to avoid dangerous situations. The folktales mentioned above also taught you "not to trust strangers that you don't know."

Kindergarten children were concerned with the literal safety of characters paralleling their own positions as young children. "Never go across dangerous bridges." Their answers reflected their developmental status as young children who are still dependent upon others for their safety and well being. Hearing literature about the plights of others has the capacity to broaden their experiential bases and make them better informed about universal laws that are operative in the world. This is typified by one 5-year-old's response when asked what the author of *The Three Pigs* was trying to teach you: "Build your house strong." This response indicated an awareness directly related to how one might achieve safety in a world of wolves. The potential of literature to broaden the background knowledge of children and to make them more sensitive to the world around them can occur in nurturing contexts where the child's perspective of meaning is encouraged and valued. Children will grow in their insights uniquely and at different rates; therefore, assessment must take this individual response input into this process and an awareness of the unique transactions that occur when a child interacts with a book. With that in mind, assessment cannot be viewed as a static process.

CHILDREN RESPOND TO A CHAPTER BOOK

In responding to picture books, the questions used in the above research guided the children's attention back toward the reading event. As students grow older, valuable interchange will occur when responses are shared: different points of view, alternative interpretations, and self-awareness along with a more worldly view. Hepler and Hickman (1982) have suggested the notion of creating "a community of readers" which will promote children's responses to literature. With this shared literacy context, children and teachers can better assess individual and collective book responses.

Within "a community of readers" children should be allowed some choices for final evaluation. To assist children's responses to literature, research indicates that various forms of response activities may be offered as choices to students: drawing, painting, writing, drama, music, and artistic creations (Anzul, 1993; Cohen, 1968; Cullinan, Jaggar & Strickland, 1974; Galda, 1993; Holland & Shaw, 1993; Weston, 1993). Thus, children can choose how they wish to enter a deeper level of response and understanding concerning what was read. Teachers should also suggest other evaluative activities, such as discussion directions and whole or small group projects.

How do teachers help readers, especially older readers, "return to, relive, savor" the literature that they read and consider alternative assessment strategies? In order to investigate this question further, 10 fourth-grade pupils were engaged in the reading of and responding to *Bridge to Terabithia* by Katherine Paterson (1977). During the first half of the 12 1-hour sessions together, the researcher (Holland) and the children concentrated on reading the book. The researcher read aloud chapters which introduced the two main characters, described Terabithia, and the sequence of one main character's death with the other character's reaction and recovery. The children read the other parts of the book during free time in school and at home.

The researcher immediatly began gathering whole group assessment materials. Children were encouraged from the beginning to respond collaboratively in many ways. Upon being introduced to the two main characters: Leslie and Jess, life-sized paper body cut-outs of one boy and one girl were made, so that the children could create a "character grafitti." That is, as the story emerged, students wrote words, phrases, or sentences anywhere on the body cut-out which described the characters or their feelings. At first the children concentrated on physical dimensions of the characters but eventually shifted to the level of the character's feelings. At about the halfway point of the book, in order to evaluate how the students were understanding and responding to the two main characters, the researcher suggested that the rest of the school might want to know Leslie and Jess by way of placing the body cut-outs in the hall with cartoon balloons introducing themselves. The girls took Leslie's collective "grafitti" body notes and wrote an introduction of her to the rest of the school:

> Hello my name is Leslie Burke. I'm the fastest kid in the fifth grade, but I don't brag about it. Me and my friend, Jess started a fort. I just moved here and I dislike my house. My parent's are writers. We don't have a T.V. I don't know why I said I don't have a T.V. in front of my class. I love to read. I have to leave now. I'm going to meet Jess. Good-by!

The boys did the same with Jess:

> Hi I'm Jess Oliver Aarons, Jr. I want to be the fastest kid in the fifth grade. But my friend Leslie is faster than me. She made up a land called Terabithia. I have four *stupid* sisters. I try to please my father. But he is hard to please. I am in *love* with Ms. Edmunds my music teacher. Janice Avery a bully took Maybelle *Twinkies* so Leslie and *I* get revenge on Janice. It is Christmas. I want to get Leslie something special.

The jotted words and phrases on the character "grafitti" served as notes for the final encapsulation of each character. By collaboratively composing these introductions, students not only shared knowledge of the two main characters, but the researcher was able to assess their strong understanding of each character's strengths and weaknesses crucial to the group's entering the climax of the book.

Another evaluative response activity occurred after the chapter describing Terabithia was shared. Would intermediate-grade children be able to consider that each reader has different pictures in his or her head about the same image within a book? Within evaluative contexts, students often compete to achieve the same outcome product. Students were encouraged to draw their own version of what Terabithia looked like in their own minds. The researcher could assess processes employed for this first independent response project. Many students reread the chapter to obtain relevant information concerning the exact elements of this secret place, while other children relied solely on their imaginations to create their illustrations. It is interesting to note that those pupils who reread the chapter chose the efferent stance, while those who imaginatively drew Terabithia chose the aesthetic stance. After this, pupils wrote brief captions for their poster size renditions of Terabithia and all where added to their burgeoning hall display. In terms of assessment, children became accepting of different opinions and visualizations about Terabithia because the researcher created an encouraging context in which various opinions and perspectives were accepted and valued.

Once the book was concluded, the researcher wanted to evaluate thematic issues before students began independent or group final response experiences. An in-depth discussion involving three topics helped students focus more deeply upon themes and personal responses. As Lehr found in her developmental study of theme, the emphasis during this hour-long in-depth discussion on open-ended questions discussed among the students was helpful in assessing children's responses.

The first topic considered how characters were different at the end of the story versus the beginning. These children talked about Jess, his father, Jess's teacher, and Janice Avery, the bully with whom the children were unexpectedly sympathetic. Students chose to list characters on the chalkboard and describe how they were different at the end of the book: Leslie—gone; Jess—closer to his father; Mother—nicer; Maybelle—Queen; Mrs. Myers—compassionate. Students decided to illustrate their findings for the hall display.

A second discussion challenged the children to consider what gifts Leslie had left for Jess. This question shifted students into consideration of continuation of life and friendship. At first, comments centered on concrete items like the books of fantasy, art paper, and paints.

Then, one child suggested that Leslie had left Terabithia and imagination as gifts to Jess. Because the discussion was not cut short, other students began to offer responses that included abstract gifts like friendship, courage, anger, and sadness. One fourth-grade child summarized this discussion beautifully, "He's like Leslie at the end more than like himself at the beginning." Two students wanted to illustrate these gifts for the group's developing hall display. Thus, not only were their responses elicited in many different ways; they were also valued enough to be shared with others.

The final discussion concerned the author's selection of "bridge" within the title. Students were asked to consider why that word appeared in the title. Again, concrete answers emerged from the group and were centered on the fact that if there had been a bridge across the gully Leslie might not have died. Students were encouraged to talk about what a bridge does, and when they realized its role as a connection between two things, they shifted to abstract levels of talk about the connections between people in the story. On their own they turned to the mathematical operation of addition and they began to discover all the people the two main characters, Leslie and Jess, each connected to within the story:

LESLIE
Leslie + Jess
Leslie + her teacher
Leslie + Janice Avery
Leslie + Prince Terrian

JESS
Jess + Leslie
Jess + Maybelle
Jess + his music teacher
Jess + his father
Jess + his teacher

In this discussion, the students were able to go beyond the surface meaning of the title and offer a response involving the universal human need to connect with others. Upon reflection of this long discussion, the researcher and students together were able to assess their new, deeper understanding of more complex thematic issues for this book. Time, acceptance of all responses, and building meaning within the group allowed these complex themes to emerge through oral discussion. That children volunteered to create posters showing their new, deeper understanding of this story demonstrated their growing pride in their collaborative efforts. The hall display was the most concrete collection of individual and collective evaluative products. But more importantly, the process leading to these evaluative products had been closely observed and recorded by the researcher.

Now the children needed to initiate their own final assessment activities. During the remaining sessions, the 10 fourth-grade children and the researcher brainstormed individual and/or collaborative response activities involving writing, art constructions, and/or drama. In allowing choice of personal response to the book, each child could explore his or her own feelings and ideas that resulted from the impact of the story events within the context of their life experiences. The uniqueness and individuality of choice were respected and encouraged the children to engage in meaningful, purposeful responses. The process as well as the final assessment product became part of the cumulative evaluation of each child. Response choices are described below for each child or team of children.

Daniel. Daniel wondered what the "Recipe for Revenge" really looked like when written out by Leslie and Jess as they plotted against Janice Avery, the school bully. He mixed a liquid drink consisting mostly of mixed paint colors and showed it to the researcher, who suggested he write out his recipe so others could use it. He reread the chapter involving the revenge plot and created the following recipe.

Revenge Potion

Ingredients:
1 Cup Mad Victim
2 Cups faithful friends
1 Quart criminal
1 Tsp. false love letter

Needed: 1 large kettle, 1 bonfire, 1 small one pint container, 1 small cup

How to make:

1. Mix the mad victim with the faithful friends until both turn yellow.
2. Sprinkle some false love letter on the mixture.
3. Then pour it into the small container.
4. Put the criminal in the kettle.
5. Pour the mixture into the kettle and let it set until cold.
6. Put it over the bonfire.
7. Cook for 48 hours.
8. Pour potion into mug.
9. Serve to criminal secretly.

Geoff. Geoff wanted to write a diary of the book's events from the point of view of Prince Terrian, the puppy. He spent considerable amounts of time rereading the book to search for events involving the puppy. His first entry indicates the gist of the diary as a whole:

> Dec. 24 Dear Diary, Today Jess gave me some food. Later he picked me up and told me we were going to Terabithia. Then we came to a gully that didn't have any water but it was still a long drop. I felt like jumping out of his arms. When we were swinging over I shut my eyes. When we were over, there was a girl sitting in a fort. He gave me to her.

Danielle and Anne. They wanted to do something that got deeper into the two main characters, so they collaborated on a book entitled *Cartoons and Poems by Jess Oliver Aarons and Leslie Burke*, in which they pooled their art and writing talents. Danielle assumed Jess's cartooning talents, while Anne took on the role of Leslie, who loved to write poetry. They reread the book to locate events where Jess drew cartoons and devised poetry by Leslie to match the artwork. In the final entry, Jess drew a queen as Tyrannosaurus Rex telling the story of *Moby Dick* to the king as a mouse, who is frightened. The poem to match this royal cartoon couple captured the essence of both main characters:

> The queen, the queen
> the Royal queen
> How big, and so brave!
> The king, so small and meak.
> And how he changed!
> We don't know.
> Now we Have a pair of two!

Beth and Anne. Beth began to redesign the cover of the book which she thought was too dark and depressing. She copied the heads of Leslie and Jess off the original cover, but she placed Prince Terrian and Terabithia between the two characters. On this cover, Leslie has a copy of *Moby Dick* next to her, and Jess has his watercolors and paintbrushes next to him. Anne watched this brighter watercolor cover design emerge and wondered if Beth would like some poetry to go with it. Both girls decided to compose a poem about friendship by each character, as follows:

> FRIENDS by Jess
> Friends are for caring and helping
> when tough times come.

They are for playing make-believe
They are for sharing good times and bad
That is what friends are for.

FRIENDS by Leslie
Friends Friends are fun to have
They are very helpful too
But sometimes
when things go wrong
they always end up as
Friends.

Sharry. Sharry wondered what things would be like later in Jess's life. She wrote a four-chapter sequel about Jess and Maybelle 5 years after the time period of the book's ending. She had to reread the ending and reflect on what Jess had learned from Leslie. In her own composition, she wrote from Jess's point of view using Katherine Paterson's dialect for the appropriate characters.

Chapter 4: Comin' Back

The next day when I finished breakfast Maybelle came in and said, "You know what you're 'sposed t' do, Jess?"
"I know," I said. I went upstairs and changed my clothes.
I got to Terabithia before Lisa [ed: Maybelle's new friend] and Maybelle. I went to the pine grove and pretended to ask the spirit to make the comeback good. Then when I got to Terabithia, Lisa and Maybelle were there. We played the game of Terabithia. Lisa was great at being princess. I think I'll let her stay. It's been a good day!

Frank. Frank hated the ending of the book where Jess let his little sister come to Terabithia. He wanted to write his own version of how it should end.

Chapter 14: Queen Maybelle

After Jess and Maybelle built the bridge, they thought that being at Terabithia alone was boring. They asked Brenda, Ellie, and their friends to be part of Terabithia and they could bring some friends. They said, "Yes!" Then, Brenda, Ellie, and their friends came to Terabithia and built their own individual forts. After that, Jess and Maybelle brought their friends and they built their own individual forts. Joyce Anne [ed.: toddler] is not allowed ever to come to Terabithia because she might tell the parents. If the parents know about Terabithia, everybody at Terabithia won't be able to go to Terabithia whenever they want. Parents and adults are never allowed to come to Terabithia.

While these examples show the uniqueness of each child's response to the book, not all children chose to do written responses. Joel, a cartoonist in his own right, drew his own version of the artwork Jess had most liked at a museum. Teresa struggled to discover her own way back into the book. She could not make up her mind until the other children were well on their way. Then she pointed out to all of us that no one had drawn the scene where Leslie had gone to church on Easter. Teresa proceeded to do so using her own stick-like figures and her own church setting. Perhaps the most amazing response came from Jeff, who simply wanted to paint. He used a long piece of computer paper and waterpaints to explore the moods of each chapter. He simply painted the emotions according to his own color guide (i.e., black = death; yellow = happy) on each computer paper sheet, on which he had written the title for each chapter. When he shared his work with the group, he pointed out that he had used two colors for the final chapter, purple for the new royalty and orange "because it's not as happy and sunny as it was when Leslie was there."

Each of the students presented his or her own individual or collaborative final project to the whole group. Students became aware of the uniqueness of each project choice, but the researcher assisted them in consideration that when put together the final projects collectively captured the essence of the whole book! Each child could trace his or her contributions to the shared meanings within the hall display response artifacts which became the basis of process and product assessment.

Children responding to *Bridge to Terabithia* were encouraged to make choices within the response processes and projects. They were able to choose with whom they would work. They were able to choose which response activities they would engage in. Before beginning these activities, however, it is important to note that oral language was encouraged during and after parts of the book were read. Flood (1977) suggests the importance of encouraging children to answer questions about what they read. In the activities described above children engaged in lengthy discussions about character's actions and how characters changed during the course of the story. Author intentions were discussed when children pondered on Paterson's choice of the word *bridge* in her title. These discussions focused the children and allowed them to reflect orally on what the story meant to them. This crucial turning point focused the students upon deeper under-standings of the book itself and of their varied yet collective responses to the story. Beyond this point of discussing, children were also given time to engage in various forms of response activities: poetry, recipes, prose, and liquid concoctions. Children often had to reread portions of the book to gather information in an efferent stance and to recapture feelings and moods in an aesthetic stance. In other words, children had "to return to, relive, savor, the experience." In these response experiences, assessment was ongoing both during and after the reading of the story.

IMPLICATIONS FOR THE CLASSROOM

Classroom teachers might consider many aspects of assessment for use with children toward preserving and balancing reader responses. First and foremost, teachers might consider that evaluation is ongoing during reader response activities and instruction. Observation and interaction with and among children are crucial. Teachers observe children's oral responses, actions, processes, and final products to maintain awareness of growth for evaluative purposes. Interactions between students and teachers, as well as among students, are encouraged and noted especially because response contexts can be varied.

Analysis and reflection on children's responses may or may not include children. Children's answers, especially within discussions about books, are to be as important as the teacher's need to develop open-ended questioning strategies which invite personal responses. Teachers may opt to keep their own anecdotal records and collections of children's work. Children may become involved in assessment processes both during and after reader response experiences. Conferences with students, allowing students to keep their own evaluative folders, and group sharing of response artifacts are other aspects of response assessment teachers might consider.

Children need to be allowed choices among modes of response: discussions, drama, art/media, and writing. Even within the choice of the mode, there might be a response occurring. Various children might lean toward art versus drama versus written responses. Within these unique response choices, children might further decide whether they want to work alone, in partnership, or in a group. Both individual and group approaches could be allowed to vary assessment contexts. And most importantly within the choice and context of response activities, children need plenty of time to move into and through their aesthetic and efferent responses to children's literature.

Finally, perhaps the most important evaluative strategy teachers might consider is the great need for more teacher-researcher activity in the area of children's reader responses. Research in children's responses to literature is only 15 years old! We would call for teacher-researchers to actively familiarize themselves with reader response theory and research. Then perhaps more teacher-researchers such as those in Holland, Hungerford, & Ernst (1993) would begin to explore oral, dramatic, artistic, and written children's responses to the wonderful literature made available to them in the classroom. Once this is accomplished, teacher-researchers might begin to broaden all of our horizons concerning the vast and complex phenomenon called children's responses to literature.

REFERENCES

Anzul, M. (1993). Exploring literature with children within a transactional framework. In K. Holland, R. Hungerford, & S. Ernst (Eds.), *Journeying: Children responding to literature* (pp. 187–203). Portsmouth, NH: Heinemann.

Applebee, A. (1978). *The child's concept of story.* Chicago: University of Chicago Press.

Bloom, B. (1956). *Taxonomy of educational objectives.* New York: Longmans, Green.

Britton, J. (1971). What's the use? A schematic account of language functions. *Educational Review, 23*(3), 205–219.

Cohen, D. (1968). The effects of literature on vocabulary and reading achievement. *Elementary English, 45,* 209–213, 217.

Cullinan, B., Jaggar, A., & Strickland, D. (1974). Language expansion for black children in the primary grades: A research report. *Young Children, 29,* 98–112.

Flood, J. (1977). Parental styles in reading episodes with young children. *The Reading Teacher, 30,* 864–867.

Galda, L. (1993). How preferences and expectations influence evaluative responses to literature. In K. Holland, R. Hungerford, & S. Ernst (Eds.), *Journeying: Children responding to literature* (pp. 302–316). Portsmouth, NH: Heinemann.

Goodman, Y., & Burke, C. (1972). Additional guide questions to aid story retelling. Revised for *Reading Miscue Inventory Manual: Procedure for diagnosis and evaluation.* New York: MacMillan.

Harding, D.W. (1977). Psychological processes in the reading of fiction. In M. Meek (Ed.), *The cool web.* London: Bodley Head.

Hepler, S., & Hickman, J. (1982). "The book was okay. I love you"—Social aspects of response to literature. *Theory Into Practice, 21*(4), 278–283.

Hickman, J. (1981). A new perspective on response to literature: Research in an elementary school setting. *Research in the Teaching of English, 15,* 343–354.

Holland, K., Hungerford, R., & Ernst, S. (Eds.). (1993). *Journeying: Children responding to literature.* Portsmouth, NH: Heinemann.

Holland, K., & Shaw, L. (1993). Dances between stances. In K. Holland, R. Hungerford, & S. Ernst (Eds.), *Journeying: Children responding to literature* (pp. 114–136). Portsmouth, NH: Heinemann.

Lehr, S. (1988). A child's developing sense of theme as a response to literature. *Reading Research Quarterly, 23,* 337–357.

Lehr, S. (1991). *The child's developing sense of theme: Responses to literature.* New York: Teacher's College Press.

Lehr, S. (1993). The princess learns a lesson: Three studies of theme in individual and interactive contexts. In K. Holland, R. Hungerford, & S. Ernst (Eds.), *Journeying: Children responding to literature* (pp. 237–249). Portsmouth, NH: Heinemann.

Paley, G. (1981). *Wally's stories.* Cambridge, MA: Harvard University Press.

Paterson, V. (1977). *Bridge to Terabithia.* New York: Avon Camelot Books.

Pearson, P., & Johnson, D. (1978). *Teaching reading comprehension.* New York: Holt, Rinehart, and Winston.

Piaget, J. (1968). *The language and thought of the child.* London: Routledge and Kegan Paul. (Original work published 1928.)

Rasinski, T. (1988, January). The role of interest, purpose, and choice in early literacy. *The Reading Teacher,* pp. 396–400.

Rosenblatt, L. (1976). *Literature as exploration.* New York: The Modern Language Association of America. (Original work published 1938).

Rosenblatt, L. (1978) *The reader, the text, the poem: The transactional theory of literary work.* Carbondale, IL: Southern University Press.

Rosenblatt, L. (1982). The literary transaction: Evocation and response. *Theory Into Practice, 21*(4), 268–277.

Rumelhart, D. (1980). Schemata: The building blocks of cognition. In R. Spiro, B. Bruce, & Brewer (Eds.), *Theoretical issues in reading comprehension.* Hillsdale, NJ: Erlbaum.

Weston, L. (1993). The evolution of response through discussion, drama, writing, and art in a fourth grade. In K. Holland, R. Hungerford, & S. Ernst (Eds.), *Journeying: Children responding to literature* (pp. 137–150). Portsmouth, NH: Heinemann.

chapter 10
Assessing Literary Understanding Through Oral Language

Joanne M. Golden

How can we learn about children's literary understanding? An alternative to traditional written tests is to observe children in the process of actively making sense of a story. One way to observe this process is to create opportunities for children to discuss and dramatize literature. The purpose of this chapter is to explore how aspects of literary understanding can be assessed by viewing how one group of children discussed and dramatized a novel.

There is a range of things it is important to consider when assessing children's literary response including enjoyment, type of response, reading ability, and interpretive skills. The type of response that is the focus of the present chapter is the interpretive response. Interpretive skills are an important means of determining how readers are linking into the literary text (Cooper, 1985; Scholes, 1985). Interpretation, according to Scholes (1985), involves the reader's ability to make sense out of the work and to thematize the work, moving from a level of specific events to a more general level.

We can assess interpretive skills in different ways, and it is important to recognize the strengths and limitations of each means of assessment. Some measures, for example, may claim to assess interpretive skills but actually focus on other aspects of response. Standardized objective tests may emphasize the "facts" in the text and score responses according to right or wrong answers. The underlying assumption of this approach is that meaning exists in the text, and that the reader must apprehend that particular meaning. This view contrasts with that of some literary theorists (e.g., Ingarden, 1973; Iser, 1978) who argue that literary texts generate multiple meanings. These differing perspectives illustrate the importance of examining the theory of interpretation which guides the assessment.

Written responses on tests or essays can provide information about students' responses to literature; however, the writing process itself may constrain how the reader elaborates upon a response. Writing employs a different set of conventions, is more planned and is more selective than spoken language (Kantor & Rubin, 1981). Written responses thus provide a different type of data for assessment purposes. In one study (Golden, 1986), for example, one student told the researcher that speaking is just a lot easier than writing. Other students stated that the advantage of oral discussion is that it allows you to work out your own responses while, at the same time, you refine and develop those responses by listening to others in the discussion. In this sense, meaning is constructed by more than one person through "cooperation and collaboration" (Collins, 1981, p. 198). Thus oral responses provide one important means of assessing how students construct meaning during interactions with other readers.

The purpose of the present chapter is to explore how it is possible to assess students' interpretation of a literary work through an examination of oral responses.

Description of the Small Group Discussion

The author worked with a group of five fifth-grade boys over a period of five sessions to prepare a dramatic interpretation of scenes from the fantasy novel *The Phantom Tollbooth* by Norton Juster (1961). The novel is filled with unusual characters, humorous incidents, and numerous plays on words. The project was a part of a larger scale program in which children from an intermediate school were brought to a university campus to participate in a Children's Television Theatre (Green & Golden, 1983).

Over the five-session period, the children actively participated in interpreting the novel and making decisions about how to transform the novel into a dramatic presentation for videotaping. In the first two sessions, the participants read and discussed the characters and language of the novel, and in the remaining sessions they made decisions about which characters and scenes they would present and how they would present them. In the final session, the scenes were videotaped and played back for the students and a discussion about the process was recorded.

In order to explore how the children interpreted the novel, the chapter is organized into three sections. The first section focuses on the literary understanding assessed in the first two sessions, in which children discussed the characters. The second section considers the discussion cn transforming the novel to drama during the third, fourth, and fifth sessions. The third section addresses how the actual performance provides information about the children's interpretation of literature.

DISCUSSION OF CHARACTERS

Generally, the teacher set the framework for the discussion in each session by designating the task or question that elicited the students' responses. Often, however, the students renegotiated the task by pursuing their own line of interest (e.g., focusing on the props they thought would be helpful). In the following excerpt, the intent of the teacher was to find out which characters the students thought were interesting and what the students discovered about the characters.

T: Well let's start and go around. Sam, let's begin with you. Which character did you find to be interesting and what did you find out about him? Maybe we can look back through our book.

Sam: Well, Officer Shrift.

T: Okay, yeah.

Sam: That's the one I read about. And I liked him because of his size—how real short and like around two feet and his you know he's real fat well it says about double the size of his height. And I like the way he—when Milo says that you need a judge to sentence somebody so then he puts on the black robe and becomes the judge. And then he says now I sentence you to 6 million years in the dungeon and then he says and then Milo says but you need a jailer to put somebody in jail so he takes off the black robe, then he gets his keys, then he takes him to the jail and he takes him down to the dungeon, puts him in the dungeon. And he's talking about being careful because of the witch and it wasn't a witch but it was a which and Milo thought it was a witch.

There are several interpretations in the above sample. Sam identified the physical attributes of Officer Shrift, paraphrasing the author's description "almost twice as wide" (Juster, 1961, p. 59) to "about double the size of his height" to illustrate this. The ability of the character to change roles from judge to jailer is an important trait and

Sam used specific incidents that reflect this. Embedded in this description is Sam's attention to the language of the character which is often exaggerated—"I sentence you to 6 million years in the dungeon." Awareness of language is also evident in Sam's statement about Officer Shrift's warning about a witch in the dungeon who actually turns out to be a which. The excerpt thus reveals how the reader identified some important traits of the character and recaptured some of the language in the text.

When Gary described the Humbug, he also focused on the language of the character as well as indicating a point of confusion he experienced while reading the passage.

Gary: I like the Humbug because he was really funny, like in the things he did. He always had the wrong thing to say at the wrong time. He always managed to say the wrong words and he always made the wrong answers and everything and um he was in the story a lot and the things that he did were just so funny that I just and some of the things I didn't believe about him like when they were stuck in the island. The thing I didn't believe was that if he was a bug—why didn't it behave—if he was a beetle in the thing when he first came in—why wouldn't he fly? Why couldn't he fly out of there?

In the first part of the excerpt, Gary depicted the character as having "the wrong thing to say at the wrong time." This trait is emphasized in the text in that the Humbug often irritates other characters because of his responses. Gary's conception of the character does not match how the "beetle-like" character behaved in one instance. Gary envisioned the Humbug as a Japanese beetle and therefore expected him to fly instead of swimming to the island. This suggests that Gary is visually imaging the character by associating it with real-world knowledge he has about beetles. He did not, however, apply this set of expectations to other character behaviors such as the Humbug talking.

At a later point, the teacher asked Gary to say more about the language of the character.

T: Can you expand a little bit on the way he used language, the kinds of things he did with words? Do you remember anything?
Gary: Umm
T: Well like when somebody said something, what would he say?
Gary: He would always
T: Humbug, he had a certain way of talking.
Sam: Oh, he would say "bah."
T: Yeah, he said certain things.

Gary: He would say like in that Christmas thing—I forgot its name. The humbug where he said bah and he didn't believe anything. He wouldn't give charity.

Tim: Like the Scrooge or something like that.

Gary: Scrooge. The Scrooge.

T: Yeah, like Scrooge. He was like Scrooge. "Bah Humbug." That's where they got that name. That's why it's so funny. "Bah Humbug."

Tim: Yeah, because Scrooge would always say "'Humbug.'"

As the discussion progressed, other students became more involved in elaborating on each other's views and joining in the interpretive process. The focus on the language used by the character led to Gary's observation of a link between the Humbug's stingy trait and his use of "Bah" and Scrooge's similar traits in Dickens' tale.

In another part of the discussion, Peter described the way the Whetherman talked and provided an example of how the character repeats things. The teacher elicited a reference to the other kind of weatherman and Sam and Tim contributed to this perspective. Gary compared this to the which/witch character that Sam had previously alluded to in his discussion of Officer Shrift.

Peter: The way the whetherman always talked like he always said—like he always kept on repeating himself like "Good day, Good day, Good day, Good day." Saying something ten times after he said something else. And Tock—in some parts when Tock came in, he really didn't talk as much like that.

T: Did he have anything to do with the other kind of weather?

Peter: Yeah, he told.

Sam: He asked, "Is it going to rain?"

Peter: Oh yeah, if it's going to rain then we'd give them an umbrella or something.

Tim: Then it rains on him.

T: Yeah, he was sort of like the other weatherman. That was a really crazy guy.

Gary: It was just like that thing with the witch—"I'm not a witch, I'm a which. I'm not a weatherman, I'm a whetherman."

The talk continued when Peter discussed another character.

T: "Well, tell us about Tock, Why was he appealing to you? Did you say Tock was the other character? What about him was interesting?

Peter: Well, the way he wanted people to never be bored. He always wanted people to do stuff with. When he came into the doldrums—he wouldn't want people to just like sit down and lay around. He wanted people to be doing stuff like reading or something. Just not sitting there and doing nothing.

Gary: Said they can't waste time.

Peter: Instead of taking four naps in one day—early morning nap and all that stuff—he wanted them to be active till 9:00 or something when they had to go to bed.

T: He was actually a watch.

Sam: He was like Officer Shrift like—he was kind of like the Sheriff of the town—the man that kept the right thing on—the man that protected the rules.

T: Oh that's an interesting point.

Sam: Trying to make rules.

T: Yeah, I never thought about that. Tock was kind of interested in keeping things right.

Sam: Yeah.

T: Yeah, that's an interesting point.

Gary: Another thing about Tock. It was neat because he was a watchdog and he had a big watch on him.

T: Yeah. That was funny.

Gary: I thought it was going just to be like...and the whetherman because I thought he was going to say not a watchdog but a watch dog and he told time. I thought that he was going to say that but he was a..."

When Peter portrayed the character of Tock, Sam drew an analogy between Tock's traits and those of Officer Shrift whom he also viewed as a character interested in rules. Thus Sam interpreted two characters by comparing traits not explicitly stated in the novel but rather what he had inferred from the behavior of the characters. At the end of the discussion segment, Gary noted the distinction between Tock, the watch dog, and Tock, the watchdog, indicating his awareness of the author's play on words.

The excerpts discussed above illustrate how discussion provides information about how students identified key character traits and how they used the language of the character and the events in the text to illustrate their perceptions of the characters. The teacher provided the framework for the discussion for the purpose of eliciting the students' perceptions of characters and the language of the text. These perceptions would serve as the basis for the transformation from written text to oral drama.

DISCUSSION OF DRAMATIZING THE NOVEL

The students' discussion of how to dramatize the novel also revealed information about how they interpreted the characters and events in the novel. One of the purposes of the discussion was to evoke students' views of the important scenes in the book. In the following excerpt, Sam indicated what he thought was significant.

Sam: But we do—there's two scenes that we're no doubt about it have to do that. Those are the two with the two brothers you know—Digitopolis and Dictionopolis. They're I mean they're like they're just like the main part of the story there.

Gary: Yeah, Dictionopolis is the main part.

Sam: Dictionopolis and Digitopolis....

T: ...Now let's consider Stan's point. In order to get the meaning of the book you have to have the two kings in there. Now what do the rest of you think about that?

Gary: Yeah, I feel the same way.

Sam: You have to have those two—Digitopolis and Dictionopolis.

Gary: Yes you do. Those are the two main cities in the whole thing.

Tim: Because they like have a fight with each other, and they don't like like each other like they have it separated, and Milo asks why, and all that.

T: Now what are they separated according to?

Tim: Because, um—I kind of forgot.

T: One thinks one is more important than the other. One thing is more important. What are they really fighting over anyway?

Sam: Umm, over words and numbers.

Sam's comments reflect his recognition of a major conflict in the story between the two warring brothers—one, king of the land of letters; and the other, king of the land of numbers. In a later part of the discussion, Sam responded to the teacher's question concerning what the brothers are fighting over, a point on which Tim was unclear. As the discussion continued, Gary elaborated on the fight, addressing the question of how the author presented the information through narrative rather than through dramatization of the actual fight.

Gary: In the beginning—in the beginning of the book they didn't have like a scene and like they didn't say like umm the two kings—Mathemagician and King Azaz got together and they fought with each other, and they didn't say all the words and stuff. They just said that—they just said that um—they just told them—just said in the book about how—about what happened that they're separated. They just said that they had a fight and Rhyme and Reason were always the ones that kept the whole—that settled their arguments until they got banished and then after they were gone they got into another fight and that separated them. But they didn't like act it out like Tock meeting up with Milo-they didn't do that.

In the novel this information is told as a history by another character. This contribution indicates that Gary is sensitive to the ways in which information about characters can be revealed in literary texts: that is, through narration of past events or through dramatic interactions between characters.

Later, Sam suggested another episode that is central to the story as well as to the dramatization of the story.

Sam: I was thinking about another good place would be the Doldrums because that uses everybody here.

Gary: Oh, we already have that down. We're going to do that.

Sam: All those little people that were laying around and that would use everybody like the Royal Banquet would use everybody.

Gary: Only Milo...

T: Okay, let's think of the audience. You're trying to turn kids on to this book. Do you feel that the Doldrums is one of the key scenes that's of interest?

Tim: Yeah.

T: Okay.

Tim: Because it's like the way Milo's attitude is.

Sam: Yeah.

Tim: Like he belongs in the Doldrums.

Sam: No kidding.

Tim: Because Milo doesn't really think that much. Like when they say "Oh God, here comes Tock, run, run, run."

T: Oh, and that's where Tock gets introduced too. And Tock gets him out of that.

Sam: Yeah, he could be the narrator.

Tim: And when Tock tells how his brother goes Tock, Tock, Tock, and his brother was named Tick.

Gary: We need to do that.

Tim: And then how Tock says, "Well, I go Tick, Tick, Tick but they call me Tock, Tock." Because their parents had it mixed up and he started to cry and you saw this little tear coming out of the top of his eye.

While Sam's reason for choosing the episode was that it uses a number of characters, Tim added that the episode reflects the main character's traits. Tim also developed the teacher's suggestion that the scene is valuable because the character of Tock is introduced, quoting some of Tock's lines and the reason for his name to provide further interpretation of that character.

The discussion shifted from the students' identification of important characters and scenes to the students' presentation of their characters informally to the group. Initially, each student portrayed a character and repeated the presentation. The second time around, other students were encouraged by the teacher to offer suggestions for further development of the character. As the session progressed then, other students become more involved in considering how a variety of characters could be interpreted. When Peter completed his presentation of the Whetherman, for example, Tim suggested that he actually repeat words as the character does, and Gary and Sam offered ways this might be accomplished. Peter incorporated their suggestions into his presentation.

Peter: My name is the Whetherman. I'm not a Weatherman but I am a Whetherman like whether or not if you're going to do something. Now here's Faintly.

Tim: I've got a question. Remember how he repeats everything—repeats everything, the Whetherman. I think may you should say well, I repeat everything, I repeat everything, I repeat everything.

T: Good touch. Do you like that?

Peter: Yeah.

T: Add on to it because I loved your introduction and that would be a great thing to have.

Gary: Okay, just put that on at the end.

Sam: Say like...say like, now I'm going to introduce Faintly, Faintly, Faintly, Faintly.

T: Oh that would be a nice touch.

Gary: No, but after he tells us why he does that...like why he does it. "I like to repeat everything," and then he says, now I'd like to introduce Faintly, Faintly, Faintly.

Tim: Now I'm introducing Faintly, now I'm introducing Faintly, now I'm introducing Faintly.

T: Okay now that would even do it better since he's repeating the whole phrase.

Peter: Okay.

T: That's fun.

Peter: Hi my name is the Whetherman. I am not a weatherman but a whetherman—like whether or not you're coming. I like to repeat everything I say, everything I say, everything I say. Now here's Faintly, Faintly, Faintly Macabre.

When it was Gary's turn to portray one of his characters, he had some difficulty in remembering the main attributes, so the teacher encouraged him to write them down. However, when Gary presented his second character, he did not have the same difficulty. This suggests the importance of sampling the student's responses over a number of times in order to assess the students' ability to interpret. Gary consistently offered insightful comments on a range of characters throughout the discussion but in one instance found it more difficult to provide a concise representation for dramatic purposes.

During this process of determining which parts of the book were important and how to represent the characters, it was possible to assess how students interpreted aspects of the book. They provided reasons for their choice of scenes central to the book and they selected key attributes of the characters to depict in their presentation.

Throughout the discussion, other participants contributed interpretations that helped the individual to refine and extend his own interpretation.

PERFORMANCE OF THE NOVEL

In the dramatic performance recorded on video camera, the students introduced their characters as planned and enacted one scene from the book. The portrayal of the characters was more detailed in the small group discussion than in the actual production. In the performance mode, some of the character traits observed in the discussion were omitted, as were lines from the characters.

This is exemplified when we recall Sam's observations about Officer Shrift noted earlier, and contrast that description with his presentation in the performance.

Sam: Hi, my name is Officer Shrift. I'm one of the meanies in the story. I'm about two feet high and four feet wide. I can turn into different things. I can be a judge, a jailer and my own self, Officer Shrift. Now I'm going to introduce the Whetherman.

This example illustrates the importance of assessing students' literary understanding by looking in on the processes they engage in rather than limiting assessment to what is evident in the performance. In this instance, the performance was not representative of the way in which the character was interpreted during the discussion. Like the description of writing as a more selective process than speaking, the performance was generally more selective than the discussion.

While the performance did not always reflect all that the students observed about the characters during discussion, the presentations provided another means of assessing character interpretation. As Gary said in the postdiscussion, drama "helped you understand the characters more when you had to act them out. When you read it, it told you about them, but it wasn't really—it didn't really—you had to act it to feel how they felt and to understand what they did and how they acted it." Tim, Sam, and Gary interpreted the characters in their sketches through verbal as well as nonverbal communication. Their use of paralinguistics conveyed the tone of the characters (e.g., Tim as Milo spoke in a plodding monotone, while Sam as Officer Shrift spoke in a mean, gruff tone). Tim slouched over and conveyed a bored facial expression. Gary said, "Bah Humbug" in the spirit of Scrooge. Peter and Ronnie relied more on language and props than on nonverbal communication in presenting their characters.

A reversal of this is evident when Ronnie's performance is examined in the second part of the presentation—the enactment of the royal banquet scene. He was reticent to participate in the discussion over the five-session period and only contributed when directly asked a question. It was not evident to the teacher whether Ronnie was tying into the process because he seemed uncomfortable in expressing himself in the discussion mode. However, in the scene from the royal banquet, he contributed key lines and provided the structure for the scene by starting the banquet scene: "Silence! Milo, what can you do to entertain us?"; setting the framework for the meals: "Now what would you like for dinner?"; reacting to individual characters: "Ugh, numbers. Never mention numbers unless we really have to"; and making the closing statement: "We always eat supper after the royal banquet." In this case, assessment of literary understanding was more evident to the teacher during the performance than during the discussion process. Ronnie's utterances reflected both the role and the actual language of the character, King Azaz.

The discussion process and the performance both provided information about how students interpreted characters and scenes. The discussion provided insights into the process of constructing character while the performance reflected the students' representation of the character for an audience. Both types of oral language provide information that is useful for assessment of literary understanding.

CONCLUSIONS

The previous discussion suggests several important functions of oral language as one means of assessing the reader's literary understanding.

1. Oral responses to teacher's questions can provide information about how students construct elements of the literary work such as character, plot, and style of language. Further, discussion permits the teacher to learn more about the students' responses by inviting clarification of observations and greater elaboration of viewpoints.
2. Oral responses may indicate the nature of the student's responses, such as whether the student focuses on physical descriptions of characters, motivations of characters, links between characters and the everyday world, and so forth. Students in this discussion noted some aspects of the word play, particularly the homonyms, but further assessment is needed to determine whether they understood other instances.

3. Oral responses enable the teacher to determine the kinds of evidence students draw upon to construct the literary text. Students, for example, may replicate the explicit text, apply real world knowledge and personal experience to make inferences, and evaluate the effectiveness of the text (Ringler & Weber, 1982).
4. Because oral discussion is a dynamic process, the teacher can observe how literary understanding evolves over time. In addition, the discussion mode enables the teacher to sample a wide range of student interpretations of the literature. As the previous discussion illustrated, a pattern of responses, rather than a single response, is needed to provide a fuller picture.
5. Because a small group discussion involved the interaction among students, the teacher can also assess how the students construct literary texts in a social situation. It is possible to determine, for example, whether students can incorporate other interpretations into their own responses. Readers' reactions to other readers thus indicates the student's receptivity to modifying and refining his or her own interpretations.
6. The oral discussion mode is important in assessing the process of text construction and this process is not tapped by examining the language performance alone. The performance as a single measure of understanding, whether oral or written, does not fully represent the students' understanding of the literary work.

IMPLICATIONS

The emphasis of the present exploration was on the value of oral language as a means of assessing how students interpret literature. There are several implications of this perspective for classroom teachers. First, it is important to create contexts in which oral interpretations can occur. Time should be provided for discussing literature in a group and for other oral response processes such as dramatization, introductions of books to class members, and panel discussions. Children should have opportunities to choose how they would like to interpret aspects of a book.

A second implication is that for assessment purposes, multiple samples of children's interpretive responses should be used to provide information. As the previous discussion demonstrated, interpretive responses of some children, like Ronnie and Gary, were more evident in some contexts than in others. An observation sheet might be constructed with headings denoting each context (e.g., group discussion, drama). This would enable the teacher to see a pattern of response for individual children. Ronnie, for example, appeared to be more comfortable speaking in the role of the character. More experiences of this kind may enable him at a later point to engage in group discussions.

A third implication relates to what to assess in children's responses. This determination is related to the teacher's theory of reader response to literature. The view consistent with the present discussion is based on the value of both reader and text factors in the interpretation of literature. In assessing children's responses, therefore, it would be important to note how children use text cues and their theory of the world to guide their responses. If the text cues are emphasized too much, readers may not derive a personal significance from the story. Recognition that the text generates multiple story meanings allows for a wider spectrum of interpretive responses.

A fourth implication, related to the third, is the nature of the literature. Because of the complexity of literature, it may be useful to have children focus occasionally on certain aspects of story such as characterization. Characterization might be explored across genres so the children could compare and contrast the flat and static characters of folktales with multidimensional, dynamic characters in other genres such as in some realistic and historical fiction works. In addition, discussions of heroes in folktales and high fantasy would enable the teacher to assess students' awareness of intertextuality. The students' interaction with the literature itself may center on certain aspects of the text. *The Phantom Tollbooth,* for example, generated comments about the language of the characters. Other books might evoke similar or different emphases.

In sum, the value of oral responses as a means for assessing students' interpretation of literature can be realized in the classroom setting by providing opportunities for students to respond to a variety of books in multiple ways.

REFERENCES

Collins, L. (1981). Speaking, writing, and teaching for meaning. In B.M. Kroll & R.J. Vann (Eds.), *Exploring speaking–writing relationships: Connections and contrasts* (pp. 198–214). Urbana, IL: National Council of Teachers of English.

Cooper, R. (1985). Evaluating the results of classroom literacy study. In C.R. Cooper (Ed.), *Researching response to literature and the teaching of literature: Points of departure.* (pp. 307–331). Norwood, NJ: Ablex.

Golden, J.M. (1986). Reader–text interaction. *Theory Into Practice, 15*(2), 91–96.

Green, J., & Golden, J. (1983). *Children's television theatre.* Unpublished curriculum project.

Ingarden, R. (1973). *The literary work of art: An investigation on the borderlines of ontology, logic, and theory of literature.* Evanston, IL: Northwestern University Press.

Iser, W. (1978). *The act of reading: A theory of aesthetic response.* Baltimore: Johns Hopkins University Press.

Juster, N. (1961). *The phantom tollbooth.* New York: Random House.

Kantor, J., & Rubin, L. (1981). Between speaking and writing: Process of differentiation. In B.M. Kroll & R.J. Vann (Eds.), *Exploring speaking—writing relationships: Connections and contrasts* (pp. 55–81). Urbana, IL: National Council of Teachers of English.

Ringler, L., & Weber, C. (1982). Comprehending narrative discourse: Implications for instruction. In J.A. Langer & M.T. Smith-Burke (Eds.), *Reader meets author/bridging the gap* (pp. 180–195). Newark, DE: International Reading Association.

Scholes, R. (1985). *Textual power: Literary theory and the teaching of English.* New Haven, CT: Yale University Press.

chapter 11
Children's Group Discussions of Literature: Fertile Ground for Informal Oral Language Assessment

Lenore Carlisle

Is it possible to point to something that isn't there? Five first graders were grappling with a question which had been raised by their teacher, Mrs. Sanderson. The question related to a book they had just read, *Albert's Toothache* (1974) by Barbara Williams. In the book, Albert Turtle's father points to his own toothless mouth in an attempt to convince Albert that, as a turtle, he cannot possibly be suffering from a toothache. The discussion, in part, went like this:

Stephen: How can there be a question about that?

Amy: No, you can't point to the teeth. But, well, like the air is there, but you can't see it. And if you walk in it, you're not going to bump into it, but it doesn't mean it's not there. There is something there in a way, but it's not teeth.... And sometimes you can point to something that's not *right* there. Like if you know somebody and they live far away, um well you can point to something that's seven hundred miles away. It's not right there where your finger is pointing to, but you, um, well you point in the direction of where they live. So you're pointing to something that's not there. Plus air.

Stephen: Oh brother.

Becky: Well, she's right. There is air.

Ben: But we're talking about, we're saying can you point to nothing.

Amy: No, it's that you're always pointing to something.
*Stephen:*Oh brother.
*Andrew:*Oh brother, oh brother, oh sister!
Becky: I think. I think we're off on the track of our answer.
Ben: He meant to point to no teeth.
Amy: Well you can't point to nothing.
Ben: He was pointing to the teeth, the tooth that isn't there.
*Stephen:*Oh brother.

Mrs. Sanderson's voice was conspicuously absent from the discussion. These five first graders owned their own discussion. They directed their responses to each other, they argued, they affirmed, they shared feelings of exasperation and exultation as they attempted to answer the unanswerable. And in the midst of doing this, their active discussion also revealed to their teacher a number of important things about their individual proficiencies as oral language users.

Given the opportunity to explore literature through small response groups, children have much to show us about how they use oral language. Unlike formal paper and pen testing situations, which limit the kinds of language children need to use in order to respond, child-centered group discussions of literature provide fertile ground for teachers to conduct informal oral language assessments.

In the following pages, I hope to offer some suggestions about how teachers can make use of ongoing response group discussions for the purpose of conducting informal assessment of oral language development. Rather than look to how children interpret texts or at how we can evaluate their comprehension of texts, I will be focusing directly on how we can evaluate children's proficiency as language users as they respond to literature.

Some Background Information

In recent years, teachers have been urged to abandon formal paper-and-pencil testing tools in favor of informal observation when attempting to assess student language development. Suggestions about what aspects of language to examine have been made increasingly explicit, with a newfound emphasis on acknowledging the importance of informal oral language assessment. The work of teachers and educators such as Loban (1976) and Genishi and Dyson (1984) have been helpful to those of us working with elementary school-aged children. But while their suggestions have given us some much needed direction in terms of areas to target when engaging in language assessment, there remains the age-old problem of trying to figure out how to accommodate one more informal observation in an already full schedule. Reading, spelling, and social skills assessments, along with required or mandated standardized testing, leave precious little time for planning and documenting yet another phase of informal assessment.

On a related note, classroom teachers are growing increasingly concerned about issues of accountability, particularly in the area of language arts, where there is currently a national focus on literacy deficiencies among our students. Hence some of the more informal observational assessments teachers might employ don't satisfy those parents or administrators who seem hungry for neatly reported and easily quantifiable assessments of their children's growing language proficiency. Yet for those of us who fervently believe that children's abilities as language users cannot be measured solely in terms of their knowledge of isolated vocabulary, their ability to draw conclusions from snippets of literature, or their ability to punctuate properly, it is critical that we continue to search for viable alternatives to paper and pen testing.

MAKING USE OF WHAT'S ALREADY AVAILABLE

With those factors in mind, the best alternative seems to be using ready-made language arts materials, which not only provide positive and productive learning experiences for our students, but also provide a rich arena for assessing language development. The best language arts materials are the vast array of children's literature. Quality children's books across all genres promote active responses from children, thus providing us with opportunities to examine and assess how children are using oral language. In the primary grades, the books of such authors as Leo Lionni, Lucille Clifton, Tomie de Paola, Vera B. Williams, Russel Hoban, Hugh Lewin, Eric Carle, Arnold Lobel, John Burningham, Brian Wildsmith, and John Steptoe all stimulate discussion among children. In this chapter, first graders' oral responses to a story from *Frog and Toad Together* (1971) by Arnold Lobel are examined. While specific materials were used to elicit the children's oral responses in this instance,[1] oral responses elicited by teacher's questions, or student-generated discussion, could as readily be used.

---

[1] The materials used to stimulate the discussion were from *Wise Owl*, (Matthews, Carlisle, & Tishman, 1987) a critical and creative thinking program published by Sundance Publishers and Distributors, Littleton, MA.

A WORD ON READER-RESPONSE THEORY

Reader-response theory (Rosenblatt, 1978, 1982) tells us that the interaction of reader and author through text creates a unique experience, and in so doing, a unique response is formed. Given an opportunity to voice those responses, children's speech can reveal a great deal to us about their unique individual oral language capabilities. As they respond both to the text and to each other's responses, numerous opportunities to assess individual language skills emerge.

Response theory also tells us that children's responses to literature change over time (Galda, 1980; Hickman, 1979), suggesting the possibility of greater depth and complexity of response with repeated readings. As children's internal responses become more complex, the demands on oral language ability needed to express those responses likewise grow in complexity. Thus observing response over a period of time allows the classroom teacher to discover whether or not a child is becoming more proficient in the ability to articulate subtle connections that might be required to explain and describe how a response has evolved or how it relates to an earlier response.

DECIDING WHAT IT IS YOU'RE LOOKING FOR

But before beginning observations of children's oral language use, it is important to identify and describe those aspects of language which seem to be important indicators of growth and/or proficiency. Fortunately for us, Loban (1976) has done a thorough job of describing goals for language use, which provide a source from which to identify appropriate goals for the children with whom we are working. His list provided me with a good starting point from which to isolate specific areas of proficiency for assessment. In addition, Genishi and Dyson (1984) have suggested some equally practical points of observation. The list which I have suggested is based on some of their suggestions and incorporates some of my own. Depending on the age of your students and what aspects of oral language proficiency you're interested in observing, you'll probably want to make your own adaptations.

From these more broadly conceived goals and points for observation, you can pinpoint those aspects that seem to be relevant to your assessment of individual students. You might, for example, want to observe certain basic competencies among all children during an informal observation early in the year. Such an observation might include the following considerations: Does the student speak too softly? Does the student rely on verbal fillers? Does the student speak clearly and enunciate well?

As the school year progresses and students have more experience with group discussions, you may want to create a new checklist for your assessments. Furthermore, you may want to begin to individualize assessments by looking specifically at aspects of oral language development that are pertinent to a particular student. For example, you might include these concerns when observing the more talkative students: Is the student reluctant to yield the floor? Is the student finding ways to finish saying what he or she wants to say and stop talking? Is the student able to listen to other opinions without blurting out his or her own response? Does the student maintain a respectful silence when other students are speaking? For the less talkative student, you might want to include such points as: Does the student speak too softly? Is the student showing evidence of using increasingly complex sentences? Does the student show more confidence in expressing a point of view? Is the student able to maintain a point of view?

You might choose to have six or eight points you'll observe for all students four times during the year. Then you can add individual points of observations for each student later on, once you've made these initial observations. I've found it helpful to have a loosely designed observation sheet and a folder for each child to make it easier to document my observations for my own use as well as to share relevant findings with parents, other teachers, and administrators.

USING CHILDREN'S LITERATURE FOR ORAL LANGUAGE ASSESSMENT

Now let's take a look at just one context which can be used for oral language assessment. In this instance, quality children's literature provides the initial stimulus so children can think critically and creatively through philosophical inquiry. Children read or are read good stories, and are then asked to engage in a discussion of several questions about the stories that have their roots in philosophy. The group discussions typically run for 4 or 5 days, during reading or a language arts block.

What makes children's literature in general especially useful in assessing language development is that it can challenge the student's ability to articulate precisely, to argue their own positions, to embrace new information, to be accepting of peer responses, and to communicate among themselves. Genishi and Dyson (1984) have stressed the importance of observing oral language as children communicate with each other, since those interactions are likely to demand conversational skills which are different from those observed in one-on-one teacher-directed discussions. When sharing children's literature with children, and when using an approach or materials that are so designed, the teacher can often assume a facilitating rather than a directing role; thus students do have ample opportunity to speak directly to each other without using the teacher as a filter for their responses. In a very real sense, the discussions stimulated by quality books such as *Frog and Toad are Friends* belong to the students. The eventual assessment of the students' language abilities is shaped by the initiative of the respondents, and the tenor of the assessment process is therefore established by the context of the particular response situation.

Language doesn't happen in a vacuum. Mischler (1979) has stressed the importance of conducting research in a natural context. As Genishi and Dyson (1984, p. 137) are quick to point out, children regard language not as "an object of contemplation, but rather as an instrument of use." It makes sense, then, to look at language on their terms and at how they use it in real classroom contexts. By using literature to stimulate response, and by recognizing that responses to literature are unique, we enable students to bring a highly personalized use of language to the assessment. Thus the assessment comes out of the interaction of student with text, student with teacher, and student with fellow students.

"COOKIES"

The group of first graders described earlier read a number of stories together. The first of the stories they read, and the questions that followed, provided a good starting point for informal assessment of language development. The story was "Cookies" by Arnold Lobel (1971). What appears to be a rather simple, albeit charming, story about Frog and Toad and their amusing antics as they do battle with trying not to eat too many cookies can also be seen as a drama in which the characters are exploring the concept of will and the idea of willpower. The philosophical roots of these notions are found in what is called the question of "weakness of the will" (Matthews, Carlisle, & Tishman, 1987).

The questions which follow the reading of the story encourage children to imagine themselves faced with situations similar to those faced by Frog and Toad, or to relate incidents in the story to similar life experiences they have had. What makes the questions particularly thought provoking is the manner in which they stimulate children to think of how the will is conceived as well as about how it is related to their own desires. Obviously, such questions demand a level of precision in language use, as well as an ability to listen carefully to subtle shades of meaning expressed by others. Because there are no right or wrong answers to the questions, the teacher is able to concentrate more fully on observing how children use language to convey their responses, rather than on the correctness of their responses.

What follows are specific examples of how some members of a group of six mixed-ability first graders responded to the questions and discussion over 5 days, and at how their responses could enable the teacher to engage in a very productive assessment of language development among the group (Carlisle, 1988). The excerpts which follow were transcribed from tape-recorded group discussions. It might be possible for you to tape-record some of your students' group discussions in order to allow you to get a sense of how the conversations flows with regard to group dynamics and turn taking, for example. However, it isn't critical that you record group discussions in order to assess language development.

Amy. One student who took part in a discussion of "Cookies" was Amy. Amy was the most proficient reader in her first-grade classroom. Her teacher, Mrs. Sanderson, had individualized the reading program in her classroom. Because Amy was in a league all her own, she often read alone. When she did have an opportunity to read with someone else, she typically read with Mrs. Sanderson or with the school reading teacher who came in to work with Amy once a week. Amy was hungry for involvement with her peers during reading time, but she had expressed her concern that she might find some of the books being ready by her peers "babyish."

During the first group discussion of "Cookies," Mrs. Sanderson's notes revealed that Amy rarely engaged in spontaneous responses to questions or to her peers. She only answered questions Mrs. Sanderson directed at her in an effort to get her involved in the discussion. She spoke softly, directed her responses to the teacher, and used a noticeable number of sentence fillers (*um* and *well*) when she spoke. On the following day, Amy began to offer more lengthy answers to questions, often getting lost in her own explanations. She did seem to get to the point eventually, sometimes as a result of the prodding of one of her classmates.

By the third day, Amy was responding with greater frequency and was more assertive when her peers tried to interrupt her. She also indicated an ability to hold onto the question, even to lead her peers back to the question at hand, as can be seen in the following episode.

Over the course of 2 days' discussions, the students spent a good deal of time thinking and talking about whether or not Frog and Toad would be able to know for certain that if they ate too many cookies and became ill, it was actually the cookies which had made them ill. Stephen and Becky insisted they could know it, because too much sugar could make you ill. Becky went on to say that too many cookies could give you cavities and make you fat. Amy tried to pull the discussion back on track.

Amy: No, No. Well, um...well.
Stephen: She's right. Becky's right.
Amy: Let me finish. You didn't let me say my turn, what I had to say. It's that, well he was concerned about getting sick, and that's different. At least in the book it says "We will soon be sick." Maybe he was worried he'd get fat or get cavities, or some other things. Maybe he was. It's possible he was, but it never says that...They would know they were sick because they ate too much cookies and that the reason was that they ate too much cookies they wouldn't feel good. And they know that cookies have too much sugar in them and they ate too many.
Mrs. S.: If they got sick would they know it was because they ate too many cookies?
Amy: Um, they could know that. They could know why they got sick because they haven't done anything else that could make them sick yet.
Stephen: Oh yeah, she gets it. That's right.

Whether or not Amy's response was ultimately right or wrong, or even whether it was the best possible answer to an unanswerable question, is not what is important here. What is important is that she was able to strike to the heart of the matter, to think it through with some logic, and then to explain her response to her peers in a way that was understandable to them.

It's clear that by observing Amy's language abilities over a few days, Mrs. Sanderson was better able to get a complete picture of exactly what Amy was capable of. If Mrs. Sanderson had limited her observation to a single group discussion, she would have had a very different picture of what Amy could do with language. Granted, the materials made some new demands and offered some much-needed group experience for Amy. But the important point to note is that Amy was able to rise to the challenge. Informal assessment revealed a breadth of ability that might have been overlooked by a more rigid assessment tool. It also revealed areas where Amy needed support.

Benjamin. Based on the results of standardized tests, as well as upon observations made by his teacher, Benjamin was one of the least proficient readers in his class, certainly the least proficient reader in the group. Yet his oral language ability was remarkable, indicating analytical skills that far exceeded those of the other group members. He was intent on expressing his point of view, even when it differed from those of his peers. Furthermore, he was usually able to find appropriate language to express those ideas, ideas that were often far more complex than responses typically observed among the other group members. For example, in response to a question about whether or not someone else can give you will power, five of the participants believed that their parents could give you will power. They were firm in their position, and were supportive as each member of the group affirmed the contention that parents could give you will power. Benjamin wasn't so sure.

Benjamin: My parents make it hard for me to push my sister. They let me know I'll get a punishment. But that isn't like they give it [will power] to me. Like they punish. Like going to my room, and thinking about it, which is weird because you can't make another person's mind think about something unless they want to. So like, if they say, "Now go to your room and think about what you've done," I just go to my room and I think about something else. I use *my* will power not to think about what they want me to think about. Then I just look real sad when I come out and they think I was in there thinking about my dumb sister... You don't understand about will power. Because like, your mother can't give you *your* willpower.

His argument was convincing to some members of the group, who openly expressed their admiration for Benjamin's "real good answer." Two members of the group disagreed with Benjamin, yet he held fast to his position without hostility.

Benjamin: Maybe your brain and my brain think it different. People don't always agree like that. Like that's why maybe you vote for bombs and I vote not for bombs, like that. I can think I'm right.

If Benjamin had strengths in the areas of clinging to a point, disagreeing without rancor, and using emphasis in an effective way, he had weaknesses that were equally noticeable.

Benjamin often became frustrated with the group dynamics or turn taking. Here we see how important it is to assess language development in real classroom contexts. Benjamin often withdrew into himself during group discussions when issues centering on turn taking weighed too heavily upon him. He sometimes subvocalized single words as a strategy for remembering his own response, but in so doing, he was often unable to remain attentive to the responses of his peers.

At one point, when Mrs. Sanderson called on Benjamin to respond to a question about will power, he suddenly realized that he still had something he wanted to say about the question previously being discussed.

Benjamin: That's not the answer I wanted to say. I wanted to say...I didn't even want to talk about that.
Mrs. S.:   We can come back to you if you want.
Benjamin: Well it's like every time you read the question, I *feel* the answer, then when it's my turn I start to try to explain it, I can't remember what is the question.

Mrs. Sanderson, an experienced classroom teacher, seized a potential teaching opportunity and responded as follows:

Mrs. S.:   I know how that feels. Would it help if I repeat the question more often? I'll do that. See if you can take a moment to think it out slowly, and then we'll come back to you.

Benjamin then mumbled to himself.

Benjamin: Ok, Ok, that's a good idea. Ok, yeah, think, think, think.

Mrs. Sanderson saw an area of difficulty for Benjamin. He lacked strategies for hanging on to his own responses while his peers spoke. By using real materials in a real group context, she was able not only to identify the difficulty, but also to immediately suggest a strategy to solve the problem. She later went on to suggest to him that he could wait for an appropriate pause in the conversation and then make a request for someone to refocus him on the question at hand.

Andrew. During the first few group discussions, Andrew's oral language development appeared to be markedly less advanced than that of his peers. However, it was also apparent that his generally agitated and somewhat hostile attitude made it difficult to get a clear picture of exactly what his capabilities were. He often digressed from the questions being discussed. His digressions were difficult to relate to the text, to his peers' responses, or to the questions being asked. For example, the group had been discussing the question, "Is there any way I could stop eating cookies unless in some way I wanted to stop?"

This was a challenging question, but one that resulted in a highly animated discussion. Andrew remained uninvolved in the discussion until Mrs. Sanderson directly solicited a response from him. Andrew replied,

Andrew: How 'bout if you have cookies and you're left around, you can tell the world how many cookies you can eat because it's round and it has chocolate chips all over it. And that's the end of that.

Andrew also tended to be argumentative. If he disagreed with a statement made by one of his peers, he typically interrupted or shouted, "No! No! You're wrong. That's not my answer." Mrs. Sanderson evidently noted these behaviors and continually offered Andrew strategies for responding more appropriately.

Mrs. S.: Andrew, it's fine to disagree. How could you do that in an appropriate way?

She then got suggestions from Andrew and the other group members about appropriate ways to express disagreement. She noted that Andrew seemed to be most successful in responding and engaging with the group when he was given the opportunity to draw parallels between his own experiences and feelings and those of Frog and Toad. Andrew could sometimes experience greater success in the group if questions were reframed for him. At some future date, Mrs. Sanderson might have wanted to see if Andrew had begun to need that sort of reframing less often.

Andrew's responses also suggested some difficulty in organization. He frequently became lost in trying to answer a question. When he realized he had lost track of his response, he would become angry and refuse to continue. When Andrew did answer a question with clarity, it was usually because he had drawn from a personal experience in forming his response. Other members of the group were very affirming of Andrew's responses in these instances:

Stephen: That was a good answer.
Mrs. S.: Why was it good? You said it was good. What made it good?
Stephen: Cause now I understand it, and like he told it good, a good story.
Amy: It's because of how he explained. He did a good job on explaining.
Mrs. S.: Yes I noticed that too. He told it like a story, and then he reminded us of how his story was connected with the question, how it was about what we've been reading.

Over the course of 5 days, Andrew's ability to discuss "Cookies" with his peers revealed a number of strengths and weaknesses. And the cumulative data gave a good indication of the full range of Andrew's oral language abilities. It's easy to imagine how, if questioned on a particularly bad day, Andrew's sometimes aggressive and hostile manner might have suggested an even more limited range of abilities. Instead, Mrs. Sanderson had the opportunity to see that Andrew did indeed have strengths upon which to build. He was a good story teller. The affirmation he received from his peers helped him in the area of self-confidence. Though he sometimes found it difficult to listen quietly without blurting out, he could do it. He relied on verbal fillers (*like, so OK so*) particularly when he was having trouble organizing his response, yet at other times he spoke without using fillers at all. He spoke in complex sentences: "If Frog had eaten so much cookies, he would have got sick for sure. Cause if he didn't eat cookies, he wouldn't get sick."

Each of the children used language in highly personal ways as they responded to literature. And the opportunity to respond to literature over time often revealed that they could call upon more advanced language usage to express themselves. Although Applebee (1978), among others, has led us to believe that very young children cannot achieve Britton's "spectator response" due to developmental constraints, for example, I recorded several instances in which children were doing just that. The fact that the language assessment took place in the context of group discussions told a great deal about specific proficiencies or lack thereof in each child: Amy was able to grasp a question with a vice grip and hang onto it for the entire group; Benjamin needed help in group discussions with regard to turn taking; Andrew had a chance to shine when he experienced the affirmation of his peers as he used story telling to answer questions.

Because each child was able to respond to literature using their unique language, a unique profile of each child as a language user emerged. Whereas a standardized test approach to language assessment lumps children whose abilities are quite diverse into the same categories of proficiency, informal assessment of oral language enables us to view the language user through a different lens. By having the assessment take place during group discussions, we are able to see the broader picture in terms of how a child functions in a group context and then zoom in to see how the child's individual abilities are taking shape. Oral language assessment, particularly that which allows the individual child's abilities to merge in a natural classroom context and where issues of right/wrong responses are not the focus, appears to offer insights which are far more useful to the classroom teacher.

A FINAL WORD

Sharing children's literature by reading to children or by having them read it themselves are by no means the only means to provide opportunities for language assessment. Many of us can create other contexts (i.e., dramatic play, storytelling, puppetry, drama, art, and media) that might be used in a similar way. It's a matter of choosing activities, materials, or instructional moments that have merit on their own as valuable encounters with literature, for example, but that also provide fertile ground for assessing oral language development.

What does seem important is that we act on our belief that time spent on paper-and-pen testing that is not rooted in the real language experiences of our students' classroom lives is time wasted. Only by looking at real language in real contexts will we be able to make worthwhile assessments of our students'' strengths and weaknesses, their proficiences as well as their needs. If we are going to be held accountable for our students' growing language proficiency, we need to know that we're being held accountable for something real. There can be no better way to assess language development than by listening to it unfold around us in real classrooms peopled by real speakers.

Table 11.1. Guidelines for Assessing Oral Language Development

1. Does he or she speak in group situations?
      too often?
      too infrequently?
2. Does he or she speak too softly?
      too loudly?
      too quickly?
      too slowly?
3. Does he or she enunciate and articulate clearly?
4. Is he or she able to stick to a point?
5. Is he or she able to follow someone else's response or to ask for clarification?
6. Is he or she able to distinguish important from unimportant information?
7. Is he or she able to detect basic assumptions?
8. Does he or she show an ability to organize thoughts?
9. Does he or she use words precisely? Does he or she have a good vocabulary?
10. Does he or she show an ability to adapt language to the needs of the listener?
11. Does he or she show ability to yield the floor?
13. Does he or she blurt out information?
14. Does he or she carry on other conversations while someone else is speaking?
15. Does he or she use complex sentences?
16. Does he or she rely on verbal fillers or stock responses?
17. Is he or she clear about time sequence (often evident in use of verb tenses)?
18. Is he or she able to further explain a response or opinion when asked?
19. Does he or she show respect in listening and responding to others?
20. Is he or she able to express a difference of opinion without becoming angry?
21. Does he or she have strategies for helping to redirect a discussion if necessary?

As stated earlier, the research of Loban (1976) and Genishi & Dyson (1984) provided most of the points of observation listed here. Based on your own student population, you will probably need to make some changes in these guidelines.

REFERENCES

Applebee, A. (1978). *The child's concept of story: Ages two to seventeen.* Chicago: University of Chicago Press.

Carlisle, L. (1988). Response to literature among first grade students: Exploring the possibilities. Unpublished doctoral dissertation, University of Massachusetts at Amherst.

Galda, L. (1980). *Three children reading stories: Response to literature in preadolescents.* Urbana, IL: National Council of Teachers of English Research Foundation. (ERIC Document Reproduction Service No. 188 131.)

Genishi, C., & Dyson, A.H. (1984). *Language assessment in the early years.* Norwood, NJ: Ablex.

Hickman, J.G. (1979). *Extending the dimensions of response to literature: Response in an elementary school setting.* (ERIC Document Service No. 189 600.)

Loban, W. (1976). *Language development: Kindergarten through grade twelve.* Urbana, IL: National Council of Teachers of English.

Lobel, A. (1971). Cookies. In *Frog and toad together* (pp. 30–41). New York: Harper and Row.

Matthews, G.B., Carlisle, L., & Tishman, S. (1987). *Wise owl.* Littleton, MA: Sundance Publishers and Distributors.

Mischler, E. (1979). Meaning in context: Is there any other kind? *Harvard Educational Review, 49*(1), 1–19.

Rosenblatt, L.M. (1978). *The reader, the text, the poem.* Carbondale, IL: Southern Illinois University Press.

Rosenblatt, L.M. (1982). The literary transaction: Evocation and response. *Theory into Practice, 21*(4), 268–277.

Williams, B. (1977). *Albert's toothache.* New York: E.P. Dutton.

Discussion: Unleashing the Potential of Children's Responses to Literature

Leslie Shaw,
Debora G. Jacque, and
Cheryl L. Taylor

In our classrooms, we continue to search for ways that help children, individually or in groups, actively construct meanings, create contexts for learning and responses, and, most importantly, encourage delight and facility in literary language. However, many types of traditional tests, especially standard objective questions and/or rigid writing prompts, seem to rely only on efferent responses. If we as teachers are truly to understand what children know, we need to provide opportunities and social contexts that support a balance of aesthetic and efferent responses to literature.

After reading the three chapters in this assessment of literary language section, we discussed ways to enhance children's diverse responses to literary texts. Since we teach at different grade levels from primary to intermediate to high school in suburban and rural public schools with predominately white populations, we tried to consider both developmental issues as well as the greater assessment challenge of creating contexts that allow both the efferent and aesthetic responses to be expressed and validated. Out of our collaborative reflection came the following reactions and responses.

First, all three chapters emphasized the importance of oral language exchanges. In the Golden chapter, the importance of process over product was demonstrated by the fact that more ideas were discussed and formulated during the preparation for the drama than in the actual dramatic production. The time spent in working through the oral process of evolving meaning for the novel was more important language usage and learning time than the actual final presentation of the drama itself. We also saw evidence of this in the Lehr research, where younger children were engaged in a process of meaning construction with the actual picture books present to aid conveyance of their ideas, feelings, and thoughts. And again in the Holland research, intermediate-aged students spent 12 sessions collaboratively sharing multiple meanings of *Bridge to Terabithia* through the process of oral language exchanges as well as art/media and written language response modes.

Within the drama/dramatic play context, we wondered what happened to this response mode between kindergarten and fifth grade, let alone by high school? Have we taught children to hide this natural response mode as they move up through the grades? Kindergarten children typically respond to literature using their whole bodies as vehicles of aesthetic expression. They don't hesitate to work through literary meanings in the drama/dramatic play modes. By the intermediate grades this natural response appears to have disappeared, although sometimes we have seen that after their reticence has been broken down in a trusting context, a "little kid" reemerges. But in high school it is harder to break through this reticence, even when the students are enthusiastic about a story. As in the Golden chapter, with older elementary children and adolescents, spending time talking and collaboratively constructing the meaning of a literary work seems to encourage the appearance of the dramatic mode.

Secondly, these chapters emphasized the social construction of literacy through a variety of shared responses, which further illustrates the notion of multiple meanings from the same text. Only through supportive group contexts that value individual expression in a variety of modes can thought processes be carried to fruition. In her chapter, Golden aptly shared the dynamic and positive struggle of a group of intermediate grade students as they shifted and changed their collaborative meanings in much the same way they might revise through editions of written work.

Responding to literature through choices—elicits not only a wide variety of expression but projects that require analysis and then a synthesis of ideas from the literary text. For example, in the Holland research, the child who constructed the mood chart had to return to the text of *Bridge to Terabithia* and not only analyze what had occurred but synthesize a color code to match the mood of each chapter. This is a perfect example of a child balancing the initial aesthetic response with a later efferent response to the same text. What greater skill can we ask of children than to create and think?

When we allow children to express experiences in oral and written language, they expand their comprehension by connecting their own past experiences with literature. When we read aloud a story to young children about a new baby, our children often connect their feelings from within their family about the theme of the story. Many times they go off on many new and interesting tangents the teacher never would have been able to capture if he or she had simply asked direct questions instead of soliciting open responses to the book. Once one child sparks a response to a story read aloud, other children often collaboratively response to that child and each other in their efforts to construct meanings to literary language. We feel that the classroom context necessary for such higher level thinking is created by the teacher. Carlisle's chapter explicitly shows teachers how to formulate and facilitate effective social contexts. The importance of building on all children's oral language strengths to improve group interaction is optimal, since even the high-achieving children need to expand their present oral language strategies.

Thirdly, because formal tests are required in our schools, alternative forms of assessment that increase our knowledge of a child's growth in literacy are vitally important to us. We continually search for viable ways to use assessment that acknowledges and values differences: increased and continual observation in natural social contexts, emphasis on patterns of response rather than isolated responses, and emphasis on and use of children's strengths in all literacy areas. The validity of arbitrary, quantitative tests used with diverse populations concerns us.

The need for evaluation within a variety of response contexts is an issue for all teachers. We agree with the Holland and Lehr chapter, which called for wider response arenas and choices. Sometimes children have more understanding than the evaluation format allows them to show. Children who write book reports may actually be holding back deeper responses to the book simply because they won't fit in the book report format. Thus, stronger and truer assessment of literary language may not occur. Rather, we have had to develop observation skills which concentrate on watching children recapture and reflect about books through talk, art/media, drama/dramatic play, and written language. We have learned through lots of practice to sit back and reflect on children's responses to literature, and to become more proficient in conveying vital evaluative information to important persons outside the classroom—parents and administrators.

Finally, each chapter emphasized the importance of teachers-as-researchers, which challenged us to observe with the eye of a researcher successful strategies which provide all children with oral language usage and development opportunities. We reflected on Carlisle's suggestion that, often in assessment, there is a lack of attention paid to oral language development. If children are asked a literal question, they may not find the means within this oral context to convey their meaning. But when children are allowed to enter oral language exchanges openly and in their own meanings, they often can find amazing things in stories to share with the whole class. Golden's emphasis on more oral language processes surrounding and supporting textual language interpretation, as well as Carlisle's suggestion that teachers become facilitators versus directors, helped us to reflect and reconsider this assessment area. Success of our students both in and out of the classroom requires both receptive and expressive language skills. As Holland and Lehr suggested, when children listen and read (or are read to) in supportive contexts where unique responses are allowed and valued, teachers garner expressions that are the result of analysis and synthesis. As we observe and hear children within the context of natural language use, deeper efferent and aesthetic responses are often elicited.

As teacher-researchers we have learned that children need to use oral and written language actively and purposively in diverse social contexts in order to learn. When children are unnecessarily restricted in expressing their ideas, meaning is stifled in the process. Consider the elementary teacher who questioned her students about the meaning of *infinity*. When one child enthusiastically shouted out, "Cream of Wheat!" he was labeled disruptive and sent from the reading group. However, when asked for further elaboration of the "Cream of Wheat" response, the child explained, "Ya know that man holding the box has a picture of the man holding the box, and that man has a picture of the man holding the box. . . ." As teacher-researchers we need to dig deeper into responses children give to literary language and go the extra mile in allowing them to connect it to their background of experience.

These three chapters have convinced us that aesthetic and efferent responses can be balanced across many classroom contexts among diverse populations with many different backgrounds of experiences. We have reconsidered applying these assessment strategies: validating multiple meanings from one text, allowing children to choose response mode(s), valuing and observing oral and written language processes surrounding and supporting literary works, and emphasizing process and patterns of response over time versus emphasis on products. We, as teachers and researchers, can no longer afford to overlook the potential and possibilities of creating alternative assessment contexts that will unleash all children's responses to literature, both efferently and aesthetically.

Author Index

Subject Index